STANDING ON THE OUTSIDE LOOKING IN

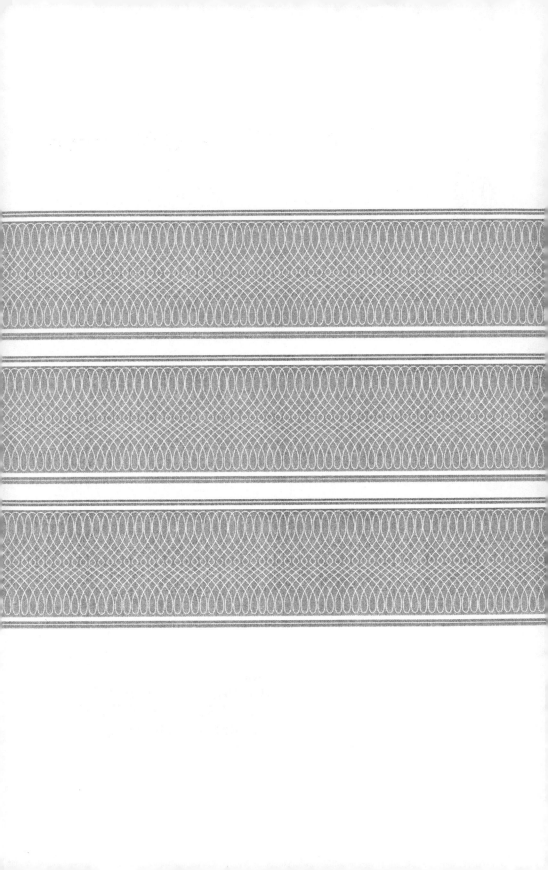

STANDING ON THE OUTSIDE LOOKING IN

Underrepresented Students' Experiences in Advanced-Degree Programs

Edited by Mary F. Howard-Hamilton,

Carla L. Morelon-Quainoo,

Susan D. Johnson,

Rachelle Winkle-Wagner,

and Lilia Santiague

Foreword by Raechele L. Pope

STERLING, VIRGINIA

Published by Stylus Publishing, LLC
22883 Quicksilver Drive
Sterling, Virginia 20166-2102

Library of Congress Cataloging-in-Publication-Data
Standing on the outside looking in : underrepresented students' experiences in advanced degree programs   /
edited by Mary F. Howard-Hamilton . . . [et al.] ; foreword
  by Raechele L. Pope.—1st ed.
      p.   cm.
  Includes bibliographical references and index.
  ISBN 978-1-57922-283-3 (cloth : alk. paper)—
  ISBN 978-1-57922-284-0 (pbk. : alk. paper)
    1. Minorities—Education (Graduate)—United States. 2.
Minority graduate students—United States—Social
conditions. I. Howard-Hamilton, Mary F.
LC3727.S73   2009
378.1′982—dc22   2008025790

13-digit ISBN: 978-1-57922-283-3 (cloth)
13-digit ISBN: 978-1-57922-284-0 (paper)

Bulk Purchases

Quantity discounts are available for use in workshops
and for staff development.
Call 1-800-232-0223

First Edition, 2009

10 9 8 7 6 5 4 3 2 1

The editors of this book and members of the Dream Team would like to thank Dr. Charlie Nelms, for investing in our research vision.

CONTENTS

I find it absolutely amazing that this book was not written years ago. *Standing on the Outside Looking In* addresses many issues that have been neglected in higher education. Although diversity and multicultural issues in higher education have a long history, the literature to help us understand these issues has had a hard time keeping up with their complexity. Despite the growing number of students of color attending college in the 1980s, little information was available for higher education professionals to fill the void left by their graduate training programs. Most of the early research on college students and, in fact, almost all of the theory-building studies of the 1950s, 1960s, and 1970s such as those of Perry (1970), Kohlberg (1981), and Chickering (1969) were based on the experiences of White men. Higher education practitioners had little option but to apply these theories and research to students of color or to make it up as they went along. The practices that resulted from these theories may have had a harmful effect on college students of color and may have affected their ability to succeed.

As a result of many criticisms, the inadequacies of the literature and ineffectiveness of higher education professionals in understanding and addressing the concerns of students of color began to be addressed in the mid-1980s and 1990s. The literature expanded to include a focus on how to make college campuses more welcoming and multiculturally sensitive and more recently on the importance of developing multicultural competence. In addition, multicultural issues in the curriculum and the need to create transformative educational experiences in higher education have been the subject of many books and conferences. Although this literature has been invaluable in addressing the concerns of college undergraduates by educating higher education professionals about the unique concerns of students of color as well as about how to increase the multicultural sensitivity of White students, research shows that multicultural efforts on college campuses continue to have mixed results. The approach to addressing multicultural issues has historically been piecemeal; however, such practices have been enhanced with the addition of the multicultural organizational development (MCOD) paradigm that emphasizes the need for systemic and systematic change efforts. Such efforts suggest the need for change to the personnel, policies, and practices of most higher education institutions.

Standing on the Outside Looking In adds a much-needed perspective by focusing on one of the most essential aspects of creating multicultural campuses. Without serious efforts toward addressing the multicultural pipeline to ensure that adequate numbers of students of color attend and graduate from college, the problems that exist on our campuses and in our society may never truly be eliminated. An essential piece of this process is to ensure that adequate numbers of college students of color not only attain an undergraduate degree but also come to view graduate education as a necessary prerequisite for career and lifelong success. In higher education we have been so focused on attracting and retaining undergraduate students of color that we have often failed to see the larger picture. Our vision should include students of color fully involved in all aspects of higher education—undergraduate education, graduate education, and professional schools. Enlarging our focus, our vision, has the potential to transform our campuses by increasing the available pool of faculty and administrators of color. Moreover, it also has the potential to transform private business, the service sector, and government in the same ways.

By highlighting the dismal state of literature on graduate and professional students of color, *Standing on the Outside Looking In* provides a groundbreaking and essential text that will allow us to take our multicultural efforts in higher education to the next level. The chapters offered by Howard-Hamilton, Morelon-Quainoo, Winkle-Wagner, Johnson, and Santiague provide a combination of specificity and universality in addressing the varied and unique concerns and realities of graduate and professional students of color. From addressing issues of access and choice to exploring the realities of a particular field such as science and engineering and to highlighting the specific concerns and needs of particular groups of students of color, this book has it all. One of the most powerful and unexpected aspects of this collection is the reliance on qualitative research by many of the authors. Such a perspective is so important to truly expand our understanding of graduate students of color, who have been so rarely studied. Qualitative research is an ideal and necessary method to represent these seldom-heard voices. These studies help the reader to understand more fully the current experiences and realities of graduate and professional students of color.

The rich voices and stories represented do more than document the experiences of graduate and professional students of color; they offer ideas, strategies, and solutions for addressing the concerns and barriers that currently exist in higher education. One common theme across much of this book is the responsibility of higher education institutions to prioritize expanding their multicultural efforts to address the needs of graduate and professional students of color. Literature on college outcomes clearly indicates that providing an education to an undergraduate student of color changes the life of that one person and her or his family. However, educating a graduate or professional student of color has the added potential to change radically a profession and even higher education by providing sorely needed role models and advocates, differing worldviews and perspectives, and cultural connections and insights.

Standing on the Outside Looking In powerfully embraces alternative intellectual frameworks including critical race theory and Black feminist thought to increase understanding of the experiences of graduate and professional students of color. What the authors emphasize in a variety of ways is that it is no longer reasonable or acceptable to sit back and do nothing. Many years ago, Jo Freeman (1979), in her study of female graduate students, suggested that a *null environment* in which the issues of an underserved and underrepresented group are ignored or minimized is just as harmful as if the environment were purposefully oppressive. Unless educators and administrators act as advocates counteracting the many negative messages and experiences from society, undergraduate students of color are less likely to find themselves confident, prepared, and inspired enough to attend graduate and professional school. *Standing on the Outside Looking In* will be of tremendous value to faculty, administrators, staff, researchers, and other higher education professionals. More than ever we need to appreciate the value of creating supportive environments and opportunities and make a commitment to the future of higher education. If everyone is not able to participate fully in higher education, its golden opportunities and transformative effect will fall short. Reading *Standing on the Outside Looking In* provides an essential first step toward ensuring that the rich diversity of society is able to participate fully in higher education. Remember, though, reading this book is not enough; words without action fall short of their promise.

Raechele L. Pope
Associate Professor
University of Buffalo

References

Chickering, A. (1969). *Education and identity.* San Francisco: Jossey-Bass.

Freeman, J. (1979). How to discriminate against women without really trying. In J. Freeman (Ed.), *Women: A feminist perspective* (pp. 217–232). Palo Alto, CA: Mayfield.

Kohlberg, L. (1981). *The meaning and measurement of moral development.* Worchester, MA: Clark University Press.

Perry, W. (1970). *Forms of intellectual and ethical development in college years: A schema.* New York: Holt, Rinehart, & Winston.

INTRODUCTION

Mary F. Howard-Hamilton

S tanding on the Outside Looking In is a project that was born of intense personal reflections, actual experiences of students and faculty, and the need for a collection of stories and empirical research that provides an exhaustive look at the campus climate for graduate students of color. Many of the studies on underrepresented students of color are concisely presented in Pascarella and Terenzini's (2005) analysis of research on the cognitive, psychosocial, and environmental impact of postsecondary institutions on undergraduate students. Literature regarding the academic experiences of graduate students from underrepresented populations, however, is comparatively meager. Although researchers, governing bodies, and policy makers are increasingly concerned about the entry into postsecondary education and the consequent retention of underrepresented minority students, the topic has been examined primarily in relation to the undergraduate experience.

This volume offers a comprehensive examination of issues of access, retention, transition, and personal experiences for students of color in advanced-degree programs. The authors researched issues with the following questions in mind:

- What factors influence underrepresented students' consideration of advanced-degree programs?
- What factors affect students' choices of programs and institutions?
- Once in graduate school, what challenges do students face as they transition into degree programs?
- What factors enable students of color to persist?
- How can colleges and universities provide the support necessary to increase persistence and matriculation among graduate students of color?

Chapter 1, "The Advanced-Degree Pipeline for Graduate and Professional Students of Color," is written by a group of scholars who successfully navigated the doctoral Higher Education Program at Indiana University–Bloomington. They became a research group called "The Dream Team," led by Carla Morelon-Quainoo and including Rachelle Winkle-Wagner, Susan Johnson, John Kuykendall, Ghangis Carter, Ted Ingram, Dwyane Smith, Lidia Santiague, and Keon Gilbert. This group began to serve some of the purposes that the research suggests are important: mentoring and supporting students, engaging in research, and creating a community of racial ethnic peers. All the authors have either completed the doctorate or are near completion (see About the Authors, p. 227). This chapter presents the results of a qualitative grounded theory study exploring the access and decision-making process of African American and Latino graduate students at predominantly White private and public institutions. The findings suggest that the following factors influence doctoral students' consideration of the feasibility of graduate school: appropriate levels of available financial aid, program and institutional reputation, access to a critical mass of students and faculty of color, religious commitment, and desire to use the degree to give back to family and community.

Linda DeAngelo, in chapter 2, "Can I Go?" examines the intersection of race/ethnicity and institutional type, exploring the influences of the culture and mission of comprehensive institutions on student aspirations and preparation for the Ph.D. Using over 100 interviews of faculty and students, this chapter explores Ph.D. preparation.

The focus of chapter 3, "Financing the Dream," is financial aid; the authors, Susan Johnson, John Kuykendall, and Rachelle Winkle-Wagner, explore the impact of financial aid on graduate/professional education in general and on doctoral and professional students from underrepresented minority populations in particular. Financial aid is one of the primary, if not the paramount, variable for African American and Latino students when considering the pursuit of graduate education.

Chapter 4, "The Path to Graduate School in Science and Engineering for Underrepresented Students of Color," by Marybeth Gasman, Laura Perna, Susan Yoon, Noah Drezner, Valerie Lundy-Wagner, Enakshi Bose, and Shannon Gary, investigates the transition from undergraduate to graduate education in the fields of science, technology, engineering, and math (STEM). In particular, the authors examine the factors that may influence students' decisions to pursue graduate work and ultimately their entrance into the professoriate.

Chapter 5, "Countering Master Narratives of the 'Perpetual Foreigner' and 'Model Minority,'" by Oiyan Poon and Shirley Hune, begins our discussion of specific racial/ethnic groups in graduate programs. The authors argue that Asian American doctoral students bear "hidden injuries of race" despite their increased numbers. Viewed not as Americans but as foreigners, and stereotyped as a "successful" minority group, they are marginalized in the academy, where their concerns and unequal treatment at all junctures of the pipeline are ignored. The chapter includes the results of a qualitative questionnaire distributed nationally to Asian American doctoral students.

Chapter 6, "Latinas in Doctoral and Professional Programs," by Juan Carlos González, examines the similarities and differences in the support systems and challenges faced by Latinas in doctoral and professional programs. Thirteen 1- to 2-hour semistructured interviews were conducted with Latina doctoral students attending public research institutions in the United States who had been in their programs for 3 or more years. Using production theory, the researchers conduct a phenomenological analytic study of Latina doctoral experiences. Findings include the importance of support systems, challenge, resistance methods, and issues with claiming their academic voice.

Terrell Strayhorn explores the experiences of African American male graduate students in chapter 7, "African American Male Graduate Students." This chapter provides a detailed analysis of factors associated with enrollment in graduate school for a nationally representative sample of African American males. Specifically, a set of noncognitive factors is included in the statistical model, as such factors may prove to be invaluable in increasing the number of African American male graduate students.

Chapter 8, "Oppositional Stances of Black Female Graduate Students," by Venice Thandi Sulé, explores the oppositional knowledge gained by African American female graduate students at predominantly White institutions. Women from varied economic backgrounds, ages, and stages in their doctoral programs were interviewed to understand their experiences, with the finding that many of the women have a powerful woman as a role model early in life and that this greatly influences the women's academic goals and their resiliency in advanced-degree programs. The women are also motivated to succeed in graduate school by social justice goals.

Chapter 9, "'God Has a Purpose and I Landed Somewhere,'" by Mary Howard-Hamilton, Kandace Hinton, and Ted Ingram, addresses the philosophical topic of spirituality and faith among graduate students of color. The findings from qualitative data collected at two institutions indicate that graduate students of color rely on their spiritual roots as they navigate through their doctoral or professional programs. Spirituality is central during the admission and selection process, sustains them during the matriculation process, and serves as an impetus for giving back to their communities.

Chapter 10, "Our Stories of Mentoring and Guidance in a Higher Education and Student Affairs Program," by Kandace Hinton, Valerie Grim, and Mary Howard-Hamilton, discusses the importance of graduate students having mentors during their educational process. The authors use a case-study approach, relating the experiences of one African American female graduate student. This chapter specifically examines the strategies applied by the student and her mentoring team in every phase of the educational process.

The book is summarized in chapter 11 by Frank Tuitt, who weaves together the various issues, cases, policies, and recommendations presented in the book for a synopsis of how faculty, administrators, and graduate programs can protect and promote graduate students of color. Moreover, recommendations are given to students of color so that they may be able to manage the barrage of challenges in their respective programs as well as within the university environment.

The editors hope that this book will be helpful for students seeking a voice that validates the day-to-day experiences and situations that they encounter on college campuses. This book is also written to share conversations, concepts, and constructive criticism that typically may not be read or heard by individuals who are leaders at our institutions so that they may begin to remove the barriers that keep marginalized students "standing on the outside looking in."

Reference

Pascarella, E. T., & Terenzini, P. T. (2005). *How college affects students: A third decade of research* (Vol. 2). San Francisco: Jossey-Bass.

I

THE ADVANCED-DEGREE PIPELINE FOR GRADUATE AND PROFESSIONAL STUDENTS OF COLOR

Issues of Access and Choice

Carla Morelon-Quainoo, Susan D. Johnson, Rachelle Winkle-Wagner, John A. Kuykendall III, Ted N. Ingram, Ghangis D. Carter, Keon Gilbert, Dwyane G. Smith, and Lilia Santiague

Over the course of several decades, the United States has been inundated with media coverage and depictions of the increasingly diverse landscape in which we live. As this country's population becomes less homogeneous, there is a pressing need to respond to the sociological, political, economic, and educational challenges that arise from this diversity. Compounding this issue is the reality that despite the increased number of racial minorities in higher education, they have not—as a group—advanced educationally (and consequently in other ways) in comparison to their White peers (Pathways to College Network, 2003). Yet, increasingly, a college degree is a requisite for social mobility (Carey, 2004).

Kingston and Clawson (1986) suggest that "graduate education provides a fast track to the most powerful and prestigious positions in the occupational distribution" (p. 314). Because graduate and professional students of color are underrepresented in graduate education, their potential for upward mobility toward desirable careers and toward high socioeconomic status is in peril. In an effort to understand this phenomenon among a population of first-generation graduate and professional matriculants, Golde (2000) believes we must "recognize that they are learning simultaneously to be professionals and successful students" (p. 200). Toward that end, this chapter delves deeper into perceptions of access and the decision-making process that students of color experience as they consider and matriculate in advanced-degree programs. Additionally, we offer suggestions for increasing the participation and educational attainment of these underrepresented groups in graduate and professional programs.

The aforementioned studies suggest that conversations about the linkages between educational attainment and career aspirations have shifted from an emphasis on a baccalaureate to a graduate degree. Although the demographics of the United States continue to shift, the educational attainment of underrepresented groups has increased to match with these trends. Warburton, Bugarin, and Nunez (2001) reported that African Americans received only 7.2% of all doctoral degrees, but three years later their representation dropped to 5.1%. Representation of Latinos is equally disturbing: associate's degree, 7.7%; bachelor's, 5.5%; master's, 4.1%; doctorate, 3.2%; and first-year professional, 4.6%. These alarming rates have generated scholars' interest in understanding the barriers to graduate and professional education for these populations and have served as the impetus for this study.

We are in agreement with two assertions that Golde (2005) proffers: relatively little research has (a) distinguished the differences between undergraduate and graduate attrition or (b) studied the institutional environment to determine its impact on this phenomenon. Our study attempts to fill this gap in the literature by exploring the manner in which institutional characteristics shape graduate students' perceptions of access and degree-program decision-making processes. With this aim in mind, it is important to determine which elements of the institutional culture and its characteristics influence students' ability to consider and matriculate into graduate programs.

Literature Review

Two elements that have strong influence on the process of choosing a college for graduate and professional students of color are the type and amount of financial aid available in relation to the costs of tuition, fees, and related expenses (Manski & Wise, 1983). In many cases, financial aid may ultimately determine not only whether a student will attend a particular college but whether the student will attend college at all. Matriculants are increasingly required to fund a greater portion of their education, which has led to increased debt for students at the end of their program. Debt management is a serious issue for all students, and it is conceivable that a student may create a debt level that outweighs the benefits associated with education. In 2002, St. John reported that African American students were carrying a lighter debt load than their White and Asian peers. His study also revealed that 69% of African Americans in college had dropped out because of high loan debt. Additionally, his study revealed that 59% of the African American student-loan borrowers felt "extremely" or "very" burdened by student-loan payments (p. 1).

The continuity choice construct conceptualizes the linkages between financial aid and the outcomes of education (St. John, Asker, & Hu, 2001). If educational outcomes are treated as a sequence of interconnected choices, it is possible to understand the significant decisions that graduate and professional students of color must consider as they progress through their educational careers. The capacity to meet financial obligations (e.g., tuition and fees, room and board, books, living expenses, conference travel, and other graduate-related fees) can often become a greater barrier than other issues such as academic preparedness (St. John, 2003). That is, even if a student is academically prepared, financial hurdles may prevent or delay educational attainment. Current shifts in institutional policy also mitigate the traditional intentions of financial aid, lessening the potential to make higher education affordable and accessible to those who might not otherwise be able to pursue postsecondary education (Arnone, 2004; Burd, 2001; Campaigne & Hossler, 1998; Mortenson, 1991).

The process of choosing a college, another aspect of access, has been primarily studied at the undergraduate level. The choice process at the undergraduate level is affected by such factors as students' social networks (Freeman, 1997; Perna, 2000), race and culture (Freeman, 1999a; Freeman & Thomas, 2002), financial capital or financial barriers (Freeman, 1997), high school experiences (Freeman & Thomas, 2002; McDonough, 1997), and the perceived economic outcomes of college degrees (Freeman, 1999b). This study adds to the college-choice literature, focusing on the choice process of students of color considering advanced-degree programs.

Some scholars contend that it is the institutional culture and climate that inevitably impress on students' desire or willingness—once they are introduced to the institution—to complete the application process or to persist once they enroll in graduate programs (Hurtado, Milem, Clayton-Pederson, & Allen, 1998). Among the factors that influence the graduate student experience are socialization (Turner, 2002), mentoring (Boice, 1992; Cosgrove, 1986), student-faculty interaction (Hancock, 2002), marginalization/isolation (Beoku-Betts, 2004; Gay, 2004; Hurtado et al., 1998; Turner,

2002), difficulty in transitioning (Davidson & Foster-Johnson, 2001), and lack of faculty or administrative support (Fox, 1984; Turner, 2002).

As access becomes less realistic and persistence becomes a struggle for a prospective student, the decision-making becomes more entangled and could possibly muddle one's vision of educational attainment, particularly at the graduate/professional level and specifically for students of color. Should this phenomenon continue to unfold as it has, this group of students will find it increasingly difficult to consider graduate/professional programs. Consequently, the pipeline could potentially become less diverse, and the American educational landscape will never become as diverse as its people. This creates a conundrum and serves as the basis for this study, whose methods are outlined in the next section.

Method

Reflecting on the way in which students of color choose their advanced-degree programs provides a unique view of students' perceptions of the socialization process. We examined the influence of institutional characteristics on students of color in graduate and professional programs as they consider and matriculate into their programs. The study was guided by the following research questions: What factors influenced students' decisions to pursue graduate school? and What role did financial aid play in students' ability to consider graduate school?

Selection of Participants and Study Site

This chapter reports data from a study of two institutions: a predominantly White, public, midwestern, research-extensive institution (Midwest University) and a predominantly White, private, northeastern, elite institution (Northeast University). The study included 28 participants.

Names of minority students within one doctoral and two professional schools at Midwest University (MU) were obtained by permission in order to contact students of color within each respective school. At Northeast University (NU), the dean granted permission for the study and assisted in the recruitment of participants. In both instances, the research team sent Institutional Review Board–approved invitation messages that detailed the purpose of the study and provided the researchers' contact information. Upon receiving responses from students, the team arranged mutually convenient times for focus groups. At least two members of the research team were present at each focus group. As one team member directed questions to the students, the other observed the interview process and recorded field notes. Interviews were tape-recorded, with the understanding that pseudonyms would be used when reporting results and that tapes would be destroyed upon conclusion of the study.

About Our Sample

MU participants consisted of 14 first-year doctoral students of color in education, law, and sociology. Because the sample is small and easily identified, we offer only general descriptions here. The sample included 10 doctoral and 4 professional students, comprising 3 Latina, 1 Dominican, and 10 African American/Black students. There were 5 males and 9 females participating at MU. Administrative offices in the various programs granted permission to investigators to contact students of color in their areas.

The NU sample included 14 participants from the following departments: computer science (2), urban studies and planning (2), technology and policy (2), chemistry (4), business (2), political science (1), and electrical engineering (1). The demographics of the participants at NU were as follows: 6 Latino/a, 1 Arab American, 1 Chinese American, and 6 African Americans; there were 8 men and 6 women. A dean provided access to the participants at this institution.

Qualitative Approach

Employing the focus group approach (Denzin & Lincoln, 2003) and semistructured interviews, we attempted to uncover several dimensions of first-year graduate and professional students' experiences when considering and matriculating into their respective graduate programs. Through direct inquiry and interaction with the study participants (Denzin & Lincoln, 2003), we attempted to capture the essence of the choice and transition process in their own words. Qualitative methods afforded participants the freedom to choose aspects of their educational process on which to elaborate. Exploratory in nature, a semistructured interviewing technique allowed for an in-depth examination of issues of access, choice, and persistence that arose while the students' considered whether to pursue and complete a graduate degree (Miles & Huberman, 1994).

Data Collection

We conducted focus groups, following Denzin and Lincoln's (2003) conceptualization of the technique, in which the interviewer "directs the inquiry and the interaction among respondents" (p. 71). Focus group interviews were used to capture the true essence of participants' experiences as they attempted to gain access to and considered completing graduate school.

Data Analysis

Constant comparative methods (Glasser & Strauss, 1967; Lincoln & Guba, 1985) were used to analyze the data collected in this study. According to Lincoln and Guba, this method "stimulates thought that leads to both descriptive and explanatory categories" (p. 341). In grounded theory work, data analysis develops in a continuous manner, and small units of data are used to develop a theoretical model. We transcribed the data verbatim and then collectively examined the transcripts to conduct open coding. In the open coding process, themes emerge from the data and are grouped together in categories (Denzin & Lincoln, 2003; Strauss & Corbin, 1998). Two members of the research team independently coded the data, and the analyses were compared. After open coding was conducted manually, the data were entered into coding software.

Trustworthiness

To ensure that participants' responses were accurately interpreted and recorded, we shared an initial draft of the interview transcriptions and findings with focus group participants. Through this process, participants later provided feedback or necessary revisions to the transcripts. Additionally, all codes were checked by the entire research team, ensuring that the codes could be re-created by others, a step that added to the trustworthiness of the analysis and elicited rich, thick descriptions.

Findings

Although there were numerous themes that emerged from the data, here we focus particularly on the perceptions of students of color that are relevant to access and choice. That is, the participants described the factors that influenced their decision to attend a particular institution: reputation and rankings, financial aid, perceptions of faculty support, and the campus climate related to diversity.

Reputation and Rankings and the Influence on Access

We learned that reputation and rankings were of primary importance to MU and NU students' perceptions of access. Both groups of students consistently explained that institutional, departmental, and faculty reputation were significant factors when selecting an institution. A professional student from

MU reported that his primary consideration in choosing an institution was "rankings, rankings, rankings." Students at MU tended to apply to public institutions ranked similarly or higher than MU; the NU students did the same, but they primarily focused on Ivy League institutions. When asked why rankings were so important, an MU student responded, "I got a job at a law firm after my first year of college, and that is all they look for, how well your school is ranked. Those are the students who get interviewed for jobs." Several students offered similar comments, illustrating the connections between rankings and external perceptions of program and faculty quality.

An NU doctoral student noted that her primary reason for choosing the institution was that "the faculty are famous here; it is the best in the country." This comment is reflective of doctoral students from both institutions who were attracted to the institution because faculty members were conducting research in the students' areas of interest. The students generally did not discuss close relationships with their professors. Yet the majority of NU students still wanted to work with the faculty, often because they were "famous" in their fields.

MU students considered equally or more highly ranked programs at other public institutions. Even though this group of doctoral and professional students considered institutional and departmental reputation as important factors, they were more likely to cite the importance of being able to pursue degrees and research in their areas of interest. A female doctoral student wanted to pursue two distinct areas, and both were located at MU. When she was deciding which institution to attend, MU was an easy choice: "It was very important for me to find a school that would allow me to do both without having to compromise one because I was just really serious about doing both of them." Even though rankings and reputation were important, it was the availability of majors that swayed her decision to enroll at MU, not the rankings alone. One of the professional MU students, Megan, offered a similar perspective in relation to rankings and availability of majors: "I want to study Internet law, and MU is one of the top programs for Internet law, and that was high on my list."

While institutional or departmental reputation and ranking were an integral component of students' decision-making processes, financial accessibility often was an additional significant factor.

Financial Aid and Perceptions of Access

Unlike the NU students, the MU students appeared to put a higher priority on access via financial support than on institutional prestige. MU students chose their final institution largely because the financial assistance package was more attractive. For example, one first-year African American female doctoral student in education at MU recalled, "For me money was very important. Whether or not I will be funded was *the* main deciding factor for coming to this school." Like many of the participants from MU, if she had been unable to secure funding, she would not have been able to attend; thus, financial assistance became a gatekeeper to her degree. So the financial package outweighed the institutional prestige for many MU students. Simply speaking, students at the public institution made an economic decision to forgo more elite institutions that did not offer financial packages that were as rewarding.

Another African American woman enrolled in her first year of law school at MU summarized her choice to attend law school this way: "I looked for a scholarship. . . . It came down to money." The ability to earn a scholarship became her only means to pursue an advanced degree; it acted as a gatekeeper. One African American professional student remembered her desire to attend a top-flight private institution, recounting, "The cost was just too much for me." Thus, real and perceived financial barriers can influence the choices of students to attend particular institutions for their advanced-degree programs.

Despite the predominant message of aversion to loans, this attitude was not as pervasive among the professional students at either institution. Although no one at either institution wanted to consider loans a part of his or her financial equation, the professional students were more likely to concede that it was a necessary part of their educational attainment goals. It is important to add, however, that students from both institutions considered their programs worth the potential incurred debt levels. Participants also spoke often about the influence that their NU and MU degrees would have on salary potential, adding that their school's academic reputation and alumni presence in the field provided additional leverage.

We also learned about the influence of pipeline programs on students' choice process. Quite a few of the participants explained that summer internships and research programs during their undergraduate years introduced them to various aspects of graduate education. Students attributed to the experience their desire to conduct research, become a professor, or pursue a certain major. One student provided an especially insightful comment: "And I got into a minority research program back home as part of the NIH [National Institutes of Health], and from that I got exposure to meetings, national meetings, and other opportunities." Another student offered a similar comment about her summer NIH experience: "You meet people who are just like you and trying to do the same things, and it shows you that you can do it." It appears, based on these and other participants' comments, that the pipeline programs expose them to the norms in their field, pair them with student and faculty with similar interests and aspirations, and instill in them the confidence necessary for academic success.

In sum, financial-aid grant packages attracted students to the institution, and summer experiences prepared them, but students mentally and comprehensively surveyed the institutional landscape, as indicated by the data presented in the following sections. It appears, based on participants' conversations, that they were looking for a "complete package." That is, it was important to the students to find an institution that expressed an interest in attracting (e.g., through financially beneficial offerings) and retaining them. In the next section, we outline students' perceptions of the relevance of institutional support structures.

Support Structures

When asked to list issues that were integral in their selection of an institution, students identified institutional, faculty, and peer support as major considerations in their eventual decisions. Fella observed that it was important "to see how the school fits. Fit, it has to do with the ability to smooch with people, and it is important to know people." He added that he chose NU rather than another Ivy League institution because of the predetermined values that people have a tendency to impose on students. At NU, he did not feel this type of pressure. Several students from NU indicated that they were surprised to see that most students at NU were "normal," which—in their own descriptions—amounted to well-rounded students who were socially and academically adept. "The environment is very important," maintained Francis, alluding to the importance of institutional support.

Both graduate and professional students expressed that being able to engage in scholarly research with faculty played a large role in their choice of academic departments and institutions. This opportunity provided a way to learn the proverbial academic ropes and interact with faculty on a social— and to some extent a personal—level. One of the most interesting revelations that emerged from our interviews was the influence that faculty had in shaping the way that students learn. For example, Cy, a professional NU student, was reflective of all participants who clearly anticipated reaping the rewards of working with or conducting research with their faculty: "When I graduated, I planned to apply for a research internship in both the industry and academia, and I think coming from a major research university makes a difference. My adviser is pretty well known in the field, and if I publish with him, I feel like I have more credibility when I apply for those types of jobs."

Cy's statement relates to the issue of faculty prestige, whereby students—particularly at NU—enjoyed the benefits of working with a professor who was well renowned.

Relying on faculty support appears to have been a phenomenon more prominent among the doctoral students than among the professional students. A comment by an NU student offers a reflection that neatly encapsulates the experience of most of our participants. Francis described the ideal type of faculty support as "an interaction that is not just business and research. An interaction where you are my colleague and we are here to work together. We are colleagues, we are friends, and we are doing research together. Rather than something where 'this is the boss, and where are my results?' That kind of an environment I would not like." Francis frames the faculty-student relationship as collegial and even personal.

Anna, a Latina doctoral student at MU, offered a similar observation: "I know the school has a strong department, but that really means nothing if I have no support." Anna had a particularly close relationship with her faculty adviser, who was also Latino. Lisa, an MU doctoral student, noted the way that she felt about the program and institution: "I want the support. It's very important. It would be the difference between me staying here and leaving." Lisa's comments intimate that faculty and department-level support of her research interests were integral to her decision to persist in her program.

On the other hand, Tony, an MU professional student, explained, "I came from a really big undergraduate research university, and we didn't get any support, and I didn't expect to get any here at the law school. I was always brought up to believe you should find your own way." Tony's summation that law school is about finding "your own way" is an illustration of the individualistic atmosphere in the law school. Another NU student offered a totally different scenario: "I think having a stipend [is good] when you have one, but you work with them [the faculty] and do what they force you to do or they will not pay you. It's better to have your own funding so you can do what you need to do." In this case, the student saw the student-professor relationship as more like a business transaction than a personal or collegial relationship.

Francis, an NU student, found that the faculty were more engaging during a recruiting trip than she anticipated. She told us that it was important to find herself in an institution where professors were "normal," indicating that she wanted to be able to interact with faculty members on a personal level. Such idealistic notions were quickly dashed for some NU students who mistakenly visited professors without scheduling appointments. Unlike the

NU students, MU graduate and professional students did not appear to be hesitant to approach their faculty to ask for help or to secure educational opportunities such as research assistantships. NU students spoke about a worry of "bothering" some of the well-known professors if they were to ask for research opportunities. Some eventually made unscheduled visits to certain professors, only to be turned away by their administrative assistants. Comments about accessibility to research projects with faculty were mixed for NU, with some participants describing their faculty as "nice," "laid-back," and "approachable." Others described their faculty as "mean" and suggested that specific faculty were only interested in furthering their own careers by overworking their graduate students. The students generally did not discuss close relationships with their professors. Yet the majority of NU students still wanted to work with the faculty, often because they were "famous" in their fields.

In addition to the necessity of faculty support, many of the participants indicated the necessity of finding support among their peers. The students of color often talked about relying on one another to succeed in their programs, as if they were not getting support from faculty or the institution more generally. It appears that even though the students developed friendships with students and faculty of all races, it is the people within their own ethnic groups with whom they felt most comfortable. Leslie found comfort in another African American graduate student: "So he understands how it is to be an underrepresented student at this institution and just have a lot of work to do." She added that she calls him whenever she needs to express frustration and relieve stress associated with her life as a graduate student. When we asked Francis where she finds support, she spoke of her Hispanic friend: "[We] speak Spanish for a while and [are] more able to express ourselves." She added that she also meets other Hispanic friends and that talking in Spanish enables them to express themselves differently, suggesting that they are able to converse more comfortably in their native language and among native friends. Probing further, we asked about the importance of speaking to other Hispanic students, and Francis responded, "You don't feel completely new. You know people have been through it and out of it and are doing a good job. It's kind of a thing where they did it, I can do it." This comment is very similar to one made by Leslie, who told us the following about her African American colleague at NU: "He understands what's going on, and he's going to have to go through it too." These comments underscore the necessity of balancing student diversity with having peer support from people with whom students racially identify. Also relevant to the issue

of diversity, the following section provides insight into the way that perceptions of diversity, or a lack of diversity, influenced students' choice of institution or department.

Diversity

For most of the MU participants, their eventual choice of institutions was
highly dependent on their perception of the presence of a "critical mass" of
students and faculty of color in the institution and/or department. Students
explained that they usually began to assess the institution's mission regarding
diversity by reviewing the institution's publications and its Web site, which
they assumed would accurately reflect the campus environment. The
doctoral students' perception of the extent to which the institution reflected
diversity was dependent on the department in which they matriculated.
Some students felt there was adequate (but minimal) representation of
minorities. One student felt that the institution's espoused mission of diversity was not one that was also enacted. An education student from MU
noted, "I expected diversity. I see some number of students of color. I don't
see too much of a *push* for embracing diversity. So, it's here, but I'm not so
sure how much it's *embraced* or how welcome it is." Leslie's analysis of NU
was similar: "In terms of, like, Black people, Hispanic people, they're not
really here and on the graduate level. They are, like, I don't really see, you
know, any Black graduate students. I probably know like 10." Renee, a
chemistry major, cited the following: "I am in chemistry, and there are 50 of
us total, and . . . African Americans are 2%. In my opinion, that is not
diverse to me." At both NU and MU, the students voiced frustration with
the lack of diversity among students.

The professional students at both NU and MU consistently mentioned
the importance of being able to interact with other students of color in their
program and mentioned the plentiful number of student activities sponsored
by minority student organizations in their professional school and at the
institutional level. Tony, an MU professional student, believed that "getting
to know other Black students" helped him to adjust to school. On the other
hand, NU students were less likely to consider diversity as important. One
student felt that attending another school filled with people like himself was
not reflective of the "real world," and he wanted to interact with all types of
people.

Among most MU participants, however, there was discussion of the
importance of institutional affirmation of their presence on campus. Even
though students made a conscious choice and a conscious sacrifice to attend
an institution located in a culturally isolated environment, they lamented the

comparatively meager social outlets and campus activities that complemented or affirmed their culture.

Another difference that we found was to whom the students delegated the ownership of diversity. Doctoral students felt strongly that their departments and the institution should proactively engage in bolstering diversity. One student even shared disappointment that Latinos seemed absent from the curriculum. She summarized, "It makes you feel like you don't exist." On the other hand, law students seemed to accept the notion that diversity was not something that they should expect in their program. NU students seemed to acquiesce to the fact that the graduate student body is not as diverse as they would desire. When we asked Monique what the lack of diversity meant to her, she responded, "Within my program, I can't really fault the institution for that. I am 25% of my class. So, we've got lots of minorities. At the level we are at, you have to be completely color-blind and country blind, everything. You have to admit people based solely on the merits of their application." This comment also connects to the discussion about rankings. In this case, the prestige of the institution seems more important to Monique than her desire for diversity. It is worth noting, however, that NU is located in one of the country's most diverse cities. Therefore, some students found it easier to ameliorate the impact of cultural isolation by immersing themselves in the large community of the city. Despite this convenience, several students lamented being the only person of color or the only female in their class or program, particularly in the sciences. One African American chemistry student at NU said, "I think there is maybe one other African American woman in the Ph.D. program." The students also acknowledged, however, that different forms of diversity (e.g., cultural, ethnic, geographical, economic) were also important.

Students' expectations of finding an inclusive environment included faculty and student support, professionalism among faculty, diversity, and a "strong minority networking group." The students believed that this type of environment would convey an institutional- and school-level commitment to their personal, academic, and professional growth. For example, Anna, a Latino education student at MU, reflected on her friendship with an African American student: "Having a friend here who . . . in a way had experienced society at one point or another . . . in similar ways . . . really has helped me, having that [friendship], that network." This comment also relates to the importance of peer support. Comments from Reginald, a professional NU student, echoed Anna's sentiments: "When there aren't that many minorities in the class, it's pretty much a tight-knit group sometimes. Everyone knows each other. We all know each other [all the Black students], and we get together once a month for dinner or a party or something. There's a bond there, even though [we have] limited numbers. There's a good social network there, and they all help each other out." In addition to expressing the need for a critical mass, these comments further perpetuate the importance of fostering spaces—either formal or informal—on campus where students of color can support one another.

At MU, the small college town added to a lack of comfort for the students of color. Citing even the most basic of needs, Tony was concerned that "there was no place to get your hair cut, there is no place that really sells, like, Black products, [and] these other little things kind of add up to be a little discomforting." For Tony, and for many of the students in this study, the lack of hair products sent a message that the business community was unaware of their needs, adding another layer of inconvenience for students who were then required to drive to a major city for such basic materials.

NU, on the other hand, is in a more diverse city, as previously stated. Thus, the lack of diversity on campus could in some ways be mitigated by the city. For example, one Latino student in chemistry noted, "There is a good Latino community here [in the city], but there are also other people from different cultures." He concluded that this was an integral factor in his decision to attend NU. He continued to reflect on the importance of having another Puerto Rican friend at NU, highlighting the importance of interacting with others from a similar ethnic or racial group.

Discussion and Implications

At the outset of this project, we were interested in understanding the graduate and professional experience related to access and choice from the perspective of students of color in advanced-degree programs. In regard to access, we quickly learned that reputation trumps type and amount of aid for students attending the elite private institution, whereas students at the highly ranked public institution were much more concerned about affordability, or perceptions of affordability. Students also attributed their potential for success to their experiences in summer internship and research programs. The choice process was additionally influenced by perceptions of the extent to which faculty support and a critical mass of people of color were evident. Finally, students' decision to matriculate into their programs was shaped by their perception of the institution's environment, whether it "fit," whether the department included "famous" and/or collegial faculty, and whether it had a diverse student body. In consideration of these emergent themes, we provide several recommendations for research and practice that reenvision the role of socialization of the student in ways that promote success and educational attainment:

1. *Facilitate access by creating holistic baccalaureate summer experiences and graduate admission financial packages.* Students from both institutions clearly benefited tremendously from their diverse summer experiences. Whether they attended summer law camps or NIH research programs, students easily made the connections between those experiences and their level of preparation for the rigors of graduate study. Institutions interested in affecting the pipeline of future faculty, administrators, and other professionals should aspire to create, sustain, or expand programs to increase access for underrepresented students. More important, institutions should create financial incentives for students who participate in such programs and then enroll in the institution. Students at NU were clearly willing to forgo more lucrative packages from equally elite institutions because they considered institutional reputation to be more important. MU students, on the other hand, chose the institution whose price tag was more palatable. When students are weighing one institution against another, perhaps it is worth studying the threshold at which students are swayed one way or another. Institutions located in cities with expensive lifestyles should consider offering affordable housing as a part of their financial award. When institutional reputation is an absolute advantage, it might behoove the institution to try to increase access by developing innovative financial-aid packages (e.g., engage in conversations about ways for students to utilize their talents, create opportunities to work in different units based on research interests, make on-campus graduate housing an attractive offer, provide conferencing packages, recruit through pipeline programs that promise financial assistance).

2. *Create an environment that introduces, promotes, and sustains interest in graduate school and research.* Because NU is an elite institution, we were alarmed to learn that students there were struggling to become academically successful in their course work. Equally alarming were the measures that students were willing to pursue in an effort to conduct research with renowned faculty. Before students become disillusioned with the process, institutions should consider reframing their environments in ways that highlight the true meaning and rewards of research. For example, faculty seeking tenure should be supported in their efforts to mentor students, and tenured faculty should be encouraged to mentor junior faculty in this respect. Academic

departments should also consider the importance of aligning new students' interests and backgrounds with available resources. As students proceed through the program, they should be encouraged to interact with faculty and students in a way that reflects students' unique contributions rather than simply repeating what they have learned. Such programming should expose students to various aspects of the culture and encourage their feedback about their experiences.

3. *Assess the impact of perceived institutional and departmental diversity on admissions and recruiting efforts.* Diversity is important to students of color; therefore, it is important that institutions better understand the impact of institutional culture on their capacity to diversify the student body, particularly because our findings indicate the necessity of minority peer-group support. Again, we suggest implementing pipeline programs with minority-serving institutions (e.g., historically Black colleges and universities [HBCUs], Hispanic-serving institutions [HSIs], and tribal colleges) and urban institutions through their undergraduate programs. In addition, institutions could reward faculty, staff, and students whose innovative ideas promote diversity at the institutional level. Because the students in our study were impressed with diverse faculty, including female professors, we suggest that institutions continue to support faculty recruitment and retention plans that diversity their professoriate. Once faculty of color are at the institution, careful attention should be paid to the responsibilities of these minority faculty: if there are too few faculty of color, students of color still will not have enough faculty of color as role models and mentors, and the faculty may burn out. We do not suggest that having a more diverse faculty is the only solution; however, it is important for all students to feel that the institution values their presence by recruiting and retaining others who look like them.

4. *Clarify the impact of faculty socialization on students of color in comparison to their White peers (research collaborations, teaching assistantships, graduate assistantships, field placements, summer intern opportunities, and the like).* In each instance, faculty support plays a critical role, in the sense that faculty are the purveyors of knowledge and disciplinary norms, they are the source of intellectual discourse and research, and they can easily avail students of professional and social contacts in

their fields. Without faculty support, many students have the potential to become perpetual students, ever revolving through institutional doors but never evolving into their full academic potential. Faculty support can be realized by encouraging and rewarding practices that can be institutionalized at the departmental level (e.g., structured student-faculty interaction, faculty inclusion of graduate students in research, social networking, social and academic mentoring). It is important for institutions to find ways to support students as they acclimate themselves into the institution and to discard practices that impose on the unique identities and experiences that students bring to their new institution.

Conclusion

Graduate students of color face multiple barriers to their academic success and educational attainment. Inadequate financial, academic, and social support proves particularly detrimental to the ability of underrepresented minority students to thrive in a sometimes uninviting graduate school environment. By understanding the environment in which graduate students of color find themselves and their consequent socialization, we can better prepare these students for their subsequent careers in academe.

References

American Association of Universities. (1998). *Committee on graduate education: Report and recommendations.* Washington, DC.

Arnone, M. (2004, January 30). 250,000 eligible students shut out of college, group says. *The Chronicle of Higher Education, 50*(21), A21.

Ayres, Q. W. (1983). Student achievement at predominantly White and predominantly Black universities. *American Educational Research Journal, 20,* 291–304.

Beoku-Betts, J. (2004). African women pursuing graduate studies in the sciences: Racism, gender bias, and third world marginality. *NWSA Journal, 16*(1), 116–135.

Boice, R. (1992). *The new faculty member: Supporting and fostering professional development.* San Francisco: Jossey-Bass.

Brazziel, W. F. Improving SAT scores: Pros, cons, methods. *Journal of Negro Education, 57,* 81–93.

Burd, S. (2001, March 2). Lack of need-based financial aid still impedes access to college for low-income students. *The Chronicle of Higher Education, 47*(25), A26.

Campaigne, D. A., & Hossler, D. (1998). How do loans affect the educational decisions of students? Access, aspirations, college choice, and persistence. In R.

Fossey & M. Bateman (Eds.), *Condemning students to debt* (pp. 85–104). New York: Teachers College Press.

Carey, K. (2004, May). *A matter of degrees: Improving graduation rates in four-year colleges and universities—Report by the Education Trust.* Retrieved August 19, 2004, from http://www2.edtrust.org/NR/rdonlyres/11B4283F-104E-4511-B0CA-1D30 23231157/0/highered.pdf.

Cosgrove, T. J. (1986). The effects of participation in a mentoring-transcript program for freshman. *Journal of College Student Personnel, 27*(2), 119–124.

Davidson, N. M., & Foster-Johnson, L. (2001). Mentoring in the preparation of graduate researchers of color. *Review of Educational Research, 71*(4), 549–574.

Denzin, N., & Lincoln, Y. (2003). *Collecting and interpreting qualitative methods.* Thousand Oaks, CA: Sage.

DesJardins, S., Ahlberg, D., & McCall, B. (2002). A temporal investigation of factors related to timely degree completion. *Journal of Higher Education, 73*(5), 555–581.

Fox, M. F. (1984). Women and higher education: Sex differentials in the status of students and scholars. In J. Freeman (Ed.), *Women: A feminist perspective* (pp. 240–247). Palo Alto, CA: Mayfield.

Freeman, K. (1997). Increasing African Americans' participation in higher education: African American high-school students' perspectives. *Journal of Higher Education, 68*(5), 523–551.

Freeman, K. (1999a). The race factor in African Americans' college choice. *Urban Education, 34*(1), 4–25.

Freeman, K. (1999b). Will college make a difference? Economic expectation and college choice. *College and University, 75*(2), 7–12.

Freeman, K., & Thomas, G. E. (2002). Black college and college choice: Characteristics of students who choose HBCUs. *Review of Higher Education, 25*(3), 349–358.

Gay, G. (2004). Navigating marginality en route to the professoriate: Graduate students of color learning and living in academia. *International Journal of Qualitative Studies in Education, 17*(2), 265.

Glasser, B. G., & Strauss, A. L. (1967). *The discovery of grounded theory.* Chicago: Aldine.

Golde, C. (2000). Should I stay or should I go? Student descriptions of the doctoral attrition process. *Review of Higher Education, 23*(2), 119–227.

Golde, C. (2005). The role of the department and discipline in doctoral student attrition: Lessons from four departments. *Journal of Higher Education, 76*(6), 669–700.

Green, P. E. (2001). The policies and politics of retention and access of African American students in public white institutions. In L. Jones (Ed.), *Retaining African Americans in higher education.* Sterling, VA: Stylus.

Hancock, D. R. (2002). Influencing graduate students' classroom achievement, homework habits and motivation to learn with verbal praise. *Educational Research, 44*(1), 83–95.

Hatch, L. R., & Mommsen, K. (1984). The widening gap in American higher education. *Journal of Black Studies, 14*(4), 457–476.

Hu, S., & Hossler, D. (1998). *The linkages of student price sensitivity with preferences to postsecondary institutions.* Paper presented at the annual meeting of the Association for the Study of Higher Education, Miami, FL.

Hurtado, S., Milem, J. F., Clayton-Pederson, A. R., & Allen, W. R. (1998). Enhancing campus climates for racial/ethnic diversity: Educational policy and practice. *Review of Higher Education, 21*(3), 279–302.

Kingston, P., & Clawson, J. (1986). Getting on the fast-track: Recruiting at an elite business school. *International Journal of Sociology and Social Policy, 5*(4), 1–17.

Kuh, G., Schuh, J., Whitt, E., & Associates. (1991). *Involving colleges.* San Francisco: Jossey-Bass.

Lincoln, Y. S., & Guba, E. G. (1985). *Naturalistic inquiry.* Newbury Park, CA: Sage.

Manning, K. (1992). A rationale for using qualitative research in student affairs. *Journal of College Student Development, 33,* 132–136.

Manski, C. F., with D. Wise. (1983). *College choice in America.* Cambridge, MA: Harvard University Press.

McDonough, P. M. (1997). *Choosing colleges: How social class and school structure opportunity.* New York: State University of New York Press.

Mehan, H., Hubbard, L., & Villanueva, I. (1994). Forming academic identities: Accommodation without assimilation among involuntary minorities. *Anthropology of Education Quarterly, 25,* 91–117.

Miles, M. B., & Huberman, A. M. (1994). *Qualitative data analysis: An expanded sourcebook* (2nd ed.). Thousand Oaks, CA: Sage.

Mortenson, T. (1991). Financial aid problems for dependent students from low income families. *Journal of Student Financial Aid, 20,* 32–41.

Myers, R. D. (2003). *College success programs: Executive summary.* Washington, DC: Pathways to College Network Clearinghouse. National Center for Education Statistics.

Office of Education Research and Improvement, U.S. Department of Education. (1999). *The condition of education.* Washington, DC: Government Printing Office.

Pathways to College Network. (2003). *A shared agenda: A leadership challenge to improve college access and success.* Washington, DC: Author.

Perna, L. W. (2000). Differences in the decision to attend college among African Americans, Hispanics, and Whites. *Journal of Higher Education, 71*(2), 117–141.

St. John, E. P. (2002). *The access challenge: Rethinking the causes of the new inequality* (Policy Issue Report No. 2002-01). Bloomington: Indiana Education Policy Center.

St. John, E. P. (2003). *Refinancing the college dream: Access, equal opportunity, and justice for taxpayers.* Baltimore: Johns Hopkins University Press.

St. John, E. P., Asker, E. H., & Hu, S. (2001). College choice and student persistence behavior: The role of financial policies. In M. B. Paulsen & J. C. Smart

(Eds.), *The finance of higher education: Theory, research, policy & practice* (pp. 419–436). New York: Agathon Press.

Strauss, A. L., & Corbin, J. (1998). *Basics of qualitative research: Techniques and procedures for developing grounded theory* (2nd ed.). Thousand Oaks, CA: Sage.

Tierney, W. (1997). Organizational socialization in higher education. *Journal of Higher Education*, 68(1), 1–16.

Trowler, P., & Knight, P. (1999). Organizational socialization and induction into universities: Reconceptualizing theory and practice. *Higher Education, 32*(7), 177–195.

Turner, C. S. V. (2002). Women of color in academe: Living with multiple marginality. *Journal of Higher Education, 73*(1), 74–93.

Turner, J. L., Miller, M., & Mitchell-Kernan, C. (2002). Disciplinary cultures and graduate education. *Emergences, 12*(1), 47–70.

U.S. Department of Education. (1999). *Enrollment in higher education.* Washington, DC: Author.

Warburton, E. C., Bugarin, R., & Nunez, A. (2001). *Bridging the gap: Academic preparation and postsecondary education success of first-generation students.* Statistical analysis report. Postsecondary descriptive analysis reports. Washington, DC: National Center for Education Statistics.

2

CAN I GO?

An Exploration of the Influence of Attending a Less Selective Institution on Students' Aspirations and Preparation for the Ph.D.

Linda DeAngelo

Just what matters for students in making the choice to pursue a Ph.D., especially if their postsecondary origins are at a less selective institution, and does what matters differ if they are underrepresented racial minority (URM) students? This question is important to consider given that students whose postsecondary education was in a research university are much more likely to earn a Ph.D. than are students with origins at less selective institutions such as comprehensive colleges and universities (National Science Foundation, 2006), even though these two institutional types educate similar proportions of the undergraduate population (Carnegie Foundation, 2001). The concentration of URM students at comprehensive colleges and universities only further compounds this disparity. In California, for example, at the flagship University of California system in fall 2002, American Indian, African American, and Latino/a students represented 16.5% of the undergraduate population (University of California Office of the President, 2002), whereas at the comprehensive California State University (CSU) system, URM students represented 33.1% of undergraduate enrollment (California State University, 2003). In addition, studies such as those of Weiler (1993) and Cole and Barber (2003) offer evidence that minority students have high degree expectations upon entering college, as high as or sometimes higher than majority students do, and yet they are less likely to enter postbaccalaureate programs.

Degree Aspirations Literature

Studies of the postbaccalaureate college choices of students receive little attention in the literature. The few studies that do focus on postbaccalaureate enrollment patterns do so without much regard to the institutional environment in which students participate (Perna, 2003; Weiler, 1993). Degree aspirations literature is also sparse, though it has been evolving in the past decade, and it does not examine aspirations for the Ph.D. directly, instead using a variable that includes both aspirations for the Ph.D. and for first-professional degrees. The early aspirations studies of Astin and Panos (1969) and Astin (1977) are useful to the extent that they identify student characteristics that are important for researchers to consider when evaluating students' aspirations, but they are less useful for understanding the role of institutional context in aspirations development. Pascarella (1984) cogently criticizes these studies for, among other things, not being able to identify "whether or not there are differential patterns of environmental influences on educational aspirations at different kinds of institutions" (p. 754).

To address this weakness, Pascarella (1984) used path analysis on a longitudinal sample of Caucasian men and women attending both selective and less selective institutions. As theorized, Pascarella found some differential patterns of environmental influences on aspirations. Notable were findings of a peer effect and a faculty effect on aspirations. In Pascarella's study, peer effect was measured by the level of academic and intellectual competition at a campus, indicating a positive relationship between competition and aspirations, although the effect is stronger at selective institutions than at less selective institutions. The faculty variable used in the study, impersonal and inaccessible faculty, had the expected negative relationship to aspirations, a finding that is consistently confirmed in studies of the relationship between student-faculty interaction and aspirations (Carter, 2001; Cole & Barber, 2003; Hearn, 1987; Oseguera, 2002).

In the first major study to examine postbaccalaureate aspirations with a focus on race/ethnicity, Carter (2001) used two longitudinal data sets to identify both individual and institutional factors involved in the development of degree aspirations for African American and Caucasian students. The study found different background predictors and substantially different strengths of some predictors for African American and Caucasian students. For instance, Carter found that socioeconomic status explains much more of the variance in the outcome for African American students than it does for Caucasian students. Caucasian students were much surer of their degree goals than were African American students, and thus, Carter suggests that the college environment might play a larger role in aspirations development for African American students. Carter also found that faculty contact and peer contact have a positive relationship to aspirations for African American students, whereas these same contacts appear less important to the aspirations of Caucasian students. In addition, large institutions were found to have a positive relationship to aspirations. Carter suggests that perhaps large institutions provide access to graduate students and knowledge about graduate study.

Cole and Barber (2003), who study career-choice aspirations rather than degree aspirations, downplay the effect of environmental and institutional context in their study of the factors that contribute to an interest in academia, attributing interest in being a college professor almost completely to college academic achievement, regardless of the race/ethnicity of the student. The researchers conclude that academic achievement is so critical to professoriate aspirations that the most important factor in URM students' interest in academia is that they attend a college or university at which they are likely to earn a high grade point average. Further, Cole and Barber suggest that given the preparation level of most URM students, the best institution is usually a less selective institution. In addition to finding that academic success, regardless of institution attended, is the single most important determinant in students' making the choice to become a college professor, Cole and Barber also have found differences in what attracts Caucasian and URM students to the professoriate. This finding about differences in attraction to the Ph.D. does not lead Cole and Barber to conclude that student mobility to advanced degrees might differ by race/ethnicity. But their finding, coupled with the findings of Pascaralla, Wolniak, Flowers, and Pierson (2004) and Carter (2001), seems to suggest that such a disparity might exist, and certainly this notion warrants further investigation.

Theoretical Framework

The study described in this chapter is guided by two theories: a theory of degree aspirations as posed by Carter (2001) and a theory of organizational and institutional socialization as discussed by Kamens (1981). The nature of much of the aspirations literature, though often interested in examining organizational and institutional influences, has focused almost exclusively on how the individual with his or her background and ability chooses to participate in the college environment. Although important in identifying students who have the propensity for advanced degrees, this theoretical framework used alone tends to ignore more systemic elements at work that may mediate student mobility and, given URM student enrollment patterns, may impede interest in and pursuit of the Ph.D. Thus, I employ both a theoretical lens with the student at the center and a theoretical lens that focuses on organizational and institutional socialization.

Degree Aspirations

Carter's (2001) aspirations model seeks to account for different degree aspirations among Caucasian and African American college students. This theoretical framework builds on status attainment theory (Blau & Duncan, 1967) by examining how and if aspirations result from social constraints or from students' fulfilling their goals without constraints. To this framework, Carter adds conceptualizations about the role of the institution that a student attends, noting that institutional characteristics and experiences need to be linked to theoretical perspectives of status attainment. Finally, Carter incorporates the premise that models of aspirations that are tested on Caucasian students are not sufficient to explain the aspirations of students of color because of their vastly different backgrounds, types of institutions attended, and experiences within those institutions. The findings of Pascarella et al. (2004) also support this conceptual underpinning. In sum, the model posits that degree aspirations are a function of students' individual backgrounds and circumstances, the institution they attend, and the influence of those institutions on students. The focus of this model remains firmly on the individual's actions and is easily reduced to variable influences that need to be accounted for (see Oseguera, 2002; Pascarella et al., 2004) and is not as useful to understanding more directly the effects and interplay of the environment.

Organizational and Institutional Socialization

A closer examination of organizational and institutional socialization complements and extends the conceptualizations of Carter (2001) so that we can understand how the institutional environment in which a student participates affects aspirations. Kamens (1981) argues that educational institutions vault students to adult status and are modern rites of passage that have replaced more localized initiation rituals. Using social allocation theory, he explains that if educational institutions are highly differentiated in their missions and in the eventual fates of their graduates, the institution itself will have a direct influence on the adult opportunities available to its graduates. Kamens goes on to state, "Students will accept in advance—and perhaps internalize—those definitions of themselves and learn those attitudes and skills appropriate for the positions they are later to occupy" (p. 113). Here the educational process or socialization function of an institution is in part about learning the likely occupational identities of graduates of an institution. When this learning is internalized, it affects student outcomes, and thus the educational experiences steer students to certain types of occupational futures.

Kamens (1981) discusses three ways that institutions might achieve these impacts: preentry effects, student-nonstudent effects, and intensification effects. Preentry effects reflect the fact that in a system in which the roles of institutions are well known, socialization can occur before a student enters. Student-nonstudent effects account for the status opportunities given to graduates and closed to nongraduates of an institution and, thus, for the socializing effects that institutions have on people who never come directly into contact with them. Intensification effects are the formal and informal socializing structures of an institution that provide information regarding the qualities that are important for future role performance.

Purpose

The purpose of this study is to examine the pathway to the Ph.D. for students who have their postsecondary origins in comprehensive colleges and universities, paying particular attention to the experiences of URM students and how they make their way within the institutional milieu in which they participate. This study is intended to expand on our understanding of aspirations development and preparation experiences for the Ph.D. at an institutional type that is much less likely to be the institution of origin of eventual doctoral degree holders and yet that holds the most promise in the near future in the further diversification of Ph.D. programs. Specifically, this study explores the interplay between the institutional environment of the comprehensive college or university and Ph.D. aspirations and asks how participation in this environment shapes interest in the Ph.D. and preparation for the Ph.D.

Methods

This study uses qualitative methodology, specifically individual interviews. The format of the interviews was unstructured, with the intention of allowing interviewees considerable leeway to structure their own account of how and when they developed degree aspirations for the doctorate and their experiences related to preparing to fulfill those aspirations. As Guba and Lincoln

(1981) describe, this format allows "interviewees [to] introduce to a considerable extent [their] notions of what [they] regard as relevant, instead of relying upon the investigator's notion of relevance" (p. 156).

Sample

Data for this study come from interviews of current master's and Ph.D. students who were registered at the University of California–Los Angeles during the winter quarter of 2002 and who hold bachelor's degrees from one of the 23 California State University (CSU) campuses, the comprehensive college/university system in California. Access to the subjects was provided by the UCLA Graduate Division, whose administration, as part of a 3-year effort titled the "CSU Outreach Project," was interested in learning how it might improve outreach efforts on the CSU campuses. In all, 122 interviews were completed between July and September 2002.

For the purposes of this study, only a subset of the interviews was analyzed. In order to isolate the experiences of students preparing for the Ph.D., only interviews of students who entered UCLA as Ph.D. students were analyzed, creating a sample of 56 students. These students represent 17 of the 23 CSU campuses, with students from the four urban Los Angeles County campuses making up 48% of the overall sample. Caucasian students make up 63% of the sample, followed by Mexican American/Latino students (22%), Native American students (4%), and Asian American/Pacific Islander students (4%). An additional 7% indicated that they considered themselves not to fit into any of those categories, and no African Americans were among the students interviewed.[1] Of the students, 35% indicated during the interview that they started their postsecondary education at a community college, and 20% stated that they were the first in their family to attend college. Students in the humanities, social sciences, life sciences, and physical sciences are about equally represented, and the sample includes a few students in education, engineering, and computer science.

Although students who had aspirations for the doctorate but were not successful in entering a doctoral program would have been a useful addition to the sample, identifying a potential pool of such subjects proved daunting. Thus, I chose to study only the success stories, in the hope that learning about successful pathways to the doctorate from a comprehensive college or university might allow for an understanding of how those pathways might be expanded to allow more students, especially URM students, to pursue the Ph.D.

Analysis

Data analysis proceeded using the constant-comparative method, as described by Lincoln and Guba (1985). During the initial read of the transcripts, I developed an informal list of codes through an inductive analytic process. Next, as themes began to emerge, and new data were added to a theme area, I compared the data to the theme as a whole. This began the process of generating theoretical properties for each theme, and the process of checking the incidents within a theme against the properties of the theme, as these properties became somewhat fixed and the analysis process became more deductive. Further, through a series of outreach events carried out by the UCLA Graduate Division, in which some of the interviewees participated, the emerging themes and conclusions were informally verified and checked.

Findings

Findings are clustered around three predominant areas: the role of faculty in aspirations development and preparation for the Ph.D., the role of research and other experiences in aspirations and preparation for the Ph.D., and the contribution of the general environment of the CSU to aspirations and preparation for the Ph.D. I discuss these three overarching areas and themes within these areas in relation to aspirations development and preparation at the individual level and then in the broader context of the college environment in which students participated at the CSU.

Aspirations Development

Among the students, there was almost an even split in when they initially gained Ph.D. aspirations. About half the students stated that upon matriculation to the CSU they already possessed some inkling that they intended to pursue an advanced degree. Caucasian students and students whose parents had attended college were much more likely to aspire to a Ph.D. at college entrance than were URM and first-generation students. Although the vast majority of the students who entered college with aspirations for the doctorate discussed experience at the CSU that had solidified their interest, the CSU experience itself was not as vital to aspirations development among these students as it was to those students who entered without degree aspirations.

For those students for whom the CSU experience was an integral part of their decision to pursue a Ph.D., the majority discussed specific encouragement and mentorship they received at the CSU that prompted them to consider themselves Ph.D. material and sparked their interest in continuing their education at that level. For URM and first-generation students, a particular type of mentorship proved important to aspirations development and, later, to preparation for the Ph.D. Students described mentors who did such things as walk up to them and tell them that they were graduate school material, approached them about special research programs and lab opportunities, and even called them at home after they had graduated to suggest that they come back and pursue further education. This type of mentorship, which I call "talent-seeker" mentorship, begins casually through a brief conversation initiated by a faculty member and develops into a full-blown mentorship relationship in which the professor guides the student and connects him or her to the types of experiences both inside and outside the campus that will prepare him or her to compete successfully for entrance into a doctoral program.

For many students, these talent-seeker mentorship relationships opened up an educational opportunity that had never before occurred to them or seemed a real possibility. Particularly illustrative of how these mentorship relationships begin are the comments of one URM sociology doctoral student who told of a professor who approached her after class and asked if she had even considered going to graduate school. The student stated, "I guess he thought I was doing well in the class." The scope of these relationships is evident in the comments of this first-generation URM student in the sciences: "She [the faculty member] approached me about the McNair Program and started off by asking me what my plans were for the summer, eventually suggesting that I apply to the McNair Program. This professor became a good mentor to me and, along with the adviser of the McNair Program, gave me a lot of support and encouragement [for the Ph.D.]. They were really helpful to me because they understood the issues I was facing." Though Caucasian faculty members did on occasion initiate talent-seeker mentorship relationships, most of these relationships were initiated by minority faculty members.

For students in the sciences and engineering, research experiences at the CSU or at another institution were often critical to aspirations development. Students stated that through these experiences they learned that they had an aptitude for research and that they enjoyed research. Common were statements such as, "As I continued to work in the lab I became more and more interested in research" and "When I got back from [research abroad program] I knew that I really wanted to pursue the Ph.D., and be involved in research. . . . If you aren't exposed to research, it is difficult to get interested in research." Internships and work experiences outside academia were also important for students in these academic areas. Through these experiences students learned that the types of positions that they could hold with a bachelor's degree were not intellectually challenging enough and that in order to enjoy their work and find it interesting they needed an advanced degree. One engineering student put it simply: "Seeing what people with a bachelor's degree did led me to want to get a higher degree."

Some students also noted that gaining an understanding from mentors or other key individuals of how to fund graduate study had increased or solidified their interest in the Ph.D. and that this information was particularly important for CSU students, who often experience financial hardships. This theme emerged mostly in student discussions of suggestions for attracting more CSU students to graduate-level work. A Caucasian student noted, "Letting students know that they would not necessarily have to pay for graduate school is real important to increasing desire to attend graduate school." Similarly a Latina stated, "Lots of students don't know about funding and that knowing this is very important for creating desire for graduate school." Students also suggested that students, particularly CSU students, often have little knowledge of what having a Ph.D. means or what you can do with a Ph.D. and need to understand the relevance of the degree and why they might want to consider continuing their education at this level. Further, a few URM students stated that they were inspired by the idea of earning a Ph.D. in a field in which there were so few other minority Ph.D. holders, and that this led them at least in part to want the Ph.D. With regard to what students hoped to accomplish by earning a Ph.D., gaining fulfillment through meaningful work was a primary motivator for many of them, as was ongoing intellectual curiosity and stimulation. One biology doctoral student noted, "At [CSU attended] I ended up taking a lot of extra math and science courses [to challenge myself intellectually]."

Preparing Academically and Intellectually

Just as talent-seeker mentors were important to aspirations development, they were equally important to experiences that the interviewed students described as paramount to preparing them for the Ph.D. and making them competitively eligible. These mentors did more than encourage potential; they fostered and engaged students in critical research experiences and through academic engagement experiences like the California Pre-Doctoral

Program, McNair Scholars Program, and various National Science Foundation (NSF) and National Institutes of Health (NIH) programs dedicated to
diversity in graduate education. For students to be competitively eligible for
entry into a top doctoral program, the importance of these experiences to
students cannot be underscored enough. Two URM students in the sciences
who worked in a lab for several years as part of an academic program state it
best: "If I hadn't had the extensive lab experience [while I was an undergrad-
uate], I would have either had to earn a master's degree before starting the
doctorate or worked in a lab for several years." Said the other, "My research
experience [at the CSU attended] spoke for itself. I would not have been as
competitive an applicant [without it]." In addition to connecting these students with vital preparatory experiences, mentors, especially talent-seeker
mentors, assisted students with selecting schools, doctoral programs, and
advisers and gave critical information about what to expect in graduate
school, how graduate school was financed, and how to put together a competitive application, including assistance with personal statements.

Another important type of mentor is the "accidental assister." This type
of mentorship relationship is initiated by the student, often after aspirations
for the Ph.D. are formed. Most students who talked about this type of mentor stated that they noted a significant change in attitude toward them once
they made it known that they were interested in graduate study. Typical were
comments such as, "I saw a real big change in him [professor assigned as her
academic adviser who later became a mentor] when I told him that I was
planning on getting a Ph.D." Like students mentored by talent seekers, students mentored by accidental assisters often found the mentor quite helpful
in their preparation academically and professionally for graduate-level work,
but the assistance and encouragement given was much more likely to leave
the student with unmet needs, compared to students mentored by talent
seekers. Characteristic of remarks of students with unmet needs were statements such as, "Professors at [CSU attended] were not at all current about
what faculty were doing in the field and the type of research that was currently being conducted. They couldn't help me pick programs and did not
give me assistance with my personal statement."

Research experiences, in addition to assisting students to be competitively eligible for graduate study, were important to preparation in other, less
tangible but equally significant ways. Students who participated in structured research experiences at the CSU or in summer research programs
at other universities reported that they learned critical information about
graduate-study experience during these activities. This information included
how to put together a competitive application, how to fund graduate school,

and how to select schools, as well as information about what to expect in the graduate school environment. One URM student who participated in an academic research program in the sciences noted, "He [her lab supervisor and mentor] would look over your grades and discuss them with you and make sure your research was coming along. They [NIH program] had seminars every Friday, and speakers would come and talk about their research. It was great to learn about the research in my field that was being done. The coordinators of [NIH program] go over funding for graduate school and how to fund your research career." Another URM student in a similar program added, "Speakers would come and talk about what graduate school was all about. When I started at UCLA I was not shocked about the hours or the devotion necessary to get a Ph.D."

Although students in the humanities and social sciences were less likely to participate in structured research experiences, mostly due to a lack of opportunity rather than a lack of interest, these experiences were no less important to them, especially in their understanding of what research in a particular field of study was about. One student in the social sciences who won a prize at a statewide CSU research competition said that her research experience was like a "research community" in which she learned about her field and was mentored on her own research. Given that structured research experiences were less available in the humanities and social sciences, gaining an understanding of the scholarly environment often proved more daunting for students in these fields. In discussing the transition to doctoral study in humanities, one student noted, "It would have been better if at [CSU attended] I had had more exposure to the research environment. . . . I would have liked to know more about the research process." A student in social science stated, "I did not have any research experience. The training I needed [and would have got in a research experience] included how to read and analyze research papers." Students in these fields were more likely to discuss the importance of scholarly interactions with faculty both inside and outside the classroom and to discuss particular course work as important to their preparation for graduate study. Overall, for students who did not participate in academic programs or structured research experiences, the support that they described getting for the Ph.D., if they got support, tended to be one-dimensional, usually coming from one particular professor or a few professors.

Role of CSU Environment in Aspirations

Students stated that the overall culture of the CSU was directed toward preparing students for employment rather than advanced degrees. They felt that faculty were concerned primarily with preparing future workers, rather than future scholars, and that this was evidenced in the practical or practice-oriented programs and the overall lack of encouragement toward research and scholarly activities, which was in itself an absence of encouragement for graduate study. Several of the students who had aspirations for the Ph.D. prior to the CSU experience noted that given the overall lack of encouragement for graduate study at the CSU, they probably would not have made it if they had not already known they wanted to pursue the Ph.D. One Caucasian history doctoral student stated, "It would have been difficult for me to get to graduate school [if I had not already known I wanted to go]." Likewise, many students indicated that administrators and staff hold the same attitude toward graduate studies. One Latino science student with a strong faculty mentor noted,

> At [CSU attended] there were a lot of barriers to the types of experiences that would get students to graduate school. Administrators and staff are not concerned about providing research opportunities and don't support research. The campus did not seem interested in encouraging graduate school. People seemed shocked when I talked about wanting to go to graduate school.

Students also noted that it could be difficult to get interested in graduate study or see any value in pursuing a Ph.D. because of the overall lack of discussion about graduate study. Typical was this comment: "It was difficult to get any real idea at all about what graduate school would be like or why you would want the degree."

In addition, many of the students noted that if their professors talked about graduate study at all, they were more likely to talk about entry into a professional school—medical, dental, or law. Students commented that they were not exposed to research advances in their professors' field of study and that there was a lack of a scholarly or an intellectually stimulating conversation both inside and outside the classroom. Three comments summarize these experiences well. A Caucasian educational doctoral student stated, "I didn't get as much socialization into the academic lifestyle or the research environment as it seems students get at UCLA [as undergraduates]." An Asian American computer science doctoral student stated, "Education at the CSU is not intended to go deep into the details in the way that would be needed for students to continue their education beyond the B.S. degree." And a Caucasian engineering student stated, "CSU does a good job of having students interact with industry, but no real interactions with the scholarly world or the academic environment. There needs to be more talk by academics about ongoing research."

Although the Caucasian students were much more vocal during the interviews about the barriers to their aspirations development at the CSU, URM students were not immune to barriers, and the barriers they faced tended to be more direct. One Latina biology doctoral student told of being steered into bilingual teaching as an undergraduate, even though she was not interested in that field and enjoyed science. She related,

> Some of the counselors there [at CSU attended] have real preconceived notions of what minority students are capable of achieving, and they steer minority students away from graduate school. They even went as far as to steer me away from being a math and science teacher. When I started at [CSU attended] they [counselors] wanted to place me in basic [remedial] courses and were really surprised by my test scores.

Eventually, as a junior, after considering dropping out of college in part because of this poor guidance, this student found a mentor, a newly hired Latina faculty member in a different department. This mentor encouraged her to pursue her interest in the sciences and fostered her engagement in research, eventually steering her into a program for minority students interested in graduate school. Although this experience was not one that was commonly related by the interviewed URM students, it is no less significant. It is especially significant because the students interviewed for the study were the success stories and because the large majority of URM students interviewed for this study were directed early on into special academic programs that encouraged their scholarship and provided them with a buffer against this type of experience. This buffer allowed them to participate in a positive environment in which they could thrive and in which graduate school attendance was the accepted norm.

The URM students in these special academic programs did address institutional constraints to aspirations, but they did so mostly through their discussion of other minority students who were just as capable as they were but were not pursuing advanced degrees. Comments in this area ranged from the importance of encouragement and mentorship to the importance of the research and scholarly environment. Said one URM student, "For Latino students you really need to interact with them and make them feel wanted. . . . They need to feel that they belong; the key is mentorship." Said another, "Students don't have the opportunity to develop ambition and drive because they are not exposed to the research environment." Caucasian students also commented on this problem. One genetics doctoral student lamented, "He [a Latino student who had just as much potential as I do] did not have the information he needed to even really know what graduate school is all about or what it would take for him financially." In addition, some students spoke about family and home commitments as impediments to graduate study and about the need to work and contribute to family income. The interviewed students indicated that for the most part these issues made the influence of the CSU environment even more important to their aspirations and preparation for the Ph.D.

An additional impediment to Ph.D. aspirations development is the relative value of the degree from the CSU as compared to a degree granted at a more prestigious college or university. A sizable number of the students indicated that it was "well known" at the CSU that earning a degree from the CSU made it much more difficult to get into graduate school, especially to top doctoral programs, and that students should not even waste their time applying. Common were statements such as "At [CSU attended] there was an overall impression that it was hard to get to graduate school [a top school in my field] from a Cal State" and "I knew that my CSU degree would not be as favorable for going on to graduate school." Some students indicated that they had been actively discouraged by faculty from applying to top doctoral programs, and other students told of rumors among students that institutions like the University of California would chop down their grade point averages because the quality of the education they received was not on a par with that of other Ph.D. applicants who had attended more prestigious institutions. Other students noted that the general stigma associated with the CSU did not apply to them because they were in a particularly strong academic program or participating in an academic program that had a good track record for advancing students to the doctorate.

In the face of these perceptions, the students applied anyway, often taking additional measures academically to ensure their success yet questioning the value of their education, their aspirations, their preparation, and ultimately their own intelligence and educational worth. Students made comments such as the following:

> I thought that it was true and that CSU students were not as good. This type of feeling really discourages students. People need to know that they are qualified to go to graduate school. Thinking you are not qualified is a barrier.

I was afraid that I would not get accepted for doctoral work because I was not smart enough. Also, my CSU professors seemed fine with my choice of [CSU attended] for the master's [indicating to me that I was not good enough to apply elsewhere]. I thought the UC was out of reach—too expensive, I would not fit in, and I was not good enough to get in.

Students indicated that these perceptions about the CSU need to be addressed and that students need to know that it is possible to get to the Ph.D. from a CSU.

Role of CSU Environment in Preparation

Overall the students stated that they felt they were well prepared to enter and succeed in their doctoral program. They cited small classes and accessible faculty members who were approachable and interested in their success and, for many of them, access to research experiences as important positive preparation experiences at the CSU. In spite of these positive characteristics, students also stated that certain aspects of the CSU environment made their preparation difficult. Many of the students, especially students in humanities, physical sciences, and engineering, stated that not having access to enough high-level academic courses had made their preparation difficult. Students felt that course offerings were especially lacking in higher-level mathematics, statistics, and theoretical courses and that the courses in these areas that were available were not usually pushed by faculty, even for students who were intending to pursue a Ph.D. An engineering student noted, "I had a steep learning curve at UCLA and really needed to have had higher-level math." An English student stated, "I did not have a lot of theory or critical analysis, and this made my transition difficult."

For many of the students, preparing for the less tangible aspects of the doctoral environment was an issue within the overall academic culture of the CSU. Students indicated that it was often difficult to get an idea of what graduate school would be like and what they needed to do to prepare to be competitive for entry into a doctoral program and, further, that there was little assistance available regarding issues related to graduate study. Typical were comments such as this statement from a student without a mentor: "It was difficult to get any real idea about what graduate school would be like. [CSU attended] did not have an academic counselor that was at all helpful about graduate school." The comments of another student were also typical: "I really did not have a good indication of how the applications [for a doctoral program] would be judged, even though I asked for assistance on this directly."

As with aspirations development, certain subcultures at the CSU tended to provide students with stronger preparation. Among students who participated in academic research at the CSU in a lab or as part of a special academic experience, as well as students who participated in a research experience at another university in a summer or bridge program, the direct research experience—the research skills they learned and the intangibles they learned about the doctoral environment—proved invaluable to preparation.

Discussion

Given current enrollment trends in higher education and the pressing need to further diversify graduate education, it is important to study aspirations development and preparation for the Ph.D. at institutions in which URM students are more likely to have their baccalaureate origins. The importance of this endeavor is made even clearer by the work of Cole and Barber (2003), which contends that affirmative action programs actually stymie efforts to develop aspirations and prepare students for the Ph.D. because these programs place underrepresented students in highly selective academic environments in which they are not able to compete, and these students therefore do not earn the grades necessary to aspire to the Ph.D. The research described in this chapter provides a preliminary understanding of aspirations development and preparation for the Ph.D. for URM students at less selective comprehensive colleges and universities and examines the environment of these institutions critically with regard to their support for graduate study and to the possibility of advancing greater numbers of their URM students to the Ph.D.

With regard to aspirations development, this study both confirms and extends past research in this area regarding the influence of faculty. It confirms past research in the sense that faculty interaction and mentoring were salient experiences for aspirations development among most of the students. Mentoring was found to be especially important to the aspirations of URM and first-generation students, who were much more likely to enter college without advanced-degree aspirations and much more dependent on mentorship as a means to acquire aspirations for the Ph.D. and the engagement necessary to pursue the Ph.D. For Caucasian students, mentorship was more important for preparation, or for solidifying their aspirations, but not as key to initially acquiring aspirations. The unique role of faculty to the aspirations of the URM students in this study confirms Carter's (2001) finding that Caucasian students' aspirations are more stable across their college experience, whereas the experience of college itself tends to be more important to aspirations for URM students. The findings of this study extend our understanding of the role of mentorship by illustrating just how talent-seeker interactions contributed to the development of aspirations among this population of URM and first-generation students.

This study also found that research experiences were important to aspirations development for the Ph.D. This finding is not surprising given the preponderance of evidence demonstrating the benefits of academic engagement to a whole host of outcomes, including aspirations (Astin, 1977, 1993; Tinto, 1993). What is important in this finding is the role of these experiences in preparing students for doctoral study. Beyond assisting the students to be competitively eligible for doctoral study, these experiences were invaluable in teaching about the graduate school environment and culture and assisting the students to see themselves as working scholars in their field with something to contribute. These experiences provided critical information about the Ph.D. that was not available in the more general college environment of the CSU and that was not provided by other external influences such as family and community. This information was uniquely available to the URM students who participated in academic research programs and to other students, both minority and majority, who participated in structured research opportunities at the CSU or at another college or university. Access to this information was something that many Caucasian students who did not have these types of experiences noted was missing for them in the development of their aspirations and their preparation.

Our understanding of the development of aspirations was also extended by other findings in this study. Of particular note is the relationship between understanding graduate school funding and aspirations development. The financing of graduate school was an important element of aspirations development for the students in this study: Knowledge of funding options increased and solidified interest in the Ph.D. Not understanding how graduate funding worked was a barrier to aspirations development, especially among this population of students, who were more likely to have financial need and less likely to have an understanding already of the funding differences between undergraduate and doctoral study. Due to external pressures and an overall lack of experience with postgraduate study as compared to their Caucasian counterparts, an understanding of graduate school funding seemed especially important to aspirations among the URM students in the study. Access to funding information, as with access to an understanding of the elements of the graduate school culture, was for the most part only available to a select group of students at the CSU who participated in structured research opportunities or academic research programs. In the past, most notably in Carter (2001), the relationship between financial need and aspirations was explored through undergraduate financial aid variables and found not to have much of an effect. Given these findings, in future studies it is important to explore this relationship through questions that get at students' understanding of funding at the graduate school level.

With regard to students' perceptions of the overall environment of the CSU, students reported that the environment was not conducive to promoting graduate study or to preparing students for graduate study and that it instead tended to socialize students to see themselves as future workers. This tendency was evidenced not only by the practical orientation of the academic programs at the CSU but also by the overall lack of discussion of graduate study and the limited exposure to the scholarly environment and rigorous course work, as well as by the administrative and other roadblocks to aspirations and preparation that these students experienced. This finding supports social allocation as discussed by Kamens (1981), indicating that the environment of the CSU prepares its graduates for a different fate altogether than the fate of future scholar. Given the high percentage of URM students who are in one way or another locked into attendance at institutions with similar missions and status allocation functions, this is a form of social reproduction that tends to keep these students tracked into less elite positions in society. As evidenced in these students' stories, access to graduate school is not altogether unavailable, and indeed strong stories of success exist, but access to the types of experiences that students say they need is limited. Given the reliance of URM students on the institutional environment itself for their aspirations and preparation, the overall culture of the CSU is much more likely to have a limiting effect on this population, as compared to Caucasian students, who seemed to continue to aspire to the Ph.D. and to prepare despite the limitations of the environment.

Social allocation also shows up in these students' stories in the form of anticipatory socialization. Among the general population of students at the CSU, there seems to be a general acceptance or at least acknowledgment that the purpose of the degree that they are earning at the CSU and its value to their future study is quite different from that of the degree earned by students at a more prestigious or selective institution. This form of anticipatory socialization seems to be both a preentry effect, in that students know it and accept it at some level when they enter the CSU, and an intensification effect, in that the environment, both generally and among some faculty in particular, reinforces this concept. Further, the strong effect that this internalization had on some of these students, even though they succeeded in making it to the Ph.D., indicates that it limits student mobility to the Ph.D.

Conclusion

This study has both practical and theoretical implications. On one hand, it paints a portrait of aspirations development and preparations for the Ph.D., providing a unique glimpse into the lived experience of students who are aspiring and preparing for this degree at a less selective institutional type, the comprehensive CSU system. It underscores the importance of faculty mentorship and interactions to aspirations of all students, and especially and uniquely to URM students, and the importance of scholarly academic engagement. The findings also demonstrate that the overall environment of a comprehensive college or university may not be as conducive to further diversifying graduate education but that in certain environments within the CSU, URM students are thriving. Although this study examines only one comprehensive university system, there is reason to believe that institutions in this category share similar characteristics and that the findings might be similar at other comprehensive institutions.

With regard to future theoretical approaches, it is important for researchers to make a concerted effort to include theory that critically examines the unique properties of the college environment and how that environment contributes to student mobility to the Ph.D. In this study, using Carter's (2001) theory of aspirations, and supplementing it with Kamens's (1981) conceptions of social allocation and anticipatory socialization, proved fruitful. Perhaps future studies might try to marry similar frameworks, or perhaps an enhanced and more comprehensive framework might be conceived. Regardless, given the findings in this study, as well as past findings (Carter, 2001; Pascarella et al., 2004), it will be important for future studies to conceptualize aspirations development and preparation for the Ph.D. differently for URM and Caucasian students.

References

Astin, A. W. (1977). *Four critical years.* San Francisco: Jossey-Bass.
Astin, A. W. (1993). *What matters in college? Four critical years revisited.* San Francisco: Jossey-Bass.
Astin, A. W., & Panos, R. (1969). *The educational and vocational development of college students.* Washington, DC: American Council on Education.
Blau, P. M., & Duncan, O. D. (1967). *The American occupational structure.* New York: Wiley.
California State University. (2003). *Statistical reports 2002–2003.* Retrieved August 5, 2003, from http://www.calstate.edu/as/stat_reports/2002-2003/FETH01.htm
Carnegie Foundation. (2001). *The Carnegie classification of institutions of higher education 2000 edition.* Menlo Park, CA: Carnegie.

Carter, D. F. (2001). *A dream deferred? Examining the degree aspirations of African American and White college students.* New York: RoutledgeFalmer.

Cole, S., & Barber, E. (2003). *Increasing faculty diversity: The occupational choices of high achieving minority students.* Cambridge, MA: Harvard University Press.

Guba, E. G., & Lincoln, Y. S. (1981). *Effective evaluation.* San Francisco: Jossey-Bass.

Hearn, J. C. (1987). Impacts of undergraduate experiences on aspirations and plans for graduate school. *Research in Higher Education, 27*(2), 119–141.

Kamens, D. H. (1981). Organizational and institutional socialization in education. *Research in Sociology of Education and Socialization, 2,* 111–126.

Lincoln, Y. S., & Guba, E. G. (1985). *Naturalistic inquiry.* Beverly Hills, CA: Sage.

National Science Foundation. (2006). *U.S. doctorates in the 20th century* (NSF 06-319). Arlington, VA: Author.

Oseguera, L. (2002, November). *Changes in degree aspirations during the college years.* Paper presented at the annual meeting of the Association for the Study of Higher Education, Sacramento, CA.

Pascarella, E. T. (1984). College environmental influences on students' educational aspirations. *Journal of Higher Education, 55,* 751–771.

Pascarella, E. T., Wolniak, G. C., Flowers, L. A., & Pierson, C. T. (2004). The role of race in the development of plans for a graduate degree. *Review of Higher Education, 27*(3) 299–320.

Perna, L. W. (2003, April). *Understanding the decision to enroll in graduate school: Sex and racial/ethnic group differences.* Paper presented at the annual meeting of the American Educational Research Association, Chicago, IL.

Tinto, V. (1993). *Leaving college: Rethinking the causes and cures of student attrition* (2nd ed.). Chicago: University of Chicago Press.

University of California Office of the President. (2002). *University of California statistical summary of students and staff, fall 2002.* Retrieved August 5, 2003, from http://www.ucop.edu/ucophome/uwnews/stat/fall2002/statsumm2002.pdf.

Weiler, W. C. (1993). Post-baccalaureate educational choices of minority students. *Review of Higher Education, 16*(4), 439–460.

Note

1. Although it is regrettable that African American students are not represented in the sample, it is not that surprising given the high proportion of African American doctoral degree holders whose baccalaureate origins are at historically Black colleges and universities (HBCUs). For instance, among African American doctorate recipients between 1995 and 1999, 20% earned a bachelor's degree at an HBCU, and only one of the CSU campuses was among the top 50 senders to doctoral programs, whereas for Mexican American students seven CSU campuses were among the top 50 senders to doctoral programs during this period (NSF, 2006).

3

FINANCING THE DREAM

The Impact of Financial Aid on Graduate Education for Underrepresented Minority Students

*Susan D. Johnson, John A. Kuykendall III,
and Rachelle Winkle-Wagner*

Academic preparation, though a key factor in persistence in college, does not guarantee an opportunity to pursue postsecondary education. Financial barriers can often trump academic preparation (St. John, 2003). Although financial aid should resolve financial limitations and increase the likelihood of attendance and persistence at institutions of higher education, current shifts in policy toward middle-income students and merit-based aid negate the traditional intentions of financial aid—to make higher education affordable and accessible to those who might not otherwise be able to pursue postsecondary education for financial reasons (Arnone, 2004; Burd, 2001; Campaigne & Hossler, 1998; Mortenson, 1991).

Over the past decade, the issue of student-loan burden on both undergraduate and graduate study has been of increasing concern to higher education. Since the reauthorization of the 1992 Higher Education Act, unmet financial need is increasingly resolved in the form of reduced grant and increased loan amounts (Pascarella & Terenzini, 2005; St. John, 2002). Currently, loans make up 58% of financial aid disbursements for undergraduate students (Witkowsky, 2002).

Some research suggests that the shift of federal and state financial aid policies from grants to loans may affect students of color differentially. Ehrenberg (1991) found that African American undergraduate students at all income levels were less likely than White students to take out college loans and were more reluctant to borrow. This difference may be due in part to disparity in wealth between African Americans and Whites. For instance, recent research indicates that African Americans generally have fewer inter-generationally transferred financial assets than Whites and that this can affect their attitudes toward debt (Shapiro, 2004). That is, those who do not have a history of taking out loans or accepting debt for longer-term benefits may be averse to doing so.

Students who have an aversion to aid in the form of loans need to find alternative ways to fund a college education such as part-time or full-time employment. Such alternatives are potentially counterproductive to persistence and degree completion (King, 1999). The shift from grants to loans affects both undergraduate and graduate education alike. Students emerging from an undergraduate education financed heavily by loans are likely to be wary of seeking graduate education, in the fear of accumulating additional debt—a warranted fear based on recent statistics (St. John, 2003). In 2003–2004, 75% of the aid received by graduate students was in the form of loans (College Board, 2004).

Need-based grant programs currently do not exist for graduate education, and conversations about the affordability of graduate school are also virtually nonexistent (Buchanan, 1997). Legislators and policy makers increasingly view graduate education as a luxury and a privilege rather than a necessity. Furthermore, despite graduate students' contribution to the U.S. job market and the academy, there appears to be little motivation for state and federal government to invest in graduate school education (Bruner, 1999; "Purdue President," 2000). This issue is increasingly salient as the educational credentials necessary to obtain employment continue to rise (Carey, 2004).

This chapter has two central purposes. The first is to draw attention to the graduate student experience, particularly for underrepresented minority students. Much of the scholarship regarding students of color in higher education is limited to the exploration of the undergraduate experience. Additional literature in this area will offer a new perspective and add to the paucity of currently existing literature on graduate education. The second purpose is to shed additional light on the financial barriers of graduate education faced by students from underrepresented minority populations. Research findings about financial barriers will address the influence of financial aid when deciding to pursue graduate education and select graduate programs.

Current Trends in Funding Higher Education

Research suggests that the decision to pursue higher education is heavily influenced by costs associated with enrollment (Heller, 1999; St. John, 2003).

For low-income and minority students, research further suggests a greater sensitivity to financial aid as compared to other students (Heller, 1997; McPherson & Schapiro, 2002; Perna, 2005). Although this research is predominantly based on undergraduate students, graduate students face similar concerns in considering graduate education.

Because federal, state, and institutional policies generally proscribe discrimination on the basis of race, only rarely can colleges, outside agencies, or governments target aid specifically for underrepresented minority students. Instead of using financial aid to increase participation of students from certain minority populations in higher education, policy makers must use indicators such as need or urban residence that nudge aid toward these students or must assume that minority students will respond more positively than other students to financial aid. Even so, minority students still seem reluctant to receive financial aid in the form of loans to finance their education (Heller, 1997; Perna, 2005).

Policy Shifts

In the 1980s, the shift from grants to loans may have contributed to the erosion in minority student enrollment at the undergraduate level, which, in turn, has had a direct effect on seeking a graduate degree because students of color have been shown to be less likely to enroll in degree programs with loans than they might be with grants (St. John, 1991, 1999). Families are also seeing larger portions of their incomes being directed toward college expenses, a trend that does not bode well for students from low-income families. For low-income families, tuition at 4-year colleges consumed 25% of their income in 2000, up from 13% in 1980 (National Center for Public Policy and Higher Education, 2002). This increase has also forced students to look for jobs while enrolled in college. The U.S. Department of Education, National Center for Education Statistics (2005) reports that three out of four undergraduates are now working while enrolled in college. Even more shocking is that these students work for 90% of the time that they are enrolled, for an average of 31 hours per week. One could surmise that if students are unable to make financial ends meet at the undergraduate level, graduate education could become more and more inaccessible, particularly for those students in the lowest socioeconomic groups.

The 1990s witnessed a policy focus shift from the public financing of higher education (state and federal appropriations and grants) to increased cost sharing, resulting in student/family financing (higher tuition and loans) (Reindl & Redd, 1999). Because of the increase in college pricing and the slow pace of grant aid, more and more students are relying on loans to cover college expenses (Davis, 2000). Ten years ago, loans constituted 47% of the total amount of financial aid that students received; by 2001–2002, loans made up 57% of a student's aid package (College Board, 2002). Even with the shift to loans, the current limits on federal lending over the course of undergraduate study is out of touch with the level of need of today's students (Morgan, 2002). Between 2001–2002 and 2004–2005, the percentage of student funding in the form of grants decreased from 50% to 46% for undergraduates and from 29% to 22% for graduate students (College Board, 2005). Over the same period, the percentage in the form of loans increased from 43% to 46% for undergraduates and from 68% to 76% for graduate students. Since the 1970s, loans have become about one half of all student aid and have created a growing "grant-loan imbalance" in federal financial aid policy (College Board, 2005; Gladieux & Hauptman, 1995). For graduate-level education, this means that more students enter graduate school with higher levels of debt.

According to McPherson and Schapiro (2002), in response to the decrease in public support, public institutions sought and attained greater authority over their tuition policies and proceeded to raise tuition to make up for the decreases in government support. This finding is also congruent with those of St. John (1991) and St. John et al. (2004), who found that public-sector tuition charges rose as a percentage of educational revenue as costs normally supported by state appropriations declined. The General Accounting Office (1998) reported that for every dollar lost in state tax revenues, in response, public institutions have raised tuition 75 cents. These are tremendous costs that are being passed on to students and make the need for an increase in government support for low-income students more urgent. Therefore, as public-sector tuition continues to rise, students from the lowest family incomes will need grant increases that keep up with these tuition increases in order to maintain access to college (Advisory Committee on Student Financial Assistance, 2001). The Institute for Higher Education Policy (2002) argues that public policies should also provide a degree of choice for African American, Latino, and low-income students. Such choice would counter the tendency for students from these populations to be highly concentrated on 2-year college campuses. The institute notes that in 1999–2000, 62% of all first-year undergraduate students were enrolled at public 2-year institutions. Thus, as an increasing number of students are unable to finance 4-year baccalaureate degrees, graduate education seems even less attainable to some students.

As evidenced by these studies, financial access is one of the greatest challenges for students of color in higher education today. Because of the lack of policies in place to ensure financial access to those students deemed academically qualified, many of them are simply not able to afford to attend college, even at the undergraduate level. As illustrated earlier, the number of people unable to afford college gets larger and larger every year. If left unchecked, low-income students will not have a vehicle by which they can escape their current financial status. It is incumbent on advocates of access for low-income students to continue to research these phenomena and make policy recommendations to counter the trend of diminishing participation in higher education for low-income students.

There is little literature regarding the impact of financial aid on access to graduate and professional-level education. From the existing literature about undergraduate access, however, one can predict that financial barriers may continue, if not increase, as students attempt to gain financial access to advanced-degree programs. If underrepresented minority students have high levels of loan debt and if they are averse to loans, as the literature suggests is the case, advanced-degree programs may increasingly become financially inaccessible to many students. This situation could have a serious impact on the diversity of human capital available to industry, higher education administration, and the professoriate. That is, if fewer and fewer students from underrepresented populations are able to pursue graduate education, it will become more and more difficult for industry, the professoriate, and higher education administration to reflect the demographics of the larger society.

Human Capital

An educational divide, or "fault line" of sorts (Geske & Cohn, 1998), is a major determinant of who will prosper in a global market. In modern society, the level of education is believed ultimately to shape the quality of life that individuals will experience. To gain a better grasp of the notion of prosperity and the economic benefits associated with higher education, scholars have framed their research in terms of human capital theory. According to this theory, individuals make investments in their economic future based on years of education and experience (Becker, 1962; Paulsen, 2001). The assumption is that the quantity and quality of education, along with an expansive skill set, will result in a variety of lifelong monetary and nonmonetary benefits (Becker, 1993).

Reports from multiple government and educational agencies suggest positive relationships among educational attainment, earning capacity (Baum & Payea, 2004), and voting rates (National Center for Public Policy and Higher Education, 2002). Along the same lines, poverty and incarceration rates tend to decline with higher levels of educational attainment

(Ingels, Curtin, Kaufman, Alt, & Chen, 2002). Building on these studies, Perna (2005) examined the benefits of higher education across gender, race/ethnicity, and socioeconomic status (SES). Her findings suggest that whereas gender differences in educational attainment were related to human capital, racial/ethnic and SES differences were related more to the availability of funds to pay for higher education. Thus, access to human capital, which will determine one's life chances, may be determined in part by financial aid or one's ability to pay for higher education.

According to the U.S. Department of Education, National Center for Education Statistics (2005), students of color (African American, Hispanic, Asian/Pacific Islander, and American Indian combined) obtained 21.9% of the bachelor's, 17.5% of the master's, and 13.6% of the doctoral degrees awarded in the 2002–2003 academic school year, while White students obtained 70%, 60.3%, and 56.2%, respectively. Most of the students of color, particularly African American students, in doctoral programs are in the field of education (Gravois, 2007). Yet many of these students have such high levels of debt while in their doctoral programs in education that they are unable to finish their degrees (Gravois, 2007). Given the disparate educational attainment of underrepresented minority students as compared to their White counterparts, and the growing evidence of financial inaccessibility for students of color, a discussion of the influence of financial aid on various levels of education seems timely. What follows is the description and results of a portion of a larger qualitative study exploring the experiences of first-year doctoral and professional underrepresented minority students and more specifically the impact of financial aid.

Research Method

The data presented in this chapter are from a larger study about the experiences of students of color in advanced-degree programs at multiple institutions. For the purposes of this chapter, we focus on the issue of finances or financial barriers described by doctoral students in education and sociology and law students at a large, public, midwestern research university that is representative of public research institutions nationally.

Participants

We drew participants for the study from three separate disciplines—education, sociology, and law—to ascertain some differences between disciplinary experiences. Given that the field of education comprises many of the underrepresented students in doctoral programs, an examination of students' experiences with these programs is merited. Sociology provides a comparison of education to another social science discipline. The law students provide a comparison between doctoral and professional education.

Employing purposeful sampling techniques, researchers contacted administrators in the schools of education, sociology, and law at a research-extensive, public, midwestern institution to obtain contact information for first-year graduate and professional students. The resultant sample was composed of 12 students—4 female doctoral students in education (3 African American students and 1 Mexican American student), 4 doctoral students in sociology (2 African American students [1 male, 1 female], 1 female Dominican student, and 1 Latina student), and 4 African American law students (2 male, 2 female).

Design and Procedure

Invitation messages with the study purpose and contact information were sent via e-mail to all first-year graduate and professional students in the aforementioned schools. As students responded, researchers arranged focus groups at times and locations convenient to the students. At least two members of the eight-member research team were present at each focus group. As one team member directed questions to the students, the other recorded field notes and observed the interview process.

The data were analyzed using the Constant Comparative Method, an inductive process for forming a categorical model to describe the data collected in a study (Glasser & Strauss, 1967; Lincoln & Guba, 1985). This method of data analysis continuously develops a process of interpreting the data from explaining individual units of information to the construction of a descriptive model. Following transcription, researchers examined interviews line by line as part of the open coding process used to identify potential themes and meaningful categories from actual text examples (Denzin & Lincoln, 2003; Strauss & Corbin, 1998). In addition, coding software was utilized to electronically process the data. Once the data were processed, researchers shared an initial draft of the interview transcriptions and findings with focus group participants as part of a member check. Each participant was asked to provide feedback on his or her focus group session, thus ensuring the correct interpretation of participant comments and responses.

Research Findings

Financial aid was one of the chief emergent themes in the study on the experiences of underrepresented minority graduate students. The amount and source of aid were found to be potential determinants for whether these students considered obtaining a graduate degree. Without firm assurances of continuing financial support from the institution, students were unlikely to attend. The following themes emerged from the study: financial aid as a gatekeeper, financial aid as a recruitment tool, and the burden of debt.

Financial Aid as a Gatekeeper

For the students involved in this study, the aspiration of attending a graduate or professional program was bounded by a financial gatekeeper. Finances worked as a gatekeeper in that if students were able to find financial assistance to fund their degree programs, then they enrolled in the program. If the students had not found financial assistance, then many of them noted that they would not have been able to attend graduate or professional school, regardless of their future aspirations.

Many of the participants described their need for financial assistance as the primary factor in their decision to enroll in an advanced-degree program—financial barriers were a gatekeeper to graduate education. In a focus group, one African American doctoral student in education agreed: "Money was extremely important. I am not able to afford graduate school by no means, so I knew I would have to get some type of scholarship, fellowship, assistantship, whatever in order to come to school. So that was like one thing that really drove me to school." Again, for this student, financial assistance became a gatekeeper that either would allow her to enroll in her doctoral program or would have inhibited her ability to attend the institution.

Students also considered the extent to which financial aid would sustain their families. Prior to entering a doctoral program, a Dominican doctoral student in sociology questioned the amount of aid: "[Would] the money they're offering [be] enough to support myself and my daughter?" Here, she points out that funding was essential not only to the pursuit of her education but also for her ability to take care of her family while in graduate school. The consideration of the need for funding to support one's family was not unusual. Many of the participants indicated the necessity of financial resources not only to pay for graduate school but also to support their families.

For some students, the financial gatekeeper also became a motivating factor. For example, a first-year doctoral student in education discussed her decision to attend this particular institution as being a long-term goal for which she had worked to gain financial access:

I was able to receive the [4-year full tuition remission] fellowship. And, I mean, that was just really important for me. And, I mean, that is something that has always kind of been a guiding force for me. Even through college. I was just so determined, like, in high school to do really well and get a scholarship to go to college. I know my parents, they would have done whatever they needed to do to get me to school. But I was just so determined that I could take the burden off of them as much as possible. In college, I knew I wanted to go to grad school. So at that point it was like, you know, very important to do as much as I can as much as possible so that you will have . . . to be able to receive some type of funding when it was time to go. Because I knew I didn't have the money and my parents didn't have it. So I just really was thankful to get that.

This student's need for financial assistance had acted as a motivating force, encouraging her to do well academically. Although the motivation of financial need was a positive influence in this case, it is worth noting that there were serious consequences for this student if she did not do well. She would be unable to attend graduate school at all because of financial barriers.

The financial burden for many students remained once they were enrolled in their graduate programs. For many of the participants, this burden became a source of stress and even a gatekeeper toward their ability to persist in their degree programs. A Mexican American woman in the first year of her doctoral program in education summarized:

I have an assistantship. And this is the second and last year of that grant. So it is a little like "ho-oh," a little nerve-wracking thinking about what next year is gonna provide me with. So I have the assistantship that covers tuition and then I have the stipend. And then I have taken out loans for my apartment and my bills and everything else. And then I have received two Hispanic Scholarship Foundation awards. And they are both for the amount of $2,500, and they are both given once a year. But I think that I would have had a list type thing with scholarship information. I think that I will go out and see exactly what is available. I think that this year has kicked my butt in terms of working and being on top of my stuff. I . . . definitely would have liked some further scholarships.

This student noted her nervousness at not knowing from where she would obtain funding in the subsequent years of her studies. She voiced frustration that the program did not have a centralized way of providing funding or of helping students to obtain the necessary funding.

The financial gatekeeper does not cease after a student has gained financial assistance in the first year of his or her advanced-degree program. Thus, the issue of financial access has implications for graduate and professional student persistence. When asked about the most important factor in being able to continue with their programs, many of the participants replied that funding would ultimately determine their fate. An African American doctoral student in education noted the permanence of her need for funding during graduate school: "I can't pay for it, again—I know I said that—but I can't pay for it." Here, this student strongly asserts that she simply would not be able to continue in her program, or even to be enrolled in the first place, without financial assistance.

Finances, or the lack thereof, acted as a gatekeeper to graduate school access for many students. Financial aid often was a primary recruitment tool, according to the participants in this study. In the next section, we discuss the participants' experiences with financial aid as they determined in which program they would matriculate.

Financial Aid as a Recruitment Tool

In the students' descriptions of their process of deciding which institution to attend and which degree to obtain, the primary factor was financial assistance in the way of scholarships, fellowships, and assistantships. According to the results of these data, financial assistance could in fact be the most important recruitment tool that an institution or program can use.

As the participants described the application process, it became clear that institutions needed to "come through" with a financial offer in order for the students to consider actually enrolling in the program. For example, an African American woman in the law school recalled her decision to attend this particular institution: "For me it came down to money and where I got money, not just enough but more than enough to get into school, and [this program] came through better than the others." In this case, the offering of financial assistance was the student's primary rationale for choosing to matriculate into this particular law school.

A first-year sociology student echoed the importance of having sufficient funding throughout her graduate educational experience: "Money was really an important factor. So, you know, I totally knocked out one school because they [were] trying to be funny about offering me money. . . . I required that [the department] had to have funding on the table that was going to be [available] for the entire program." In this way there is a national competition between programs, and the program that is able to offer the best financial package wins.

In the law program at this institution, there was a statewide scholarship program that covered tuition expenses. This program became an integral component in the recruitment of students to the law school. One African American woman in the first year of her law program described receiving this fellowship: "I was in a [statewide scholarship program] fellow, and that just gave me no reason to go anywhere else." Like the doctoral students in education and sociology, financial aid became *the* primary reason for choosing this particular institution or program.

Institutions that were perceived as "too expensive" were considered inaccessible to many of the participants. In fact, some participants did not even apply to institutions that were perceived to be expensive, regardless of the financial packages that may have been offered or the rankings of the programs within the institution. For example, one African American law student was particularly interested in an Ivy League school because of its program in Internet law. However, she reflected, "The cost really kept me from applying." She did not apply for this institution because of a perception that it was too costly, regardless of the potential financial aid packages or the high prestige of the institution. In these cases, finances reduced the options available to these students.

Some of the participants in doctoral programs in education considered the funding opportunities to be noncompetitive with other institutions. A Mexican American female doctoral student who had attended another institution for her master's degree made this comparison:

> I mean, [another state college] system is a little bit different. So, with them, I had pretty much guaranteed funding from the time I was there. And it was up to 30 or 33 hours per year. I could go full-time all year long if I wanted to. And they gave me a stipend of like $11,000 on top of that. Because they don't have department funding. The school in general just offers it. And I thought that was how [it] was [here]. Why would it be any different? I didn't do my homework. And so, at [this institution], even with an assistantship it might not cover the out-of-state [tuition]. It is more iffy here.

Given the importance of financial assistance in the recruitment and retention of underrepresented minority students, this perception that funding is not guaranteed could be a problem as the institution attempts to recruit more diverse populations. As the perception becomes public that this institution may not offer enough financial assistance, the recruitment of students could become increasingly difficult.

The Burden of Debt

Consistent with the literature on undergraduate students of color, the participants in this study were generally resistant to taking out loans (Campaigne & Hossler, 1998). This resistance seems well founded given recent statistics showing that doctoral students who borrow more take longer to finish (Council of Graduate Schools, 2007). In addition, graduate students in the social sciences, the humanities, and education—disciplines with the highest number of African American enrollments—borrow the most (Council of Graduate Schools, 2007; Gravois, 2007). Therefore, the toll of loans can be quite severe, particularly for underrepresented minority students.

Nearly all the students expressed a severe aversion to loans and the indebtedness associated with them. For example, a first-year female law student explained, "I hate to take out loans because I hate to have debt." On the other hand, they viewed scholarships, assistantships, and fellowships as more positive sources of aid. A first-year doctoral student in education noted,

> I have the Dean's Minority Fellowship, and basically with the fellowship they couple it with an assistantship. So you have to work the 20 hours a week in order to get financial assistantship. It covers everything: it covers my tuition; it provides me with a stipend every month to live on. Even though it's not an abundance of money, but [laughs] I can still live on it if I really budget. So I am blessed to not [have] to take out any loans for school.

Here, there is a subtle mention of an aversion to loans, corroborated by many of the participants, and the desire not to use loans to finance graduate education.

An African American law student described her aversion to loans, maintaining, "I don't want to [spend] years paying off degrees." There was some correlation between the future earning potential of the degree and the participant's desire to avoid debt. For example, students in education generally knew that they would not make enough to pay off a high amount of debt. That said, law students, who would generally have a higher earning potential, also felt the pressure of carrying a high loan debt. An African American woman in the first year of law school noted, "I hate to take out loans because I hate to have debt because regardless if I make more money, I will be spending a lot more also. So I try not to take out loans if I don't have to." In this case, even though this student knows that she will most likely have a high earning potential, she is still resistant to taking out loans.

Other students had decided to place a cap on the amount of debt that they were willing to incur during advanced-degree programs. For example, an African American man in law school had decided to attempt not to worry about his loan debt as long as it did not grow too large: "I am trying not to think about it that much. I do have a set amount that I want to take out. I think $80,000 is the number, as long as I can keep it under that amount." In this case, the student has decided on the loan debt that he feels he will be able to repay and feels that he cannot go over this set amount.

For other law students who desired to work in nonprofit or less lucrative law professions, the burden of debt was especially heavy. An African American law student who desired to work in the nonprofit sector admitted the way in which her loan debt affected her: "It affects me in a huge way because I know I won't have that salary that is typical of attorneys, so I won't be able to pay them off in a decent amount of time." This student feels resistant to taking out loans because she fears that her future profession will not allow her to pay off a high loan debt.

Another reason that many of the participants voiced a resistance to loans was the accumulation of earlier debt. Many of the participants discussed having to take out loans to pay for their undergraduate degrees. In this way, they entered graduate school with debt already looming in their future. The additional loans needed for graduate school became a particularly heavy burden for these students. An African American law student worried, "I had to borrow for law school, but I also have a huge undergrad loan, so it affects me a lot." In this student's case, the combination of her undergraduate loan debt threatened to affect her career aspirations: "Hopefully I don't let my loans deter me from doing the work that I really want to do in law, and it does not make a lot of money." Although she has career aspirations to be in a less lucrative field of law, her loan debt looms as a potential deterrent to this goal.

Discussion and Implications

Both policy-related and practical implications emerged from this study. Ultimately, the data in this study indicate that financial aid is one of the most important factors in providing access to graduate and professional education. From this study, there are implications for the access, recruitment, and retention of underrepresented minority students in graduate and professional programs.

According to the results of this study, financial aid can act as either a gatekeeper or a barrier to graduate and professional education. The extent to which graduate students from underrepresented minority populations expressed the need for financial support was pervasive. Financial assistance opened the doors of the academy to these students. However, the type of financial assistance was vital. Students voiced a severe aversion to loans. Thus, if institutions of higher education are to make graduate and professional programs more available, consideration must be given to the *type* of financial assistance that is being offered. Given the results of this study, underrepresented minority students are much more likely to perceive advanced-degree programs as accessible if the financial assistance comes in the form of fellowships, scholarships, and assistantships.

Coupled with the type of funding available to students, there are implications for the recruitment of minority students into advanced-degree programs. Policy makers, faculty, and administrators need to give serious consideration to the types and amounts of financial aid they offer if they want to recruit underrepresented minority students and consequently to increase the number of faculty of color in the academy. As institutions attempt to compete nationally for rank and prestige, there is a serious need to consider what at times seems to be a crisis in graduate student funding. The data here indicate that regardless of the prestige offered by a program or particular institution, a student may self-select out of the institution or program if it is perceived to be financially inaccessible. If programs are unable to offer full tuition remission and stipends to incoming students, the students will find an institution that can offer this assistance, meaning that institutions' inability to offer financial assistance could cause them to lose good students. This outcome could have serious implications for attempts to increase diversity in advanced-degree programs—regardless of the excellence offered in a program, financial accessibility and the perception of that accessibility may be the most important factors in recruiting and retaining many underrepresented minority students into these programs.

Limitations

We recognize several limitations of this study, namely, the number of participants, the higher number of female participants, the inclusion of only one institution, and the ethnic composition of the focus groups. Although qualitative research allows a researcher to delve more deeply into a topic with a smaller sample size, a larger number of respondents would provide more significant evidence and thereby enhance current findings. Small sample size makes it difficult to provide conclusions and suggestions that would be applicable to a wide range of institutional types. The study of this institution,

however, provides a foundation on which to build research regarding graduate education access for minority and low-income students. In addition,
there may be findings that are transferable to other students' experiences.
Because of the relative lack of diversity in the selected graduate and professional programs at the chosen institution, most students in the study were
African American and female. To discuss underrepresented minority graduate students adequately and thoroughly, a more diverse sample of students,
including various racial/ethnic groups and a more balanced sample of
women and men, is needed.

We are currently in the process of including additional graduate and professional schools in the study of this institution, as well as visiting other colleges and universities of varying Carnegie classifications. In addition, White
students will be included in subsequent studies for comparative purposes.
Supplementary data will undoubtedly increase the importance of this study
and expand our knowledge base and ability to disseminate additional findings on issues of access, choice, and retention as they pertain to underrepresented minority graduate students.

Conclusion and Future Direction of Research

This study suggests that adequate student financial aid can help equalize the
opportunity for students to gain access to and persist in graduate education.
Literature indicates that increasing state grants helps balance opportunities
for undergraduate students (St. John, 1999), but what helps balance opportunities for graduate students? Certainly graduate programs can consider need-
based grant aid as one way to provide and maintain equal opportunity.

Further, the findings of this study raise an important question about
higher education financial policy. As this study suggests, financial aid is
imperative for minority graduate and professional students. Therefore, graduate programs should coordinate their financial resources with policies on
the institutional, state, and federal level to help support minority students
to this end. Institutions could also play a larger role in providing financial
opportunity for students by offering scholarships, research assistantships, or
grants.

Finally, this study is merely a beginning; there is clearly room for additional research in this area, exploring different disciplines and students' experiences within them. Further investigation is necessary to address the
multitude of variables that potentially affect access to graduate education for
underrepresented minority students. Perhaps a better understanding of this

issue will inform optimal ways to increase the number and retention of minority graduate and professional students.

References

Advisory Committee on Student Financial Assistance. (2001). *Access denied: Restoring the nation's commitment to equal education opportunity.* Washington, DC: Author.

Arnone, M. (2004, January 30). 250,000 eligible students shut out of college, group says. *Chronicle of Higher Education, 50*(21), A21.

Baum, S., & Payea, K. (2004). *Education pays 2004: The benefits of higher education for individuals and society.* Washington, DC: College Board.

Becker, G. S. (1962). Investment in human capital: A theoretical analysis. *Journal of Political Economy, 70*(5), 9–49.

Becker, G. S. (1993). *Human capital: A theoretical and empirical analysis with special reference to education* (3rd ed.). Chicago: University of Chicago Press.

Bruner, A. M. (1999, July 22). Lacking post-baccalaureate incentive. *Black Issues in Higher Education, 16*(11), 44–45.

Buchanan, P. (1997, June 13). The burden of massive debt on graduate students. *Chronicle of Higher Education, 43*(40), B6.

Burd, S. (2001, March 2). Lack of need-based financial aid still impedes access to college for low-income students. *Chronicle of Higher Education, 47*(25), A26.

Campaigne, D. A., & Hossler, D. (1998). How do loans affect the educational decisions of students? Access, aspirations, college choice, and persistence. In R. Fossey & M. Bateman (Eds.), *Condemning students to debt* (pp. 85–104). New York: Teachers College Press.

Carey, K. (2004, May). *A matter of degrees: Improving graduation rates in four-year colleges and universities—Report by the Education Trust.* Retrieved September 1, 2007, from http://www2.edtrust.org/NR/rdonlyres/11B4283F-104E-4511-B0CA-1D3023231157/0/highered.pdf.

College Board. (2002). *Trends in student aid* (Report No. 995972). Washington, DC: Author.

College Board. (2004). *Trends in student aid* (Report No. 040341320). Washington, DC: Author.

College Board. (2005). *Trends in student aid* (Report No. 050341687). Washington, DC: Author.

Council of Graduate Schools. (2007). *Ph.D. Completion Project.* Washington, DC: Author.

Davis, J. (2000). *College affordability: Overlooked long-term trends and recent 50-state patterns.* Indianapolis, IN: USA Group Foundation.

Denzin, N., & Lincoln, Y. (2003). *Collecting and interpreting qualitative methods.* Thousand Oaks, CA: Sage.

Ehrenberg, R. (1991). Decisions to undertake and complete doctoral study and choices of sector of employment. In C. Clotfelter, R. Ehrenberg, M. Getz, & J. Seigfried (Eds.), *Economic challenges in higher education* (pp. 174–210). Chicago: University of Chicago Press.

General Accounting Office. (1998). *Tax administration: Potential impact of alternative taxes on taxpayers and administrators* (Report No. GAO/GGD-98-37). Washington, DC. Author.

Geske, T. G., & Cohn, E. (1998). Why is a high school diploma no longer enough? The economic and social benefits of higher education. In R. Fossey & M. Bateman (Eds.), *Condemning students to debt* (pp. 19–36). New York: Teachers College Press.

Gladieux, L. E., & Hauptman, A. M. (1995). *The college aid quandary: Access, quality, and the federal role.* Washington, DC: Brookings Institution Press.

Glasser, B. G., & Strauss, A. L. (1967). *The discovery of grounded theory.* Chicago: Aldine.

Gravois, J. (2007, April 6). Trapped by education: How the discipline became the predominant one for Black scholars and what it's costing them. *Chronicle of Higher Education, 53*(31), A10.

Heller, D. E. (1997). Student price response in higher education: An update to Leslie and Brinkman. *Journal of Higher Education, 68*(6), 624–659.

Heller, D. E. (1999). The effects of tuition and state financial aid on public college enrollment. *Review of Higher Education, 23*(1), 65–89.

Ingels, S. J., Curtin, T. R., Kaufman, P., Alt, M. N., & Chen, X. (2002). *Coming of age in the 1990's: The eighth-grade class of 1988 12 years later* (NCES Report 2002-321). Washington, DC: Office of Educational Research and Improvement.

Institute for Higher Education Policy. (2002). *The policy of choice: Expanding student options in higher education.* Washington, DC: Author.

King, J. E. (1999). *Money matters: The impact of race/ethnicity and gender on how students pay for college* (Report No. HE 033129). Washington, DC: American Council on Education. (ERIC Document Reproduction Service No. ED443364)

Lincoln, Y. S., & Guba, E. G. (1985). *Naturalistic inquiry.* Newbury Park, CA: Sage.

McPherson, M. S., & Schapiro, M. O. (2002). Changing patterns of institutional aid: Impact on access and education policy. In D. E. Heller (Ed.), *Condition of access: Higher education for lower income students* (pp. 73–94). Westport, CT: Praeger and the American Council on Education.

Morgan, R. (2002, November 8). Are federal grants taking a back seat to student loans? *Chronicle of Higher Education, 49*(11), 11a.

Mortenson, T. (1991). Financial aid problems for dependent students from low income families. *Journal of Student Financial Aid, 20*, 32–41.

National Center for Public Policy and Higher Education. (2002). *Measuring up 2002.* San Jose, CA: Author.

Pascarella, E., & Terenzini, E. (2005). How college affects students: A third decade of research. San Francisco: Jossey-Bass.

Paulsen, M. B. (2001). The economics of the public sector: The nature and role of public policy in the finance of higher education. In M. B. Paulsen & J. C. Smart (Eds.), *The finance of higher education: Theory, research, policy, and practice* (pp. 95–132). New York: Agathon Press.

Perna, L. W. (2005). The benefits of higher education: Sex, racial/ethnic, and socio-economic group differences. *Review of Higher Education, 29*(1), 23–52.

Purdue president challenges universities to increase fellowships for minority graduate students. (2000, December 7). *Black Issues in Higher Education, 17*(21), 16.

Reindl, T., & Redd, K. (1999). *Institutional aid in the 1990s: The consequences of policy connection.* Paper presented at the 16th annual Research Network Conference sponsored by the National Association of State Student Grant and Aid Programs and the National Council for Higher Education Loan Programs, Savannah, GA.

Shapiro, T. M. (2004). *The hidden cost of being African American: How wealth perpetuates inequality.* New York: Oxford University Press.

St. John, E. P. (1991). A framework for reexamining state resource-management strategies in higher education. *Journal of Higher Education, 62*(3), 263–287.

St. John, E. P. (1999). Evaluating state grant programs: A case study of Washington's grant program. *Research in Higher Education, 40,* 149–170.

St. John, E. P. (2002). *The access challenge: Rethinking the causes of the new inequality* (Report No. 2002–01). Bloomington: Indiana Education Policy Center.

St. John, E. P. (2003). *Refinancing the college dream: Access, equal opportunity, and justice for taxpayers.* Baltimore: Johns Hopkins University Press.

St. John, E., Chung, C., Musoba, G., Simmons, A., Wooden, O., & Mendez, J. (2004). *Expanding college access: The impact of state finance strategies.* Indianapolis, IN: Lumina Foundation for Education.

Strauss, A. L., & Corbin, J. (1998). *Basics of qualitative research: Techniques and procedures for developing grounded theory* (2nd ed.). Thousand Oaks, CA: Sage.

U.S. Department of Education, National Center for Education Statistics. (2005). *Postsecondary institutions in the United States: Fall 2003 and degrees and other awards conferred: 2002–03.* Retrieved August 15, 2007, from http://nces.ed.gov/fastfacts/display.asp?id=72.

Witkowsky, K. (2002). Debating student debt. *National Cross Talk, 10*(4), 8–9.

4

THE PATH TO GRADUATE
SCHOOL IN SCIENCE AND
ENGINEERING FOR
UNDERREPRESENTED
STUDENTS OF COLOR

Marybeth Gasman, Laura W. Perna, Susan Yoon, Noah D. Drezner, Valerie Lundy-Wagner, Enakshi Bose, and Shannon Gary

O ver the past decade, the number of Black, Hispanic, and American Indian/Alaska Native students attaining bachelor's degrees in science and engineering fields has increased substantially. In 2004, 13.9% of all bachelor's degrees in science and engineering fields were awarded to students from these three groups, up from 11.2% in 1995 (Hill & Green, 2007). Although Blacks, Hispanics, and American Indians continue to be underrepresented among bachelor's degree recipients in science and engineering fields relative to their representation among all bachelor's degree recipients (13.9% versus 16.9% in 2004, Hill & Green, 2007), these trends suggest that progress is being made.

Less progress, and greater underrepresentation, is present at the master's and doctoral degree levels. Table 4.1 shows that students from underrepresented minority groups (i.e., American Indians/Alaska Natives, Blacks, and Hispanics) received only 6.9% of all master's degrees awarded in science and engineering in 2004 (up from 5.3% in 1995). Only 4.2% of all doctoral degrees in science and engineering were awarded to these students in 2004, a slight increase from the share awarded in 1995 (3.2%, Hill & Green, 2007).

TABLE 4.1

Representation of Underrepresented Minorities Among Degree Recipients in Science and Engineering, 1995 and 2004

Degree and field	Total		Underrepresented minorities			
			1995		2004	
	1995	2004	Number	% of total	Number	% of total
Bachelor's degrees						
All fields	1,174,436	1,407,009	158,432	13.5%	237,697	16.9%
Science & engineering	192,836	234,911	21,506	11.2%	32,728	13.9%
Master's degrees						
All fields	399,428	555,537	38,401	9.6%	76,699	13.8%
Science & engineering	57,918	75,399	3,069	5.3%	5,219	6.9%
Doctoral degrees						
All fields	41,750	42,155	2,673	6.4%	3,399	8.1%
Science & engineering	19,228	18,808	623	3.2%	797	4.2%

Source: Hill & Green (2007).

Notes: "Science and engineering" includes the following fields: science (agricultural sciences; biological sciences; computer sciences; earth, atmospheric, and ocean sciences; mathematical sciences); physical sciences (astronomy; chemistry; physics; other physical sciences); and engineering (chemical engineering; civil engineering; electrical engineering; mechanical engineering; other engineering). Although the National Science Foundation also includes psychology and social sciences in "science and engineering" fields, we do not consider psychology and social sciences degrees in this category.

Underrepresented minorities are American Indians/Alaska Natives, Blacks, and Hispanics.

This decline in the representation of American Indians/Alaska Natives, Blacks, and Hispanics along the pathway from bachelor's to doctoral degree completion in STEM (science, technology, engineering and mathematics) fields has important implications for the representation of these groups in STEM careers that require a doctoral degree, particularly college and university faculty positions. Thus, these data suggest that one critical mechanism for raising the representation of these groups among faculty in STEM careers is to improve their transition to and success in graduate school.

Degree attainment in science and engineering for Blacks, Hispanics, and American Indians/Alaska Natives is limited by the absence of appropriate preparatory courses, insufficient experiences with science-oriented activities, and a lack of same-race role models and mentors (Clark, 1988; Hanson, 1996; Leslie, McClure, & Oaxaca, 1998; Seymour & Hewitt, 1997).

This chapter describes how colleges and universities can promote graduate school enrollment and degree attainment for undergraduates from underrepresented groups in science; engineering; and, more broadly, STEM fields. Drawing on a comprehensive literature review, this chapter identifies four institutional approaches for improving the educational attainment of undergraduate students of color in STEM fields. It should be noted that the literature pertaining to students of color in the STEM fields is problematic in several ways. First, there are very few empirical studies. Instead, the articles tend to be personal accounts by both majority and minority faculty. Second, most of the articles related to this topic are relegated to journals pertaining to women and minorities. It is rare that an article can be found in a mainstream journal, leading us to speculate whether the topic and students of color themselves remain at the margins of the STEM fields. Third, most of the literature related to students of color in the STEM fields pertains to the undergraduate level, revealing a substantial gap in the literature at the graduate level. Finally, although the approaches discussed in this chapter are the most prevalent in the literature and have the most empirical support, there are other approaches that may be equally helpful to underrepresented students of color in STEM fields.

Traditional Approaches to STEM Education

Increasing the presence of students of color in STEM education can be framed as a social justice issue (Treisman, 1992). Because of past injustices committed against racial and ethnic minorities in this country, some faculty and administrators have believed that the nation has a moral obligation to provide opportunities to students of color. More recently, increasing the educational attainment of Blacks, Hispanics, and American Indians in STEM fields has also become an institutional priority, both to create future faculty and researchers and, as an economic imperative, to create a competitive workforce in a global economy. This economic justification for increasing opportunities and attainment for students of color in STEM education appears to be more acceptable to those who are made uneasy by affirmative action or social justice rationales (Treisman, 1992).

Traditional approaches to STEM education emphasize "survival of the fittest." Such approaches assume that the lack of attainment in STEM fields for underrepresented minorities is attributable to the students' background characteristics, including socioeconomic status, parental education, family support, preparation in high school, and even genetics (Armstrong & Thompson, 2003; Elliot, Strenta, Adair, Matier, & Scott, 1996; Leslie et al., 1998; Seymour & Hewitt, 1997; Treisman, 1992). In short, these approaches attribute failure in STEM to student characteristics, leaving the institutional or cultural practices of colleges and universities largely free from blame and responsibility.

In contrast, more recent approaches emphasize the institutional role in empowering students by drawing on students' strengths. Rather than questioning whether students of color *can* excel, these strategies focus on institutional changes that promote success in STEM fields for students of color (Hanson, 1996; Hanson & Johnson, 2000; Jordan, 1999; Treisman, 1992). However, myriad college and university STEM programs continue to assume that weeding out the weak is an optimal strategy (Seymour & Hewitt, 1997), despite the fact that a review of the research suggests that strategies that focus on empowering students of color in STEM are more effective than traditional approaches (Hanson & Johnson, 2000; Treisman, 1992). This chapter focuses on institutional strategies and approaches for empowering students of color to gain access to and complete graduate STEM programs.

Institutional Strategies for Promoting Attainment in STEM for Underrepresented Students of Color

Our review of available research suggests four institutional approaches for increasing access to and completion of graduate education for students from underrepresented minority groups: developing integrated support systems, ensuring inclusive curricula, promoting interactive classrooms, and increasing the availability of role models and mentoring.

Integrated Support Systems

One strategy for promoting the success of students of color in STEM graduate education is to develop an integrated support system. On many campuses, support programs for students in STEM are typically disconnected from the curriculum, for example, study skills workshops (Seymour & Hewitt, 1997; Treisman, 1992). One reason for this disconnect is that support programs are designed not by faculty but by administrators, who do not have an accurate understanding of course content or activities (Treisman, 1992). Consequently, most study skills programs are planned separately from the curriculum, with no consideration of the types of assignments given in classes. In effect, students are mastering skills that do little to promote their achievement in STEM classrooms and labs. Furthermore, the availability of other types of support programs—for example, tutoring in STEM fields—is insufficient to meet real needs (Seymour & Hewitt, 1997).

Treisman (1992) and Kane, Beals, Valeau, and Johnson (2004), based on their qualitative study, including observation and interviews, of Hartnell Community College, recommend that STEM faculty members at both the undergraduate and graduate levels work with academic advisers and program support systems to create student programs that address the kinds of assignments and exams given in STEM classes. These researchers also encourage the use of an early alert system, in which academic advisers and faculty identify students of color who are struggling academically. Identifying and addressing academic problems early in the program prevents students from falling behind and becoming disillusioned and overwhelmed with STEM education and may ultimately increase the number of students of color entering STEM graduate programs (Kane et al., 2004). Although the argument could be made that early identification of problems is important in any degree program, falling behind is particularly difficult in the STEM fields because of the steep learning curve and the sequential nature of learning as courses and assignments build on prior knowledge (Kane et al., 2004; Seymour & Hewitt, 1997). Moreover, falling behind during the undergraduate years makes it particularly difficult to pursue graduate study.

Compounding the problem of disconnected support systems is the low rate of usage of such systems by students of color and, in particular, Black and Hispanic students (Treisman, 1992). Research suggests that some students view support systems, especially those specifically for students of color, as remedial and inappropriate. Based on a qualitative study of African American and Latino students at the University of California at Berkeley, Treisman

(1992) describes how one such support system was viewed by these students. After being accepted to the university, students of color in STEM received a "welcome" letter that stated, "Dear Minority Student: Congratulations on your admission to Berkeley. Berkeley is a difficult institution. You are going to need a lot of help and we are here to help you" (Treisman, 1992, p. 367). Students typically ignored the letters, as many viewed them as insulting or degrading, given that most of the admitted Black and Hispanic students were academic leaders in their high schools and were viewed by their peers as role models. Thus, it is believed that the a priori assumption of low academic abilities affected students' self-esteem (Treisman, 1992).

In contrast, a more successful institutional strategy for increasing use of support systems by students of color is to establish nonremedial integrated support systems. Instead of merely providing tutoring, time management, and study skills, nonremedial support programs emphasize group learning driven by problem solving and a community life focused on a shared interest in STEM (Armstrong & Thompson, 2003; Kane et al., 2004; Treisman, 1992). These programs often invite all students, regardless of race/ethnicity, to participate, although programs in which students of color constitute a critical mass or a slight majority show the best outcomes for students of color (Treisman, 1992). For example, participating colleges and universities have found that through working with the Posse Foundation, an organization that organizes a critical mass of students of color to enroll at particular institutions and in particular majors, students are more successful and more likely to persist in college (www.possefoundation.org).

An integrated support system for students of color in STEM should also include attention to other university services, particularly housing and financial aid. Although STEM programs do not have administrative authority over such services, STEM administrators can work with administrators around the university to ensure that the academic progress of students of color in STEM is not derailed by housing, financial aid, and other nonacademic challenges (Armstrong & Thompson, 2003; Treisman, 1992). On the basis of an evaluation study using quantitative analyses, Armstrong and Thompson (2003) argue that STEM program faculty members and administrators need to "hasten students' acclimation to the university environment by introducing them to social, bureaucratic, and administrative hurdles that they must deal with as college students" (p. 161). For example, regardless of degree field, many Black, Hispanic, and American Indian/Alaska Native students are operating on extremely tight budgets and consequently depend on the timely posting of financial aid dollars to their accounts. In addition, at least in part because of financial need, about three fourths of traditional-age undergraduates (regardless of race/ethnicity) work while they are enrolled (Perna, Li, & Cooper, in press). Many students hold off-campus jobs that require them to work on average about 24 hours per week (Perna et al., in press). Although the academic performance and progress of students in all fields may be impaired by working long hours while enrolled, the negative consequences may be greatest for students in STEM fields, given the stringent academic standards and performance requirements in these fields.

Inclusive Curriculum

A second institutional strategy for promoting access and success in graduate programs in STEM fields for students of color is creating an inclusive curriculum (Armstrong & Thompson, 2003; Green, 2001; Seymour & Hewitt, 1997; Tobias, 1992). Research shows that African Americans and Latinos, in particular, often feel alienated by and fearful of STEM education curricula (Anderson, 1990). The four main reasons that students of color find STEM classes disaffecting are the "gatekeeper" approach to learning, the scarcity of diverse perspectives in the curriculum, the perceived lack of social relevance of STEM course work, and the use of pedagogies that fail to engage students of color in STEM course work.

Many STEM education programs feel that "gatekeeping" is useful and necessary for guaranteeing quality control after the admission process. As such, programs typically use gatekeeper courses to "weed out" students during the first two or three years. At the beginning of such courses, the teacher usually lays out the *failure* parameters, and in such settings, cooperation among a few students does not evolve naturally but instead results from desperation (Anderson, 1990, p. 352). Gatekeeper courses "send a message to students that being admitted to the program is not enough" (Busch-Vishniac & Jarosz, 2004, p. 270). Students must continually work to justify their presence in the program, and as Busch-Vishniac and Jarosz (2004) suggest, "It is difficult to think of something more discouraging than these gatekeeper courses, both for the students taking the courses and for the faculty members teaching them" (p. 270).

For students of color, the gatekeeping rationale discourages them from pursuing STEM degrees in several ways. First, Blacks and Hispanics are less likely to risk rejection and failure than their White counterparts are (Buncick & Horgan, 2001; Busch-Vishniac & Jarosz, 2004; hooks, 1994; Treisman, 1992). Second, to survive these gatekeeping courses, many students form classroom work groups. While Whites and Asians often work together in groups, students of color are often excluded from these groups because of their perceived inferior academic ability (Seymour & Hewitt, 1997). Finally, gatekeeping courses stress memorization over other forms of learning, particularly problem solving. Researchers who want to reform these crucial courses claim that there is a difference between a student's ability to memorize and his or her ability to solve problems (Anderson, 1990). As solving problems is the modus operandi of science and math disciplines, it is the key to success in STEM courses and should be recognized in the classroom.

In addition to the issue of gatekeeping, a second reason that students of color find STEM classes to be disaffecting is the perception that STEM curricula are gender biased and Eurocentric (Anderson, 1990; Riley, 2003). Some critics argue that technical courses within the STEM fields "are known for their White male bias" (Busch-Vishniac & Jarosz, 2004, p. 261). Researchers have found that textbooks for these courses fail to consider the contributions of females, and when they do, they fail to name the contributors (Busch-Vishniac & Jarosz, 2004; Marshall & Dorward, 1997). Thus, even if the scientific discoveries are made by women, the scientific heroes are all men.

With regard to race and ethnicity, textbooks rarely identify authors by race and few faculty members mention race during class discussions (Anderson, 1990; Busch-Vishniac & Jarosz, 2004). As a result, faculty and students seldom discuss the historical influence of non-Western civilizations (e.g., African, Indian, Chinese, and Mayan) on STEM fields (Anderson, 1990; Riley, 2003).

"Decentering" Western civilization requires an examination of the history of science literature for examples (Riley, 2003). Diversifying the curriculum is possible, as ample information describes non-Western origins of astronomy, physics, math, chemistry, and fundamental ideas in engineering (Anderson, 1990). To address this need, some STEM faculty members include a history of their discipline in introductory classes to show the diverse origins of math and science. For example, in a calculus or physics class, students of color may be inspired by faculty efforts to "show how early mathematics and science led to the building of the pyramids, the Great Wall of China, and the road to Katmandu" (Anderson, 1990, p. 355). Efforts to create a more inclusive curriculum are designed to "shatter the myth" that STEM fields of study are a "White man's thing" and to show students that "all civilizations, though they differ and develop at different paces, have always been bound inextricably to each other" (Anderson, 1990, p. 355).

The use of a curriculum that draws on the multifaceted history of the STEM fields is at the center of the success of many historically Black colleges and universities (Gasman, Baez, Drezner, Sedgwick, & Tudico, 2007). As such, these institutions are disproportionately successful in educating African

American students. For example, Xavier University of Louisiana, using a curriculum rooted in African American history and success, places 100 students in medical school each year (American Medical Association, 2005). This contribution is greater than that of any other institution in the United States and is especially impressive given Xavier's minimal resources and meager endowment (Gasman, Baez, Drezner, et al., 2007).

A third reason that students of color find STEM courses to be alienating is the absence of clear social relevance. In addition to wanting to see themselves in the curriculum, students of color are looking for a curriculum that shows the impact of science on the larger world (Busch-Vishniac & Jarosz, 2004). Busch-Vishniac and Jarosz (2004) argue that students of color and women tend to choose majors that they see as clearly beneficial to society and that they think involve a high level of interaction with other people. Students of color are also interested in exploring issues that are relevant to their own racial or ethnic subgroup (Busch-Vishniac & Jarosz, 2004).

To make the curriculum more diverse, relevant, and engaging, STEM programs must retool the curriculum from the ground up. According to Busch-Vishniac and Jarosz (2004), "There has been a strong tendency to use minor changes and additions rather than wholesale revamping [of the curriculum] to achieve diversity. The result is not surprising. Gains are modest at best and cannot be sustained without constant diligence" (p. 256). The authors suggest revamping STEM curricula to emphasize the many examples of how STEM course content can be used to help humanity.

A final component of an inclusive curriculum is the use of pedagogical approaches that engage students of color in learning. Seymour and Hewitt (1997) stress the need to use teaching styles that are inclusive and that foster learning for diverse populations, stating, "The most effective way to improve retention among women and students of color, and to build their numbers over the longer term, is to improve the quality of the learning experience for all students—including non-science majors who wish to study science and mathematics as part of their overall education" (p. 394).

The most successful instructional reform efforts in STEM education show the value of connectivity, engagement, and inclusivity (Buncick & Horgan, 2001; Busch-Vishniac & Jarosz, 2004). *Connectivity* means that the curriculum makes links to students' concrete life experiences (as noted earlier) and that the course concepts are not taught solely in isolation or in the abstract (Busch-Vishniac & Jarosz, 2004). In other words, connectivity requires an integrated curriculum and faculty attention to drawing connections between concepts. *Engagement* means that students do not sit passively in class but actively work with faculty or peers to solve real-life problems.

bell hooks's (1994) experience and research confirm the benefits of engagement. She found that women, in particular, are more engaged in learning
when instructional techniques require action and collaboration rather than
passive reception of knowledge. One way to promote engagement may be to
require students to take fewer classes and to ensure that these classes provide
a more in-depth approach to learning (Treisman, 1992). Group and collaborative learning opportunities may also promote engagement. On the basis of
quantitative analyses and qualitative interviews with STEM undergraduate
students, Seymour and Hewitt (1997) note that, although most students,
regardless of race or gender, attach importance to collaborative learning and
active engagement in the STEM classroom, students of color and women
"sought-after, used, [and] appreciated" group learning more than other students (p. 174). Opportunities to talk and interact with other students helped
the students of color to engage more closely with the course material (Seymour & Hewitt, 1997). As in the earlier discussion of diversity in the curriculum, *inclusivity* means that *all* students are actively engaged by the course
material and the professor (Buncick & Horgan, 2001). By embracing a curriculum that encourages students of color to see themselves as future scien-
tists, mathematicians, and engineers, programs increase the likelihood that
students pursue graduate degrees in these fields (hooks, 1994; McKeachie &
Svinicki, 2006).

Programs that adopt the three instructional approaches of connectivity,
engagement, and inclusivity are better able to prepare students of color for
graduate education in STEM. For example, at Eastern Illinois University,
with the support of the National Science Foundation, administrators created
a transfer degree program with a tribal college in Minnesota. The program
aimed to increase the number of American Indian computer science and
engineering bachelor's degree recipients by focusing on indigenous culture
and tribal relevance and using a culturally based education model. Within
two years of the program's inception, participating students were winning
national computer science and engineering competitions and receiving competitive scholarships from agencies such as the National Aeronautics and
Space Administration (NASA) (Busch-Vishniac & Jarosz, 2004).

Three-two programs (i.e., articulation agreements between two institutions) offer another model for addressing issues of connectivity, engagement,
and inclusivity. Three-two programs acknowledge that students of color can
benefit from the nurturing educational environments at historically Black
colleges, tribal colleges, and women's colleges and that students attending
these institutions can obtain a strong academic foundation in core math and

science classes (Gasman, Baez, Drezner, et al., 2007). Articulation agreements for three-two programs specify that students take the first two or three years of their studies—the time in which many drop out of STEM majors—at the nurturing liberal-arts-focused institution before moving to a larger, more technical institution to acquire discipline- and major-specific skills. Examples of institutions participating in these programs include Texas Women's University, Texas A&M University, Mills College, the University of Southern California, Morehouse College, Spelman College, and the Georgia Institute of Technology (Busch-Vishniac & Jarosz, 2004). Although these programs are, for the most part, at the undergraduate level, they are vital to success at the graduate level and typically act as an impetus for interest in graduate study.

Interactive Classrooms

A third institutional strategy for promoting access and attainment in STEM education for students of color is to shift the instructional culture from competitive to interactive. Several researchers observe that the undergraduate and graduate academic experience in science and engineering course work is typically competitive rather than collaborative (Armstrong & Thompson, 2003; Busch-Vishniac & Jarosz, 2004; Zhao, Carini, & Kuh, 2005). All too often, students in STEM courses see themselves in an adversarial relationship with their professors and in competition for good grades with their peers, especially because of curved-grading practices (Seymour & Hewitt, 1997). The typical STEM college classroom is designed so that individuals must "compete ruthlessly with each other for knowledge" (Anderson, 1990, p. 352). An emphasis on competition over collaboration is troubling because of the negative implications of this approach for both student persistence in STEM fields and student preparation for STEM careers. Most companies, especially those in science and technology fields, now want employees who can work in teams collaboratively (Busch-Vishniac & Jarosz, 2004). In addition, for women in particular, the perceived masculine culture of both STEM education and careers, with associated social and academic processes that, in addition to competition, stress the disconnected, objective rational pursuit of knowledge, conflicts with the preferred learning styles of women (which are typically more collaborative and situated), thus presenting further obstacles for access and success (Zhao et al., 2005).

When a few students, typically White males, dominate classrooms, other students may feel neglected and, worse yet, that they are not "right" for STEM fields, especially for future graduate study (Buncick & Horgan, 2001). To involve and support all students in STEM fields, Riley (2003) argues for an "engaged pedagogy" that "respects students in the classroom as authorities" (p. 147). On the basis of her theoretically driven research, Riley claims that "creating a community of scholars in the classroom is the goal, and if students and instructors can each bring knowledge and experience to share, it demonstrates that students have valuable contributions to make and that everyone deserves to be heard" (p. 147). Drawing on the work of hooks (1994) and Freire (2000), Riley encourages the use of liberatory, feminist, and radical pedagogies to create democratic classrooms. Specifically, she recommends that students participate in teaching in the classroom, creating in-class activities for other students, using technology, and gathering supplemental materials for course lectures.

Anderson (1990), a math professor, also suggests alternative approaches to teaching STEM. In his opinion, the teacher should take on the role of confidence builder. For example, Anderson explicitly tells all his students that they begin with an A grade but must struggle to keep it. He believes that this strategy communicates the assumption that all students "have the intellectual capabilities to understand the material" (p. 354). Anderson further explains that he attributes students' lack of understanding of course concepts to his own or the textbook's failure to communicate the material clearly.

One of the most effective approaches to creating interactive classrooms is to move more of the "class" from the classroom to the laboratory. This approach is particularly important in creating future researchers in the field, as students are socialized into the kind of work they will eventually do as scholars. According to Buncick and Horgan (2001), active learning includes discovery labs, in which students listen to engaging lectures and then respond within the laboratory setting. Within the lab, the goal is to have a "highly collaborative, hands-on, computer-rich, interactive learning environment" (p. 1240). This approach may be especially effective for African American and Latino students, as these students tend to respond better to exercises in which they have to "think things through" rather than shout out solutions (Buncick & Horgan, 2001). When faculty members call on students from different groups to predict results and interpret lab experiments, "everyone can be a star" (p. 1251). Buncick and Horgan conclude that, with this approach, "the sense of competition is diminished, and students who might be less aggressive experience a greater sense of membership in the joint teaching and learning enterprise" (p. 1251).

Instructors may also create interactive classrooms by focusing on student collaboration. Although few STEM programs emphasize student collaboration, researchers have found that learning about study practices from other students is beneficial, particularly for the amount of time they spend studying (Treisman, 1992). For example, in a study of undergraduate students enrolled in calculus, Treisman (1992) found that African American and Latino students spent between 6 and 8 hours per week studying alone for their calculus class. In contrast, Asian American students studied 14 hours per week, with 8 to 10 of these hours spent alone and 4 to 6 hours spent in a group. Group studying activities included checking one another's work and learning from one another, as well as eating meals together. In short, the Asian students created a type of "academic fraternity" (Treisman, 1992, p. 366).

Because calculus is a course that typically acts as a gatekeeper for most STEM fields, the absence of collaborative study techniques among African Americans and Latinos may be particularly problematic to the educational attainment of these groups in STEM fields. If faculty and administrators simply describe the potential benefits of collaborative study practices, it may encourage more Blacks and Hispanics to engage in these behaviors. However, faculty and administrators are more likely to encourage these potentially effective behaviors by actively facilitating positive student interactions with peers and faculty, creating and supporting effective study groups, and developing and promoting an atmosphere that encourages students to work together to help one another rather than compete with one another (Treisman, 1992).

Role Models and Mentoring

A final institutional approach to encouraging attainment for Blacks, Hispanics, and American Indians/Alaska Natives in STEM education pertains to role models and mentoring. Over the past decade, several studies have described the lack of faculty mentors for students of color (Armstrong & Thompson, 2003; Cheatham & Phelps, 1995, Davidson & Foster-Johnson, 2001; Ellis, 1997; Robertson & Frier, 1994). At the graduate level, the lack of faculty mentors for students of color is particularly salient because graduate work often requires working closely with faculty members on research projects.

Researchers consistently note that the shortage of Black, Hispanic, and American Indian/Alaska Native faculty in colleges and universities across the country results in insufficient mentoring for students from these groups (Blanchett & Clarke-Yapi, 1999; Hood & Freeman, 1995; Linthicum, 1989). These researchers suggest that students of color are more likely than their White counterparts to experience alienating instances of discrimination and

stereotyping, as well as other attitudes and behaviors that impede their educational success, and are less likely to have a faculty mentor to help them
avoid or cope with such experiences (Armstrong & Thompson, 2003; Cheatham & Phelps, 1995; Davidson & Foster-Johnson, 2001; Ellis, 1997; Robertson & Frier, 1994). "Stereotype threat"[1] and such forms of oppression as
racism, classism, and sexism also create unique challenges for students of
color (Spencer, Steele, & Quinn, 1999; Steele, 1999). Students confronted
with discrimination in their educational programs often need someone
with whom they can talk regarding these issues (Gasman, Gerstl-Pepin,
Anderson-Thompkins, Rasheed, & Hathaway, 2004).

The absence of faculty role models may be especially problematic for
female students of color in STEM fields. Female STEM participants, especially Black and Hispanic females, often come from families in which the
mother worked outside the home and in which students were urged to
develop independence (Hanson & Johnson, 2000). When these women
enter college, however, they encounter STEM faculties that are overwhelmingly White and male. As such, many students of color cannot find mentors
who share their cultural backgrounds and perspectives (Hanson & Johnson,
2000).

A review of the national data confirms the paucity of faculty of color in
many core STEM fields. Comparing the data in Tables 4.1 and 4.2 shows the
severe underrepresentation of Blacks and Hispanics among faculty at 4-year
colleges and universities relative to their representation among bachelor's
degree recipients, regardless of field. But the underrepresentation is especially
high in science and engineering fields. Table 4.2 shows that, among full-time
faculty at 4-year colleges and universities in fall 2003, Blacks represented only

TABLE 4.2
Distribution of Full-Time Faculty at 4-Year Colleges and Universities by Race/Ethnicity in Selected Fields, Fall 2003

Field	Total	Black	Hispanic	Asian	White	Other
Total	100.0%	5.1%	3.0%	9.7%	80.3%	2.0%
Engineering	100.0%	4.9%	2.4%	21.7%	69.3%	1.8%
Natural sciences	100.0%	3.4%	2.6%	15.7%	77.1%	1.3%
Business	100.0%	4.3%	1.9%	13.9%	76.9%	3.1%
Education	100.0%	6.6%	3.3%	4.1%	83.1%	2.9%

Source: Cataldi, Fahimi, Bradburn, & Zimbler (2005).

4.9% of faculty in engineering and 3.4% of faculty in natural sciences. Similarly, Hispanics represented only 2.4% of faculty in engineering and only 2.6% of faculty in natural sciences (Cataldi et al., 2005).

The importance of mentoring relationships is clear, as higher education research consistently shows positive effects of mentoring on undergraduate persistence and graduate school matriculation (Armstrong & Thompson, 2003; Cheatham & Phelps, 1995; Davidson & Foster-Johnson, 2001; Ellis, 1997; Robertson & Frier, 1994). Finding faculty members who appreciate the perspectives of students of color and who respect and value the contributions of scholars outside the White male canon can have a positive influence on the undergraduate experience and encourage the pursuit of a graduate degree. According to Smith (2000), "It is especially important for black female students to have early and extensive exposure to black women employed in the sciences, both in teaching and in research" (p. 351).

Must mentors be of the same ethnic or racial group as their mentees? Can Black and Hispanic students benefit from mentoring relationships with White professors? Given the grim statistics related to the racial/ethnic composition of faculty in science and engineering fields, majority faculty, in addition to faculty of color, must serve as mentors for Black and Hispanic students, and Black and Hispanic students must seek mentors regardless of the race/ethnicity of faculty. Even at minority-serving institutions, the majority of STEM faculty members are White and Asian (Gasman, Baez, & Turner, 2007).

Promoting student-faculty mentoring relationships at the undergraduate level probably has many benefits. Strong faculty relationships may foster the self-confidence and support that students need to enter and complete future graduate study. Such relationships also provide students of color with opportunities to observe research approaches and skills that they can later emulate in graduate school. Strong mentoring relationships may involve in-depth conversations about graduate school, further acclimating students to the culture of science and engineering education. Finally, through mentorship relationships, faculty may introduce students to their academic and professional networks, networks on which students may later draw during graduate school.

Conclusion

Preparing and encouraging undergraduate students of color to pursue graduate education in the STEM fields is a persisting problem. We know that students of color are not completing undergraduate degrees in STEM fields and entering and completing graduate degree programs in STEM programs at the same rate as their White and Asian counterparts are. That said, how can we solve the problem? This chapter summarizes four broad approaches that researchers and practitioners recommend: developing integrated support systems, ensuring inclusive curricula, promoting interactive classrooms, and increasing the availability of mentoring.

In addition to pursuing these four approaches, we must develop greater understanding of the educational experiences of graduate students of color in general and graduate students of color in STEM fields in particular. Many questions are currently unanswered. For instance, how does the transition from bachelor's degree programs in STEM to graduate STEM programs vary based on characteristics of the undergraduate and graduate institution? What mechanisms most effectively ease the transition from undergraduate to graduate STEM programs for students of color? Why are students of color leaving the STEM pipeline between the master's and Ph.D.? How do experiences in STEM fields vary among students of color? Addressing these and other questions requires rigorous research using a range of methodologies. Existing research relies primarily on descriptive analyses of students' experiences at single institutions. These descriptive analyses must be supplemented by more sophisticated statistical analyses that control for other explanations for the observed relationships, as well as rigorous qualitative work that probes the experiences of students of color in the STEM fields. Such research is required to understand more completely the most effective strategies for promoting educational attainment of students of color in STEM fields and ensuring that pathways to graduate study for students of color in STEM are accessible. In closing, as researchers and practitioners, we must remember that a society in which scientific knowledge is limited to the few cannot be an enlightened society.

References

American Medical Association. (2005). Retrieved from www.ama-assn.org.

Anderson, S. E. (1990). Worldmath curriculum: Fighting Eurocentrism in mathematics. *Journal of Negro Education, 59*(3), 348–359.

Armstrong, E. E., & Thompson, K. (2003). Strategies for increasing minorities in the sciences: A University of Maryland, College Park model. *Journal of Women and Minorities in Sciences and Engineering, 9*(2), 119–135.

Blanchett, W., & Clarke-Yapi, M. (1999, Fall). Cross-cultural mentoring of ethnic minority students: Implications for increasing minority faculty. *Professional Educator, 22*(1), 49–62.

Buncick, M. C., & Horgan, D. D. (2001). Using demonstrations as a contextual road map: Enhancing course continuity and promoting active engagement in introductory college physics. *International Journal of Science Education, 23*(12), 1237–1255.

Busch-Vishniac, I. J., & Jarosz, J. P. (2004). Can diversity in the undergraduate engineering population be enhanced through curricular change? *Journal of Women and Minorities in Science and Engineering, 10*(2), 255–281.

Cataldi, E. F., Fahimi, M., Bradburn, E. M., & Zimbler, L. (2005). *2004 National Study of Postsecondary Faculty (NSOPF:04) report on faculty and instructional staff in fall 2003* (NCES 2005-172). Washington, DC: National Center for Education Statistics.

Cheatham, H., & Phelps, C. (1995). Promoting the development of graduate students of color. In A. Pruitt & P. Issac (Eds.), *Student services for the changing graduate student population: New directions for student services, 72*(4), 91–99.

Clark, J. V. (1988). Black women in science: Implications for improved participation. *Journal of College Science Teaching, 17*(3), 348–352.

Davidson, M. N., & Foster-Johnson, L. (2001). Mentoring in the preparation of graduate researchers of color. *Review of Educational Research, 71*(4), 549–574.

Elliot, R., Strenta, A. C., Adair, R., Matier, M., & Scott, J. (1996). The role of ethnicity in choosing and leaving science in highly selective institutions. *Research in Higher Education, 37*(6), 681–709.

Ellis, E. M. (1997). *The impact of race and gender on graduate school socialization, satisfaction with graduate study and commitment to completion of the degree among Black and White doctoral students.* Unpublished doctoral dissertation, Pennsylvania State University.

Freire, P. (2000). *Pedagogy of the oppressed.* New York: Continuum. (Originally published 1970)

Gasman, M., Baez, B., Drezner, N., Sedgwick, K., & Tudico, C. (2007, January/February). The state of Black colleges. *Academe* (www.aaup.org/AAUP/pubsres/academe/).

Gasman, M., Baez, B., & Turner, C. S. (2007). *Understanding minority-serving universities.* Albany: State University of New York Press.

Gasman, M., Gerstl-Pepin, C., Anderson-Thompkins, S., Rasheed, L., & Hathaway, K. (2004). Developing trust, negotiating power: Transgressing race and status in the academy. *Teachers College Record, 106*(4), 689–715.

Green, R. (2001, Winter). Closing the achievement gap: Lessons learned and challenges ahead. *Teaching and Change,* 215–224.

Hanson, S. L. (1996). *Lost talent: Women in the sciences.* Philadelphia: Temple University Press.

Hanson, S. L., & Johnson, E. P. (2000). Expecting the unexpected: A comparative study of African-American women's experiences in science during the high school years. *Journal of Women and Minorities in Science and Engineering, 6*(2), 265–294.

Hill, S. T., & Green, M. M. (2007). *Science and engineering degrees, by race/ethnicity of recipients: 1995–2004* (NSF 07-308). Arlington, VA: National Science Foundation.

Hood, S., & Freeman, D. (1995). Where do students of color earn doctorates in education? The top 25 colleges and schools of education. *Journal of Negro Education, 64*(4), 423–436.

hooks, b. (1994). *Teaching to transgress: Education as the practice of freedom.* New York: Taylor & Francis.

Jordan, D. (1999). Black women in agronomic science: Factors affecting career development. *Journal of Women and Minorities in Science and Engineering, 5*(2), 113–128.

Kane, M. A., Beals, C., Valeau, E. J., & Johnson, M. J. (2004). Fostering success among traditionally underrepresented student groups: Hartnell College's approach to implementation of the math, engineering, and science achievement (MESA) program. *Community College Journal of Research and Practice, 28,* 17–26.

Leslie, L. L., McClure, G. T., & Oaxaca, R. L. (1998). Women and minorities in science and engineering: A life sequence analysis. *Journal of Higher Education, 69*(3), 239–276.

Linthicum, D. S. (1989). *The dry pipeline: Increasing the flow of minority faculty.* Annapolis, MD: National Council of State Directors of Community and Junior Colleges.

Marshall, J., & Dorward, J. (1997). The effect of introducing biographical material on women. *Journal of Women and Minorities in Science and Engineering, 6*(2), 279–294.

McKeachie, W. J., & Svinicki, M. (2006). *McKeachie's teaching tips: Strategies, research, and theory for college and university teachers* (12th ed.). Boston: Houghton Mifflin.

Perna, L. W., Li, C., & Cooper, M. (in press). Improving educational opportunities for students who work. *Readings on Equal Education.*

Riley, D. (2003). Employing liberative pedagogies in engineering education. *Journal of Women and Minorities in Science and Engineering, 9*(2), 137–158.

Robertson, P. F., & Frier, T. (1994). Recruitment and retention of minority faculty. *New Directions for Community Colleges, 22*(3), 65–71.

Seymour, E., & Hewitt, N. (1997). *Talking about leaving: Why undergraduates leave the sciences.* Boulder, CO: Westview Press.

Smith, N. C. (2000). Empowering African Americans in the sciences. *Journal of College Science Teaching, 30*(3), 156–157.

Spencer, S. J., Steele, C. M., & Quinn, D. M. (1999). Stereotype threat and women's math performance. *Journal of Experimental Social Psychology, 35*(3), 4–28.

Steele, C. M. (1999, August). Thin ice: "Stereotype threat" and Black college students. *Atlantic Monthly,* 44–54.

Tobias, S. (1992). *Revitalizing undergraduate science: Why some things work and most don't.* Tucson, AZ: Research Corporation.

Treisman, U. (1992). Studying students studying calculus: A look at the lives of minority mathematics students in college. *College Mathematics Journal, 23*(5), 362–372.

Zhao, C., Carini, R., & Kuh, G. (2005). Searching for the peach blossom Shangri-la: Student engagement of men and women SMET majors. *Review of Higher Education, 28*(4), 503–525.

Note

1. Steele (1999) argues that stereotype threat, a self-evaluative threat, negatively influences performance by shifting an individual's focus from performing a particular task to worrying that low performance will confirm a negative stereotype about a group to which the individual belongs.

5

COUNTERING MASTER NARRATIVES OF THE "PERPETUAL FOREIGNER" AND "MODEL MINORITY"

The Hidden Injuries of Race and Asian American Doctoral Students

Oiyan A. Poon and Shirley Hune

It's as though race is [a Black] issue, and no one else's. Sometimes it's a Latino issue, but it definitely never is an Asian American issue.

—Asian American doctoral student

The contradictions of multicultural inclusion for Asian Americans are acute in ways that emerge from both a history of racial and political exclusion and a history of being "foreign" to the national cultural terrain.

—L. Lowe (1996, p. 30)

One might ask, What is a chapter on Asian American doctoral students doing in a volume on underrepresented minority graduate students? Aren't Asian Americans well represented in higher education? Moreover, as a "success story," they must encounter little if any racism on U.S. campuses. This chapter counters such presumptions. The observation quoted in the first epigraph is from our survey and is representative of the frustration that Asian American students endure in having their encounters with barriers to educational advancement rendered invisible by a race relations framework that excludes them as a legitimate minority group. The second quotation, by a noted Asian American scholar, speaks to the challenges that Asian Americans face, past and present, even among those who are enfranchised, because they are consistently left out of the national racial and political discourse and are still treated as "foreigners" in the United States.

Advocates for racial equity often argue that "critical mass" is vital to reducing the marginalization and isolation experienced by students of color (Anderson, Daugherty, & Corrigan, 2005). They contend that a significant number and diversity of students, or at least proportional parity and representation of different racial groups, on a given campus can reduce or eliminate incidents of racial isolation. Although Asian Americans[1] as a panethnic aggregate have reached parity in many sectors of the educational pipeline, they continue to suffer significant daily incidents of racial marginalization and isolation (Sue, Bucceri, Lin, Nadal, & Torino, 2007). In recent publications, some scholars have called these incidents "racial microaggressions" (Solórzano, 1998). For Asian Americans, Osajima (1993) has named these daily affronts "hidden injuries of race," borrowing from the classic Sennett and Cobb (1972) book *The Hidden Injuries of Class*. Hune (1997, 1998) utilizes feminist critiques of "everyday inequities" to identify the costs of racialized and sexualized mistreatment of Asian American women in higher education, costs that limit their full participation. Like racial disparities in enrollments along the educational pipeline, these daily experiences are symptomatic of encounters that people of color experience within a social system of White supremacy.

As visible to casual observers as Asian American students have become on campuses, they remain dangerously invisible and excluded in discourses about race in education studies (Osajima, 1991). This exclusion maintains a process of racial triangulation, which silences and ostracizes Asian Americans from being actively engaged in political discourse and participation, dismissing ways by which they continue to be racially marginalized. Simultaneously, this process valorizes Asian Americans as a "model minority" in relation to other people of color (Kim, 1999). Racial triangulation, under the cover of color-blind discourse and racial power, reinforces the status quo by deflecting attention away from root causes of racial oppression and White privilege (Kim, 2000). The invisibility and exclusion of Asian Americans from studies on race in education ultimately maintains what Lipsitz (1998) calls a "possessive investment in whiteness," which manipulates people of color through institutional policies and practices.

In this chapter, we challenge the notion that the perceived critical mass of Asian American students has ended their racial isolation and marginalization in academia. The continued privileging of White men negatively affects Asian American doctoral students, in spite of their increased presence along the Ph.D. pathway. Moreover, the doctoral pathway is critical for diversifying faculty and administrative leaders in higher education. In 2005, only 0.7% of 4-year-college presidents were Asian American (*The Chronicle of Higher Education*, 2005). That they are so underrepresented at this level further contests the notion that Asian Americans are a successful minority group.

Understanding that racial diversification of faculty ranks is necessary, Davidson and Foster-Johnson (2001) propose methods and strategies for White, senior faculty to effectively mentor graduate students of color. The authors argue that mentoring is critical to the recruitment, retention, and persistence of graduate students of color and offer different strategies to be effective in these areas. Davidson and Foster-Johnson, however, base their characterizations of Asian American graduate students on literature that discusses cultural values in Asia, not in the United States.

When talking about Asian American students, it is important to differentiate between Asian students, those who grew up in Asia, and Asian American students, who have lived the majority or all of their lifetimes in the United States. Much of the literature on this topic refers to Asian cultures rather than Asian American cultures. An overemphasis on cultural explanations can dangerously reify stereotypes of these populations and do not provide critical insights into understanding and supporting Asian American and other marginalized populations in Ph.D. programs. The tendency of individuals and institutions to conflate international student data (i.e., Asian students) with domestic student data (i.e., Asian American students) is a disservice to both groups and distorts what we know about the opportunities and experiences of Asian Americans per se as doctoral students (Hune, 1998).

With regard to race, Asian American students are unique in their opinions and attitudes. Inkelas (2006) contends that although Asian American college students' views and perspectives on race are more akin to those of other minority students than they are to White students, their perspectives are significantly different from those of other racial groups because of their position of being neither Black nor White. They also do not fit the traditional definition or framework of what a racial minority is in education (Villenas & Foley, 2002). Inkelas also finds that Asian Americans' racial attitudes become more positive about racial diversity as they mature in age and advance toward completion of their bachelor's degrees.

Critical Race Theory: Countering the Racial Stereotypes of Asian Americans as "Perpetual Foreigner" and "Model Minority"

Asian Americans confront two principal forms of racialization. The oldest is that they are the "perpetual foreigner" or exotic Oriental, a characterization that dates back to European and U.S. efforts to dominate the Asian continent. Despite nearly two centuries of participation in U.S. history, Asian Americans still are seen as Asians and not truly American. U.S.-born Asian Americans find this response to be common in their daily interactions. Stereotyped as foreigners, they are viewed as incapable of being fully integrated into U.S. society because of cultural differences and, therefore, as less worthy of benefiting from what the nation has to offer. This stereotype can manifest itself benignly, as when Asian Americans are frequently asked to explain where they were born and how they speak English so well. When pernicious, it is a form of racial profiling. The leap to judgment in the media in 1999 that Chinese American scientist Wen Ho Lee must be a spy for China, a crime of which he was later acquitted, and the violation of his civil and human rights by the U.S. government is a fresh reminder of Asian Americans' fragile place in the nation's social and political fabric (Lee, 2001). Being viewed as a foreigner also has implications for the way Asian Americans are treated in educational institutions and challenges their sense of belonging as students, faculty, and administrators in higher education (Hune, 2006; Suzuki, 2002).

A second racial form, the "model minority," has its roots in the pre–Civil War era, when U.S. capitalists imported Chinese indentured laborers to counter White labor-rights movements and to replace Black slave labor, positioning Asian Americans as the "middle-man" (Aarim-Heriot, 2003). The term *model minority* within the context of education is the invention of William Petersen (1966) and other conservative public intellectuals, offered in response to the urban uprisings in the 1960s and manipulating a narrow sample of Asian Americans as an antithesis to African American claims of racial oppression. As a stereotype, it is a tool to exploit Asian Americans for the benefit of the elite in the racial hierarchy (Kim, 2000; Osajima, 2000). The dominant racial discourse reinforces ideologies that African Americans, Latinos, and American Indians suffer from cultural deficiencies by portraying Asian Americans as a "successful" racial minority, absolving institutions of racism for educational difficulties experienced by other non-White students. In addition to reinforcing the cultural deficiency argument, the application of the "model minority" concept silences and marginalizes Asian Americans.

Critical race theory (CRT) research interrogates race and racism as defining and organizing constructs in U.S. society, culture, and institutions.

It challenges dominant racial ideologies that create and reinforce structural hierarchies and analyzes how these hierarchies affect the experiences of minority group members. Most important, through an interdisciplinary approach, CRT privileges the perspectives, voices, and lived experiences of women and men of color in challenging dominant discourse (Solórzano, 1998). In this chapter, the perspectives of Asian American doctoral students are highlighted to describe ways in which White supremacy, through a process of racial triangulation, operates to marginalize this population.

Hidden Injuries of Race and Asian American Doctoral Students

The purpose of this chapter is to contribute to the research literature on the Asian American education pipeline by focusing on the experiences of Asian American doctoral students, an understudied group. In the new racism of the post-civil-rights era, many racial attacks on Asian Americans and other racial/ethnic groups are more covert. Whether the occurrences are verbal, behavioral, or embedded in the operations of hierarchical structures and organizations, racialized mistreatments of Asian Americans take place every day, are commonplace, are often brief, but definitely are harmful to their educational, professional, and personal development and well-being. We build here on the findings of three studies.

Osajima (1993) conducted interviews with Asian American undergraduates and identified their internalized racial oppression and conflict, including self-doubt about their worth and ethnic identity, as "hidden injuries of race." Finding themselves one of only a few Asian Americans and contending with stereotypes, such as "nerdy," or being orientalized—that is, the embodiment of all things Asian—for example, reinforced their difference, contributed to their isolation, and complicated their efforts to belong as a student. Osajima found their self-silencing, which contributes to the racialization of Asian Americans as quiet and passive, to be not a cultural norm but a survival or resistance strategy against racism that is adopted for the classroom and elsewhere.

A study by Hune (1998), which involved interviews and focus groups with Asian American female students, faculty, and administrators, highlights the ways in which women frequently are diminished, silenced, and made to feel unwelcome in academe, which hinders their academic and professional advancement and oftentimes subjects them to racialized sexual harassment. The "everyday inequities" that Asian American women encounter were manifested in racial and gender stereotypes about their intellectual abilities and language, accent, cultural, and communication-style biases that privilege

White males and their cultural values and norms. The women found especially exasperating the overattention they received as a symbol or token and the underattention given to Asian American issues and barriers. Hune's study argues that the Black/White framework of race relations is reproduced in higher education, where policies, practices, and programs marginalize Asian American students, whether it is in the curriculum, mentoring, or other areas of campus life, and continue on in their faculty and administrative lives.

Sue et al. (2007) also used focus groups to analyze the experiences of 10 Asian Americans, 8 of whom were students and 2 of whom were working professionals. Using the concept of racial microaggressions, the researchers identified eight major themes: (1) being considered aliens in their own land (i.e., perpetual foreigner), (2) having intelligence ascribed to them (e.g., math whiz), (3) the denial of racial reality (Asians do not experience discrimination), (4) the exoticization of Asian American women (primarily viewed and treated as sexual objects), (5) the invalidation of interethnic differences (all Asians are the same), (6) the pathologizing of cultural values that are not Anglo-American, (7) being treated as second-class citizens (i.e., as inferior), and (8) being treated as invisible. All these microaggressions negatively affect the lives of Asian Americans. That these microaggressions came from friends and neighbors as well as colleagues, coworkers, and teachers compounded the participants' feelings of anger and alienation. Sue et al.'s themes, many of which were also identified by Osajima (1993) and by Hune (1998), discussed previously, suggest that some Asian American racial experiences are similar to those faced by other racial minority groups, whereas others are distinct.

We use the term *hidden injuries* in this chapter because of the common dismissal of Asian Americans as a racial minority in higher education. We argue that the racial microaggressions that they face are injurious, but because of generalizations of Asian Americans as foreigners and as a "model minority," these injuries are invalidated and continue to be hidden. The remainder of the chapter describes the survey method implemented for this study, provides an overview of the national Asian American educational pipeline, discusses the characteristics of the respondents, and presents four forms of hidden injuries of race experienced by Asian American doctoral students. Finally, we discuss implications of the survey's findings.

Survey

We prepared a questionnaire[2] that was adapted from a survey instrument developed by Watford (2007) in order to assess graduate student experiences of belonging and marginalization in the academy. Watford's survey focused on gender equity in Ph.D. programs and explored ways in which women, despite being the new majority in some academic fields, continue to be marginalized. Watford challenges the notion that a critical mass, without other significant interventions, can counteract structural and cultural sexism. Similarly, through our survey we sought to explore racial marginalization, if any, among Asian American doctoral students, including those in academic departments in which they are well represented. Our survey instrument examined six areas of doctoral student experiences: the academic department, curricula and pedagogy, student networks, professionalization, personal responsibilities, and academic responsibilities. There were 48 questions in the survey, in addition to questions about the respondents' demographic background and status in their Ph.D. programs. What distinguishes our study from the previous research of Osajima (1993), Hune (1998), and Sue et al. (2007) is that we focus specifically on doctoral students and primarily on their experiences within their doctoral studies.

The survey was distributed over a 3-week period in August 2007 through various email listservs, whose members were primarily Asian American educators, students, and graduate students of color. Recipients were asked in the recruitment email to assist in further distributing the recruitment email and link to the Web-based survey. A recruitment message was also posted on two popular Asian American community blogs: Angry Asian Man (www.angry asianman.com) and Sepia Mutiny (www.sepiamutiny.com). These blogs collectively report a largely Asian American readership of over 450,000 each month.

Our data collection has some limitations. The survey was available for only a short time and may have been biased toward students who read blogs. Although we sought to cast a wider net by going outside a single institution, a focus that is typical of many studies, 114 surveys remains a small number for a national survey. Thus, we view our survey as a pilot study to identify and generate themes for future research on the experiences of Asian American graduate students. In using a CRT approach, we sought to create opportunities for Asian American doctoral students to speak for themselves about racial injustices in academe. But before describing the results of the survey, we need to place our survey respondents in a context: What does the Asian American pipeline to the doctorate look like?

The Pipeline: Asian American Degrees Earned and Major Choice, 1993–1994 to 2003–2004

The Asian American education pipeline in recent years is a story of growth, as depicted in Figure 5.1. From 1993–1994 to 2003–2004, Asian Americans

FIGURE 5.1
Asian American degree attainment, 1993–1994 to 2003–2004.

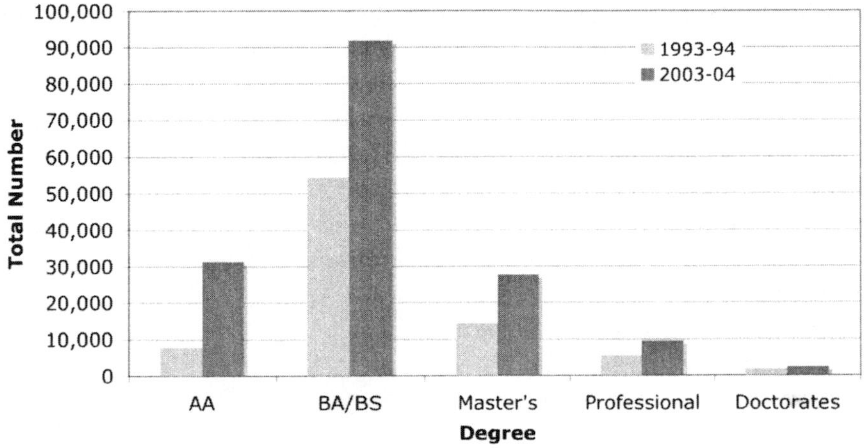

Source: Cook & Córdova, 2006

showed gains in all degree categories. Figure 5.2 demonstrates that Asian American women are driving this growth at every level, a finding that is consistent with the recent record participation of women among all racial and ethnic groups. Asian American females gained parity with their male counterparts in undergraduate education in 1990, much later than women in other racial/ethnic groups. By 2003–2004, they were earning 58% of Asian American associate's degrees and 55% of Asian American bachelor's degrees. In 2003–2004, business was the leading B.A./B.S. major for both Asian American women and men, followed by social sciences/history. In a larger context, Asian Americans represented 4.7% of total associate's degrees and 6.3% of total bachelor's degrees earned in 2003–2004 (Cook & Córdova, 2006, Tables 14, 15, 22).

Looking at graduate trends in this period, one can see that total master's degrees earned by U.S. citizens and residents increased by 46.1%. Minority students contributed much of the growth, with the number of master's degrees earned by minority students increasing 114% over this decade, compared to 22% for Whites. Asian Americans represented 4.9% of total master's degrees (27,759) earned in 2003–2004, compared to 3.8% (14,457) in 1993–1994. Women earned 53% of all Asian American master's degrees in 2003–2004, an increase from 46% in 1993–1994. In 2003–2004, business was the major most often selected by both Asian American men and women. The next most popular majors differed by gender. Engineering was the next most

FIGURE 5.2
Asian American degree attainment, by gender.

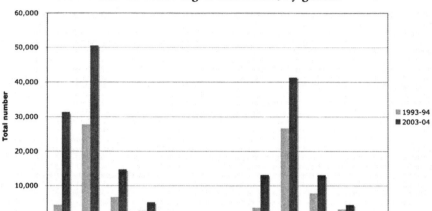

Source: Cook & Córdova, 2006.

popular major for Asian American men, and education was the next most popular major for their female counterparts, followed by the health professions (Cook & Córdova, 2006, Tables 16, 23).

The percentage of total professional degrees and doctoral degrees awarded to U.S. citizens and residents from 1993–1994 to 2003–2004 increased modestly, to 10.1% and 12.6%, respectively, largely because of a drop in degrees earned by men in both areas. Of the total number of professional degrees earned, the proportion that was earned by Asian Americans increased from 7.6% (5,758) to 11.5% percent (9,518) over this decade, the largest gain in numbers of any group. The most significant growth was made by Asian American women, increasing from 45% to 54% of total Asian American recipients of professional degrees during the decade (Cook & Córdova, 2006, Tables 17, 24).

There were 48,398 doctoral degrees and 83,041 professional degrees conferred to U.S. citizens and residents in 2003–2004. Here, Asian Americans demonstrated a modest gain, earning 4.5% (1,934) of doctorates in 1993–1994 and 5.1% (2,464) in 2003–2004. Asian American women held 51% of total Asian American doctorates in 2003–2004, up from 48% a decade earlier. Clearly more Asian American female first-year college students are aspiring to pursue doctoral degrees than are their male peers, and since 1971, there has been an overall increase in Asian American first-year college students planning to pursue a doctorate (Chang, Park, Lin, Poon, & Nakanishi, 2007). The leading doctoral field for Asian American men in 2003–2004 was engineering (271), followed by biological/life sciences (236) and humanities (174). That same year, Asian American women most often selected biological/life sciences (233), followed by health professions (195) and humanities (160), as their doctoral field (Cook & Córdova, 2006, Tables 18, 25).

Why are so many Asian American men and women drawn to professional degrees as opposed to doctorates? One explanation is that professional degrees offer a kind of job security, high earnings potential, and status among a largely immigrant community that doctorates do not. Moreover, women who were previously closed out of law, medicine, dentistry, and related fields are finding more opportunities in those fields (Hune, 2006). Also, in the view of students of color, professional degrees provide a more direct means to serve their communities. The distribution of Asian Americans across different Ph.D. fields is notable for the diversification of doctoral education; however, their numbers, though increasing, tell only part of the story. What is the quality of their doctoral experience? What can we learn about race in higher education from the voices of Asian American doctoral students as they navigate their Ph.D. programs? How does a deeper understanding of their daily encounters illuminate departmental experiences with peers and faculty? How do their insights contribute to the discourse on diversifying higher education, including future faculty, and to addressing the necessary changes required to ensure a welcoming and supportive environment for Asian Americans and all students of color?

Characteristics of Survey Participants

Overall, there was significant diversity among the 114 survey respondents in gender, ethnicity, generation in the United States, field of study, and enrollment status. Because national data sets that report the demographics of graduate students combine Asian American ethnic groups together as one racial category, it is difficult to know whether the ethnic demographics of our sample mirrors that of the national population of Asian American Ph.D. students. To participate in the survey participants had to identify as Asian American and had to be enrolled in a Ph.D. program at a university in the United States currently or within the past 3 years. Of the 114 respondents, 51.8% were female and 48.2% were male. A large proportion identified as Chinese/Taiwanese (44.7%), followed by Korean (13.2%), South Asian

(12.3%), Southeast Asian (9.6%), Hapa[3]/mixed race (9.6%), Filipina/o
(7.9%), and Japanese (6.1%).

In the United States today, approximately two thirds of all Asian Americans are immigrants. Most of our respondents, however, reported that they
were born in the United States, the majority being second generation
(59.1%), the children of immigrants. The next largest group was the 1.5 generation (30.9%), who came to the United States when they were under the
age of 12. A small number (7.3%) had parents who were both born in the
United States, making them third generation or beyond. Although the
majority of the respondents were U.S. born, only 41.2% said that English
was their first language; 30.7% stated that their first language was not
English. Slightly more than one quarter (28.1%) learned English and another
language simultaneously when they were growing up. About one third
(32.5%) stated that they were first-generation college students. Geographi-
cally, the respondents attended universities from all over the United States,
but the majority were in California and Hawaii (36%), the Midwest (24.6%),
and the Northeast (22.8%). Most (44.7%) were in the age group of 25–29
years old, but a significant number were 40 and over (18.4%). The vast
majority (88.5%) had no dependents.

Field of Study and Enrollment Status

There is a stereotype of Asian Americans as engineering or life/physical sciences majors. Our respondents, however, showed a diversity of academic disciplines: social sciences (30.7%), life/physical sciences (23.7%), education
(18.4%), arts/humanities (14.9%), engineering (7.9%), and ethnic studies/
interdisciplinary field (4.4%).

At the time of the survey, 25 respondents (21.9%) were no longer
enrolled in a Ph.D. program. Of the three respondents who did not finish
their doctorates, one left to pursue a career change, another to support family, and the third because of a lack of mentorship. Eighty-nine respondents
(78%) were currently enrolled in a Ph.D. program. Thirty-four students
(38.2%) were either preparing for their written examinations or completing
their course-work requirements. Twenty-one (23.6%) were preparing for
their dissertation proposals or oral examinations. Thirty-three (37.2%) were
in the dissertation phase of their program.

Hidden Injuries of Race and Asian American Ph.D. Student Experiences

Although the majority of the questionnaire used Likert scales, many respondents included rich descriptions of their experiences of marginalization

throughout the survey. Initially we sought to code the qualitative responses using the eight themes of racial microaggressions articulated by Sue et al. (2007). Upon closer examination, however, we found many of the themes to be interconnected, and so we focus on four forms of hidden injuries of race. By no means are the themes that we discuss a conclusive listing of all the hidden injuries endured by Asian Americans.

We found "invisibility" to be the overarching descriptor to characterize the racialized experiences of the Asian American doctoral students in this study. They are made invisible in academe when they experience being the "only one" in their departments, when treated as foreigners, when dismissed as not experiencing racial marginalization by White and other minority peers and faculty because they are neither Black nor Latino, and when others assume that "all Asians are the same" in disregarding differences by ethnicity or presuming that international Asian students and Asian American students are interchangeable.

Hidden Injury: "I'm the Only One"

Despite the perception of overrepresentation in higher education, the most articulated hidden injury of race experienced by Asian American doctoral students in the study was racial isolation. For successful Ph.D. students, collegiality and peer support is critical (Jaschik, 2007). Many respondents discussed the challenges of being the only Asian American in their program. A Chinese American female student shared, "Asian American issues occasionally come up in class, but I am sometimes uncomfortable with it because, as the only Asian American in my program, I feel like everyone's looking at me." Others found alternative ways to benefit from peer mentorship and support, as indicated by another Chinese American female student: "I am the only Asian American in my program. Non-Asian students of color are the most important support for me as they are in my program. Asian American peers are folks I meet at conferences or through other friends, so we have weaker ties." Although being the "only one" can present opportunities to develop relationships across racial lines with other students of color, for some respondents there were no other students of color in their programs, which can lead to intense racial isolation.

In addition to the lack of Asian American or other peers of color in their departments, some respondents noted the lack of faculty of color in their units. A Korean American male student shared, "For the first 3 years of my program there were no people of color on my faculty—Asian American, Black, Latino, or Native American." For some students the lack of faculty of color can be very detrimental. One Desi[4] American female student said,

"Sometimes I get the distinct feeling that White faculty may feel more comfortable with White students, hence be more likely to mentor White students vs. students of color."

Although having a fellow Asian American as a faculty advisor does not always lead to an empowering student-advisor relationship, a handful of students described their positive experiences with Asian American faculty advisors. A Southeast Asian American male student revealed, "My advisor, who is Asian American, is well-respected enough in my field (which is typically an old-White-men humanities field), [so I feel] that I am well-protected." That this student indicates a need to be protected in an all-White male setting is particularly interesting. A Korean American female student exclaimed, "I have an Asian American advisor who is the *best!* [She is] very supportive of my work and personal life. We work very well together." A Japanese American male student shared, "My ability to talk personally with my advisor is due to the fact that she is of similar ethnic background as me. I do not think I could do that with a non-Asian advisor." For this student, a shared racial background supports the positive relationship with his advisor.

Not many Asian American graduate students have the opportunity to have faculty advisors who are also Asian American, especially in the humanities, education studies, and social science fields, but overall experiences with non–Asian American advisors varied. As one Chinese American male student pointed out, "The training offered at my department was extremely uneven. I suppose it all depends on the advisor." Another Chinese American female student stated, "I think that faculty agree in principle to support Asian American research, but," in her experience, "they don't provide enough support or they treat it in an Orientalist manner." The importance of faculty supporting and mentoring students with research interests in Asian American studies has been expressed widely by students elsewhere (Hune, 1998), as well as in this study.

Hidden Injury: Being Treated or Mistaken as a Foreigner

Among the students who discussed experiences of being the "only one" in their programs, many also pointed out that there were Asian international students in their departments. As one Chinese American female indicated, however, "The depth of [our] interactions is fairly limited." Another Chinese American female student stated, "There are many Asian international students in my department. [But] my relationships with Asian American students in other disciplines is [*sic*] how I have been able to survive graduate school." A Korean American female student shared, "I am the first and only Asian American Ph.D. student in the history of my program. There have been and are currently many Asian international students, and the faculty has often misidentified me as an Asian international." Mistaking Asian Americans for Asian students simply on the basis of phenotype and treating them as foreigners further silences and dismisses their experiences of isolation as "the only one." Such a racial injury is a disservice to both Asian American and Asian students, who tend to have separate academic needs and concerns. Hence, neither group is well served by its departments.

Several students discussed their discomfort with being mistaken for an international student, who as a foreigner cannot claim the rights of citizenship. One Chinese American student, even though she was born and raised in the United States, noted, "Unfortunately, my previous advisor (a White female) was given to making racist comments about my 'English as a Second Language' grammar." For some reason, this faculty member found it acceptable to make racist and nativist comments. Perhaps faculty feel comfortable making such comments because, according to many respondents, students' grievances are rarely taken seriously. Many students said that actions were rarely taken against faculty who committed racist or sexist acts and that their complaints of anti-Asian racism were often dismissed as not truly being racist.

Although some departments have Asian professors, Asian American students explained that they were not a substitute for Asian American professors. As one Korean American male student described his disconnection, "There are no Asian American faculty members in my department. There are four Asian professors (two from China, one from Korea, and one from Taiwan), but they are foreign nationals and do not publish or conduct research on issues that are relevant to Asian America."

As the "perpetual foreigner," Asian Americans are also ostracized from discussions on race (Kim, 1999). In identifying themselves as the only Asian American student in their programs, respondents explained that people rarely viewed them as legitimate racial minority group members because they had Asian international peers. Although Asian American and Asian international students may share a common phenotype, they rarely share a common culture. As children of immigrants, Asian Americans, unlike Asian international students, have developed "hybrid" cultures (Lowe, 1996).

Hidden Injury: "Lumped" With Other Asian Americans

Students also described being grouped together with other Asian Americans and having their ethnic differences dismissed. One Filipino American male student commented, "I often find that I am lumped with other Asian Americans and therefore do not have my voice or experience heard, specifically as a Filipino American." Because some people assume that "all Asians are the same," Asian Americans often go through having their ethnic identities disregarded or having to explain their distinctions. A Desi American male student exclaimed in frustration, "Being Asian American at a predominantly White institution has its own challenges! Like being the spokesperson for the entire pan-Asian Diaspora. Explaining that I cannot really be the go-to person for how to cook Sushi or Kimchi, and folks don't understand how this can be covertly racist!" In this example, a South Asian American student is expected to know about foods associated with Japanese and Korean culinary traditions.

Historically, the term *Asian American* has its roots in the civil rights movement and is a positive affirmation of Asian Americans' belonging in the United States; it replaces the negative imagery of the "Oriental," which was created by the dominant White racial order (Espiritu, 1992). It is erroneous, however, to assume that there are no differences, including socioeconomic ones, among Asian American groups. Figure 5.3 provides data on the levels of educational attainment among Asian American groups.

Asian Americans insist on attention to their ethnic differences because of great disparities by ethnicity and class. The proportions of Hmong, Laotian, Cambodian, and Vietnamese individuals who are college educated are much less than the proportion of the overall U.S. population with a college degree or more. At the same time, the proportions of Hmong, Laotian, Cambodian, Vietnamese, Thai, Bangladeshi, and Chinese individuals with less than a high school diploma also exceed that of the overall U.S. population. Although the aggregate Asian American college attainment level surpasses the college attainment levels of several Asian American ethnic groups, most institutions treat all Asian American ethnic groups as one homogeneous group. Asian Americans are a population of contrasts and diversity of experiences and disparities. Treating them as a single monolithic "model minority" is an injustice, especially for those who experience the most disadvantages.

Hidden Injury: The "Model Minority"

Respondents also described encounters in which their inclusion as students of color was questioned through everyday experiences in their programs. A Desi American male student shared, "The entire gamut of 'the Asian American experience' is skipped in our program and college because of the perception of no struggles." According to this student, the stereotype of Asian Americans as a "model minority" leads others to neglect and dismiss their racialized experiences. A Chinese American male student went so far as to say, "Many 'students of color' believe that Asians are 'the other White

FIGURE 5.3

Asian American education attainment for population 25 years and older.

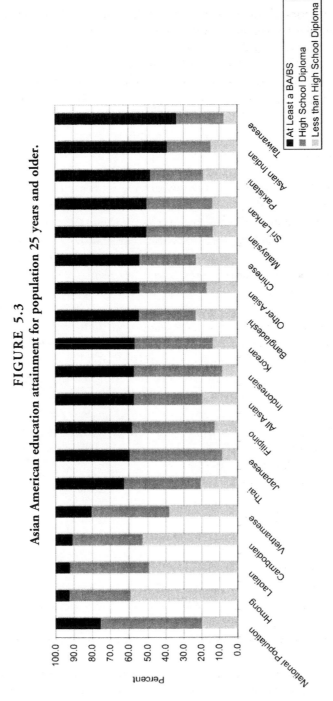

Source: Census, 2000.

meat.'" A Chinese American female described the experiences of Asian Americans this way:

> There has been widespread notice (by grad students) of preferential treatment for White students, offensive things said in class, and some of this has been brought to the attention of administration, with no change. Particularly, as an Asian American, I am treated as a minority when it's useful and as essentially White otherwise. Also, being interested in issues pertaining specifically to urban populations, I am made to feel that I am not "colored enough" to do such work.

In this student's lived experiences as a minority, she is treated as near White, but without the preferential treatment of being White, whether her experiences are akin to those of Whites or not, or she is treated as "not colored enough" to do work in urban communities, as if Asian Americans do not live in cities and confront urban inequalities as people of color.

As people of color, Asian Americans are harmed by a society that privileges Whites. Other people, however, often question their unique experiences as a racial minority group excluded from full participation (Hune, 1998). Invalidation that leads to invisibility and silencing was a common experience among the respondents. Although a racially diverse setting provides opportunities for developing multiracial coalitions and working relationships, a Chinese American female student described in great detail how her experiences of marginalization are invalidated:

> I feel like my African American peers invalidate my experiences as an Asian American. It's as though race is their issue, and no one else's. Sometimes it's a Latino issue, but it definitely never is an Asian American issue. I'm told with confidence by my African American peers that I'll get everything accomplished and all will be fine. I'm met with skepticism when I voice my concerns with an issue, because, after all, I have it "all together."

Another Hapa/mixed-race Asian American female student was shocked by the prevalence of racism in her experiences: "I was so surprised at how racism was such a big obstacle in my first year of the doctorate program. It was so evident that White students carried a sense of entitlement and also a few professors were openly discriminatory against doing projects focused on Asian Americans." Not only has this student endured racist incidents, but her desire to conduct research on Asian Americans is also not encouraged. These experiences may hinder Asian American students from developing multiracial work relationships and projects and may isolate them further in settings where they are the only Asian American student.

The deracialization of Asian Americans in higher education stems from the superficial assumption that they are overrepresented and from the dominant framework of deficiency in the commonly accepted definitions of *non-White* or *minority,* which further silences them and reinforces their invisibility. A Chinese American female student explained, "Many of my peers, conditioned by the idea that Asians are overenrolled in higher education, generalize this to every aspect of society and perceive that Asian Americans do not have challenges worthy of discussion or research. This is quite frustrating. The faculty do not discuss Asian Americans or the Asian American experience in the same detail as our Black and Brown counterparts." Another Chinese American female stated, "There is an overgeneralization that Asian Americans are well represented in all areas of academia. Women are subjugated to further silencing under this notion." In this student's opinion, while Asian Americans are silenced in general, Asian American women may experience a more profound silencing because of the intersectionality of racism and sexism.

Implications

Although the underrepresentation of Blacks, Latinos, and American Indians on campuses must be aggressively addressed, one must ask, What happens when parity is reached? Are the jobs of universities and scholars interested in racial equity done once the numbers are there? Watford (2007) explored gender equity in the academy "beyond equal representation" and found the persistence of disparities. Similarly, this chapter begins to explore racial equity after a presumption of equal representation.

Our findings contradict assumptions of success among Asian American doctoral students and show that there are many ways in which they experience the persistence of racism. In highlighting four experiential themes of hidden injuries of race in the respondents' comments, we expand on existing research and call attention to the need to reexamine institutional practices toward Asian Americans. First, many students in our study reported that they are the only Asian American in their program and described the isolation they experience among their peers and in their relationships with faculty advisors when there is a lack of racial diversity among faculty. Asian Americans, therefore, may not be as well represented in higher education as commonly presumed. Second, Asian American doctoral students are viewed as the "perpetual foreigner" and as interchangeable with Asian international students, despite differences in culture and nationality. Third, Asian Americans' ethnic differences are overlooked, which leads to institutional neglect of real educational disparities of some Asian American ethnic groups. For universities that claim a commitment to diversity, ethnically disaggregated data for Asian Americans can greatly inform institutional leaders in their considerations of racial equity. Finally, despite the racial microaggressions described by Asian Americans, their experiences as a racialized minority are dismissed because they are not viewed as a "legitimate" population of color and instead are viewed as a "model minority."

For doctoral students, financial funding is critical. That Asian Americans are too often declared ineligible for scholarships and fellowships aimed at increasing racial diversity is an unjust penalty. As one Korean American female student said, "I have been extremely frustrated that I never qualify for being a minority in regards to fellowships, etc. There are few Asian Americans in the social sciences and yet I am 'overrepresented' in grad school at large." To counter the invalidation experienced by Asian Americans, universities should include in their consideration for scholarships and fellowships aimed at addressing racial equity and opportunity Asian Americans who are the first to pursue higher education in their families, are from low-income backgrounds, or are pursuing fields in which there are few Asian Americans.

In research, race and education scholars often focus on the underrepresentation of Blacks and Latinos, but how do they address issues of racial equity in education and Asian Americans? We conclude that Asian Americans continue to face racial barriers to full participation in education and that their doctoral experiences require more attention from researchers and policy makers. Because these barriers may look different from those of Blacks and Latinos, they are dismissed as illegitimate concerns. The master narratives of Asian Americans as "model minority" and "perpetual foreigner" bring a certain level of visibility to them, but in the end these narratives also render Asian Americans invisible and silent in academia, marginalizing their perspectives and the issues they deem important. Thus, the hidden injuries of race endured by Asian Americans and the overall structures of White supremacy are maintained in the academy.

References

Aarim-Heriot, N. (2003). *Chinese immigrants, African Americans, and racial anxiety in the United States, 1848–82.* Champaign: University of Illinois Press.

Anderson, G. M., Daugherty, E. J. B., & Corrigan, D. M. (2005). The search for a critical mass of minority students: Affirmative action and diversity at highly selective universities and colleges. *Good Society, 14*(3), 51–57.

Chang, M. J., Park, J. J., Lin, M. H., Poon, O. A., & Nakanishi, D. T. (2007). *Beyond myths: The growth and diversity of Asian American college freshmen, 1971–2005.* Los Angeles: UCLA, Higher Education Research Institute.

The Chronicle of Higher Education. (2005). *Special report: The Chronicle survey of presidents of 4-year colleges.* Retrieved November 27, 2007, from The Chronicle of Higher Education Web site: http://chronicle.com/weekly/v52/i11/president surveytables.htm#background.

Cook, B. J., & Córdova, D. I. (2006). *Minorities in higher education: 22nd annual status report.* Washington, DC: American Council on Education.

Davidson, M. N., & Foster-Johnson, L. (2001). Mentoring in the preparation of graduate researchers of color. *Review of Educational Research, 71*(4), 549–574.

Espiritu, Y. L. (1992). *Asian American panethnicity: Bridging institutions and identities.* Philadelphia: Temple University Press.

Hune, S. (1997). Higher education as gendered space: Asian-American women and everyday inequities. In C. R. Ronai, B. Z. Zsembik, & J. R. Feagin (Eds.), *Everyday sexism in the third millennium.* New York: Routledge.

Hune, S. (1998). *Asian Pacific American women in higher education: Claiming visibility and voice.* Washington, DC: Association of American Colleges and Universities.

Hune, S. (2006). Asian Pacific American women and men in higher education. In G. Li & G. H. Beckett (Eds.), *"Strangers" of the academy: Asian women scholars in higher education.* Sterling, VA: Stylus.

Inkelas, K. K. (2006). *Racial attitudes and Asian Pacific Americans: Demystifying the model minority.* New York: Routledge.

Jaschik, S. (2007, July 17). *Why and when Ph.D. students finish. Inside Higher Ed.* Retrieved July 20, 2007, from Inside Higher Ed Web site: http://www.inside highered.com/news/2007/07/17/phd.

Kim, C. J. (1999). The racial triangulation of Asian Americans. *Politics & Society, 27*(1), 105–138.

Kim, C. J. (2000). *Bitter fruit: The politics of Black-Korean conflict in New York City.* New Haven, CT: Yale University Press.

Lee, W. H. (2001). *My country versus me: The first-hand account by the Los Alamos scientist who was falsely accused of being a spy.* New York: Hyperion.

Lipsitz, G. (1998). *The possessive investment in whiteness: How white people profit from identity politics.* Philadelphia: Temple University Press.

Lowe, L. (1996). *Immigrant acts: On Asian American cultural politics.* Durham, NC: Duke University Press.

Osajima, K. (1991). Challenges to teaching about racism: Breaking the silence. *Teaching Education, 4*(1), 144–152.

Osajima, K. (1993). The hidden injuries of race. In L. A. Revilla, G. M. Nomura, S. Wong, & S. Hune (Eds.), *Bearing dreams, shaping visions: Asian Pacific American perspectives.* Pullman: Washington State University Press.

Osajima, K. (2000). Asian Americans as the model minority. In M. Zhou & J. V. Gatewood (Eds.), *Contemporary Asian America: A multidisciplinary reader* (pp. 449–458). New York: NYU Press.

Petersen, W. (1966, January 9). Success story: Japanese American style. *The New York Times,* V1–V20.

Sennett, R., & Cobb, J. (1972). *The hidden injuries of class.* New York: Vintage.

Solórzano, D. G. (1998). Critical race theory, race and gender microaggressions, and the experience of Chicana and Chicano scholars. *International Journal of Qualitative Studies in Education, 11*(1), 121–136.

Sue, D. W., Bucceri, J., Lin, A. I., Nadal, K. L., & Torino, G. C. (2007). Racial microaggressions and the Asian American experience. *Cultural Diversity and Ethnic Minority Psychology, 13*(1), 72–81.

Suzuki, B. H. (2002). Revisiting the model minority stereotype: Implications for student affairs practice and higher education. In M. K. McEwen, C. M. Kodama, A. N. Alvarez, S. Lee, & C. T. H. Liang (Eds.), *New Directions for Student Services, Vol. 97: Working with Asian American college students* (pp. 21–32). San Francisco: Jossey-Bass.

Villenas, S., & Foley, D. E. (2002). Chicano/Latino critical ethnography of education: Cultural productions from *la frontera*. In R. R. Valencia (Ed.), *Chicano school failure and success: Past, present, and future*. New York: RoutledgeFalmer.

Watford, T. (2007). *Looking beyond equal representation: Perspectives of gender equity from the new majority in doctoral education*. Unpublished doctoral dissertation, University of California, Los Angeles.

Notes

1. Asian Americans are U.S. residents and citizens with ethnic and national origins in East, South, and Southeast Asia, including the Philippines.

2. For a copy of the questionnaire prepared for this study, contact Oiyan Poon at oiyan.poon@gmail.com.

3. *Hapa* in the Hawaiian language means "a portion, part, or fragment." In reference to people, the term generally refers to someone who is part White in Hawaii. It has also become a term for a mixed-race person.

4. *Desi* is the term often used by South Asian Americans in place of *South Asian*. Desi Americans are people with ethnic origins in the Indian subcontinent.

6

LATINAS IN DOCTORAL AND PROFESSIONAL PROGRAMS

Similarities and Differences in Support Systems and Challenges

Juan Carlos González

As of July 2006 there were an estimated 44.3 million Hispanics[1] in the United States (14.7% of the U.S. population, U.S. Bureau of the Census, 2007a). This number makes Latinas/os[2] the largest "minority" group in the country. Latinas/os are also the fastest growing minority group—projected to grow to 102.6 million by 2050 (24.4% of the 2050 U.S. population, U.S. Bureau of the Census, 2004). Despite this growth, the number of Latinas/os in the college-student population is not expected to grow significantly because of the massive leaks within the educational pipeline (Chapa & De La Rosa, 2006).

A look at the pipeline shows that in 2006, of the 23.5 million Latinas/os that were 25 years or older, 40.7% had less than a high school diploma, 41% had graduated high school, 5.9% held associate's degrees, and 8.8% held bachelor's degrees (see Table 6.1; U.S. Bureau of the Census, 2007b). Starkest was the attainment of graduate degrees: only 2.4% held master's, 0.4% doctorates, and 0.7% professional degrees. Latinas (women) had slightly higher attainment of associate's and master's than Latinos (men) and slightly lower attainment of doctoral and professional degrees (U.S. Bureau of the Census, 2007b). It is from these data that we begin our understanding of the "why?" and search for answers within Latinas/os' doctoral and professional school experiences.

This dismal situation for Latinas in the academy is one reason why many of them utilize their doctorates for employment outside the academy. Other

TABLE 6.1
Educational Attainment of Latinos and Latinas 25 Years and Over, 2006 (in thousands)

	Less than HS diploma	HS Grad	A.A.	B.A.	M.A.	Doctorate	Professional	Total
Men	4,992	4,999	616	1,001	266	57	110	12,042
Women	4,574	4,647	763	1,067	300	40	66	11,457
Total	9,666	9,646	1,379	2,068	566	97	176	23,499
	40.7%	41%	5.9%	8.8%	2.4%	0.4%	0.7%	100%

reasons that Latinas do not enter academe relate to the inherent racism that systematically excludes them (Olivas, 1988; Reyes & Halcón, 1988). Presently, in our era of immigration "reform" and the advancement of racist policies against Latinas/os, it is also important to understand differences between native and foreign-born Latinas. Native Latinas bring a particular educational experience and consciousness to the educational enterprise because of their K–12 educational socialization, whereas foreign-born Latinas may not. This difference may also be highlighted by class differences: native Latinas may enter academia with working-class backgrounds, and foreign-born Latinas may come from well-to-do families that could afford to send them to the United States for an education. In 2006, native Latinas earned 58.5% of the graduate degrees earned by Latinas (mostly master's degrees), and foreign-born Latinas earned 41.5% of the graduate degrees earned by Latinas, including 42% of the professional degrees (see Table 6.2; U.S. Bureau of the Census, 2007b).

In sum, the data show Latinas' lack of educational attainment leading up to doctoral and professional degrees. This lack of educational attainment led to the general questions that guide this research: How are the educational experiences of Latina doctoral and professional students similar and different? and How do they navigate and survive their doctoral and professional education?

Purpose

The purpose of this chapter is to qualitatively examine the similarities and differences in the support systems and challenges faced by Latinas in doctoral and professional programs. Few empirical studies exist on the experiences of Latinas in higher education, and the near nonexistence of Latinas/os in the ranks of U.S. faculty has made it difficult to create an impetus to explore this

TABLE 6.2
Graduate Degree Attainment of Native and Foreign-Born Latinas 25 Years and Over, 2006 (in thousands)

	M.A.	Doctorate	Professional	Total
Native[a]	192	22	24	238 (58.5%)
Foreign born	109	18	42	169 (41.5%)
Total	301 (74%)	40 (9.8%)	66 (16.2%)	407 (100%)

[a] Born in the United States but may be from native, foreign, or mixed parentage.

issue—particularly—because it is mostly Latina/o scholars who are interested in researching these issues. Where Latina/o research exists, it can be in a catch-22: on one hand, researchers who conduct research on Latinas/os are perceived as biased; on the other hand, researchers whose research is not considered "exotic" have a tenuous existence in the academy.

This chapter adds to the existing research on the Latina experience in academe, in both doctoral and professional programs. It is, ultimately, the responsibility of the Latina/o research community to inform aspiring academically talented Latinas about (a) the pitfalls that exist in the process of pursuing doctoral and professional degrees and (b) the benefits and rewards of pursuing such degrees. With this said, it must be noted that it is the responsibility of the Latina/o community to engage in research endeavors, such as this one, aimed at understanding how to succeed and advance in higher education, endeavors that will advance the political, economic, and educational interests of Latinas/os in the United States.

Review of the Literature

Because there is a dearth of research on the experiences of Latinas in academe, to set the context for this study I reviewed the bodies of literature about the experiences of doctoral and professional students more generally. The following review of the literature first highlights studies that address graduate students and then discusses studies involving professional students. Although this discussion does not by any means provide an exhaustive list— the search, for example, was limited to the past 15 years—these are some of the most critical pieces that have helped to shape our understanding of the Latina graduate experience. Furthermore, these studies all raise important issues that need to be addressed if institutions are to secure a pipeline for the production and success of Latina doctoral and professional students, an endeavor that is critical for the cultural and economic future of the United States.

Latina Graduate Students

Since 1992, most of the empirical research on Latina doctorates that has emerged from the social sciences has focused on Chicanas,[3] a subgroup of Latinas. Cuádraz (1993) interviewed 40 first-generation working-class Chicanas/os who earned their academic doctorates. Her interviewees recounted experiencing racism, sexism, and classism during their doctoral studies. It was their commitment to social justice in America, however, that helped them to persist in academe. Building on this study, Solorzano (1993) published a study in 1993 on Chicana/o doctoral students and found that although most of the students attained their doctorate, they quickly hit a glass ceiling when it came to using their degree to get an academic position. Solorzano also found that although the 66 Chicanas/os whom he interviewed had some support (particularly mentoring and research opportunities), the struggles (lack of financial support, lack of mentors, additional familial responsibilities, tokenism, and discrimination) far outweighed the support.

In another key study, Gándara (1995) interviewed 50 Mexican American graduate and professional students. Looking at the influence of family on educational success, Gándara found that the Chicana/o family is no different from a typical White family when it comes to teaching hard work, achievement, and success in school. The problem is that society does not understand this familial similarity. In a 1996 study with a different focus, Ibarra (1996) interviewed 77 college administrators, faculty, and graduate students to get a multidimensional understanding of the Latina/o graduate experience. He found that although Latinas/os have the desire to succeed and a lot to contribute, the American higher education system does not do a good job in educating them.

In addition to these seminal pieces, a few others add to the discussion on Latina/o graduate students. González et al. (2001) found that although an emerging generation of Chicana/o scholars has more support (such as mentors and a critical mass at the national level), these scholars are still extremely isolated at their respective institutions. Castellanos, Gloria, and Kamimura's (2005) edited volume adds that the doctorate for Latinas/os cannot be studied in a vacuum and that all the levels of education prior to the doctorate need further examination. That same year, Solorzano, Rivas, and Velez (2005) found that community colleges can be more detrimental than beneficial for Latinas/os in reaching the doctorate because many Latinas/os go there but few transfer to 4-year institutions. Finally, in 2006, I published a study on the academic socialization that occurs at the doctoral level, some of it good and necessary but a large part of it oppressive (González, 2006).

Latina Professional Students

Little research on Latina doctoral students exists, but even less has been written in the past 15 years about Latina professional students, particularly those in the health professions. This research is important because according to the most recent data available from the Association of American Medical Colleges (AAMC, 2007a), of the 17,845 women applicants to medical school in 2006, only 1,448 (12%) identified as Hispanic. Of the 7,804 women who were accepted and enrolled in 2006, only 641 (12%) identified as Hispanic (AAMC, 2007b). Whereas only 62% (8,114 out of 13,136) of all non-Hispanic women who were accepted actually enrolled, 97% (641 out of 663) of all Hispanic women who were accepted enrolled (AAMC, 2007c). And of the 7,746 medical students who graduated from U.S. medical schools in 2006, only 542 (14%) identified as Hispanic (AAMC, 2007d).

My search identified six key publications on the subject of Latina professional students since 1992. In the first, Grijalva and Coombs (1997) interviewed 20 Latina medical students and physicians and found that many of them experience stress, lack of confidence, sexism, and ethnic bias. But Latinas also do a good job coping with their challenges through positive thinking, being assertive, and developing social supports. Despite challenges, it is these types of coping strategies that have helped Latinas maintain a presence in medical school, where they are sorely needed because of their bilingualism and desire to work with the underserved Latina/o community (Treviño, Sumaya, Miranda, Martinez, & Saldaña, 1993).

In the second key study, Maville and Huerta (1997) investigated the effects of stress and social support on the academic achievement of Hispanic nursing students. Unsurprisingly, the researchers found that the less stress (due to a hostile academic climate) that Latinas/os experience, the higher their academic achievement. In addition to addressing academic stress, schools of nursing need to do a better job providing academic and social support. In the third study, by Villarruel, Canales, and Torres (2001), the researchers found that Hispanic nurses suffered from financial burdens, perceived discrimination, and prescribed gender roles. Not all was negative, however: some of the 37 interviewees also received support from peers, faculty, and family.

In addition to these three studies, three others have helped in understanding the experiences of Latina professional students. First, Taxis (2002) added that part of the problem that Latina professionals (in this case, nurses) face is that few professional programs offer culturally specific knowledge that is attractive to Latinas. Second, in a 2006 publication on Latina nurses, Taxis found the same challenges for Latinas that were found in the Villarruel et al. (2001) study. Taxis (2006) also found that Latinas in professional school have difficulties maintaining bicultural and authentic relationships, particularly when they are raised in exclusively Latina/o neighborhoods. Finally, Rivera-Goba and Nieto (2007) interviewed 17 Latina nurses. The researchers not only replicate the Villarruel et al. (2001) and Taxis (2006) findings but add that the main reason that Latinas do not develop authentic mentoring relationships is that there are not sufficient Latina nursing faculty with whom they can connect.

Theoretical Framework

In using theory to understand the Latina doctoral and professional school experience, it is as important to explain the incompleteness of certain frameworks as it is to show the most appropriate frameworks. Therefore, although critical theory offers tools by which to understand Latinas in higher education, cutting-edge frameworks such as critical race theory (CRT) and Latina/o critical theory (LatCrit) offer a greater degree of specificity and understanding.

CRT is best suited to explore the issue of Latinas in higher education because its basic premise is that institutional racism is the primary culprit plaguing American higher education. In addition, CRT is concerned with understanding relationships among race, racism, and power. According to Delgado and Stefancic (2001), some basic tenets of CRT are that (a) racism is ordinary (racism is common and part of the everyday experience of most people of color in the United States); (b) racial hierarchy exists and has a purpose (there exists in society a system of racial hierarchy, in which Whites are at the top of the power structure, which serves mostly the interests and purposes of Whites); (c) race and racial superiority are socially constructed and not objective, inherent, fixed, biological, or genetic (the concept of racial superiority is a type of White social "invention" of hierarchy that purports to explain racial differences in things like personality, intelligence, and moral behavior); and (d) people of color have a unique voice (a "unique voice of color" exists and explains how people of color can have histories and experiences with oppression that are completely foreign to many White people). These four themes of CRT are helpful in advancing an examination of racism and institutional racism, as it relates to education, and how educational institutions practice the subordination of racial and ethnic minorities.

LatCrit is an addition to and an enhancement of CRT. Although CRT and LatCrit are compatible and not in competition, LatCrit has been developed to highlight issues that are critical to a pan-Latina/o populace. That is, "LatCrit is supplementary and complementary to critical race theory" (Johnson & Martínez, 2000; Valdes, 1996). Because CRT does not specifically address some important issues in the Latina/o community, such as language rights, immigration, and citizenship, LatCrit has become popular as a comprehensive theoretical framework to understand Latina/o issues. So as not to "reinvent the wheel" in our understanding of historical subordination (Johnson & Martínez, 2000), LatCrit draws from both Chicana/o studies and the civil rights literature and theoretical bases, in areas such as (a) discrimination, (b) White-Black-Brown relations, (c) language issues/rights, (d) immigration and citizenship, (e) race/ethnicity, (f) culture and cultural preservation, (g) identity, (h) phenotype, and (i) sexuality.

To get a sense of the breadth and depth of LatCrit, Solorzano and Delgado Bernal (2001) describe it in the following manner: "LatCrit elucidates Latina/Latino multidimensional identities and can address the intersectionality of racism, sexism, classism, and other forms of oppression" (p. 312). Furthermore, "LatCrit theory is conceived as an anti-subordination project that attempts to link theory with practice, scholarship with teaching, and the academy with the community" (p. 312). Solorzano and Delgado Bernal describe five basic LatCrit themes. The four that are used as the analytical framework for this chapter are (a) the centrality of oppression based on race, class, gender, language, and immigration status (i.e., the layers of oppression that are important to understanding the pan-Latina/o experience); (b) the challenge to dominant ideology (i.e., the resistance to educational and societal subordination frameworks that have traditionally been used to "explain" Latina/o educational inequality and cultural inferiority, such as "objectivity," "meritocracy," "color-blindness," and "equal opportunity"); (c) the commitment to social justice (i.e., the responsive measures to the layers of oppression); and (d) the centrality of experiential knowledge (i.e., lived experiences as "legitimate" knowledge toward the understanding and advancement of the pan-Latina/o educational and societal condition).

Methods

For this qualitative study, 29 semistructured interviews were conducted with Latinas in doctoral and professional programs across the United States, 13 doctoral students and 16 in professional programs. Semistructured interviews began with general questions or topics used to create a more conversational dialogue between the interviewee and interviewer (Merriam, 1998). In addition, the semistructured interviewing allowed for the interviewers to build rapport with the interviewees by starting with questions about their background, their family, and how these contributed to their educational successes and challenges. In addition, the semistructured interviewing method allowed for a great deal of probing.

The interviewees needed to satisfy three selection criteria to be interviewed. First, they needed to be enrolled in a degree-attaining doctoral or professional program in the United States and working toward the attainment of their degree. The majority of the doctoral students had been in their program at least 3 years. The majority of the professional students were from the health field (particularly nursing, medicine, and public health), and few had been in their program more than 3 years. Second, they needed to self-identify as Latina, Mexican American, or Chicana. Third, interviewees had to be raised and educated in the United States to ensure a sample that understood the educational experiences of U.S. ethnic minorities. All the doctoral students satisfied this criterion. A few of the professional students were raised in Mexico, but because of their extensive professional training and education in the United States, they understand the conditions, struggles, and aspirations of U.S. Latinas and identify with them.

Two types of sampling methods were used: snowball and quota. Snowball sampling was used to identify doctoral interview participants. With this method, interviewees can be identified "from people who know people who know . . . rich information" (Marshall & Rossman, 1999, p. 78). During initial interviews, interviewees were asked if they knew other potential Latina interviewees, and many interviewees were found through this method. Quota sampling, popular with pollsters, is mostly used in survey research involving interviews when it is not possible to list all the members of the population of interest (Gay, 1996). This method was used mostly to identify the Latina professional students. Because a database of U.S. Latina professional students did not exist, quota sampling was effective, especially given the extensive interest that this study generated and the number of Latinas nationwide who emailed me to participate in the study.

I initially set the limit for the number of doctoral and professional students involved in the study at 10 and 15, respectively, but ultimately 13 and 16 interviews were conducted because of the extensive interest that was generated through the snowball sampling. All the doctoral-student interviews were conducted in person in 2005, and all the professional-student interviews were conducted over the phone in 2006. After identification and selection of the doctoral students through snowball sampling, the participants were interviewed at four national conferences throughout 2005. As in the initial identification of the doctoral students, the professional students were identified through contacts in the Latina/o community; and once these initial contacts were informed of the study, I sent email advertisements to listservs from national health organizations to Latinas.

Before interviewing began, a consent form was presented and explained to the participants, and then interviewees were asked to complete a short survey to provide some basic information, such as (a) years at present institution and as faculty and graduate students, (b) the degrees and fields of study completed, (c) previous institutions of employment, and (d) racial/ethnic self-identification. After completing the surveys, interviewing began.

All the interviewees were recorded with a digital recorder and transcribed with a digital transcriber. Data analysis was done with the N6 qualitative data analysis software (QSR International, 2006), which is used by researchers doing code-based analysis of complex data. N6 helps to organize data in a hierarchical treelike form, which allows for the ability to connect concepts and make relationships between different parts of the data.

Description of Interviewees

Although all the interviewees were Latinas, the two samples were different in some respects. Throughout the interviews, many of the interviewees revealed information about themselves that gave a sense about their background. Some interviewees found it necessary to talk about their educational history as far back as elementary school so that their purpose and drive would be better understood. Because of the sensitivity of some of this information, it was not asked for; it was voluntarily given. Table 6.3 shows a general glimpse and some key characteristics of the profiles of the interviewees.

Overview of Findings

The findings from the analysis of the 29 interviews can be seen through the lens of the LatCrit concepts. First, the concept of the "centrality of oppression" helps to explain the ways in which Latinas are marginalized, tokenized, and excluded based on differences such as race/ethnicity, class, gender, and language. Second, the concept of "challenging dominant ideology" helps to explain the ways in which students resisted and challenged different modes of dominant ideology that existed in the curriculum, the campus environment, discourse, and other forms of Eurocentric domination. Third, the concept of "commitment to social justice" helps to explain why students remained in the academy despite challenges; such a commitment included some students' desire to advance the Latina/o community intellectually. Finally, the concept of "centrality of experiential knowledge" helps to explain how students survive academia by finding their unique Latina/o

TABLE 6.3
**Description, Background, and Education Characteristics of
29 Latina Interviewees**

	Doctoral	Professional	Total
Self-Identification[a]			
Latina	7	11	18
Mexican American	6	7	13
Mexican[b]	3	5	8
Chicana	5	2	7
Hispanic	0	3	3
Other	2	2	4
General Field of Study			
Education	8	0	8
Humanities	3	0	3
Sociology	2	0	2
Nursing	0	7	7
Public health	0	5	5
Medicine	0	3	3
Dentistry	0	1	1
Type of Institution			
Public	11	14	25
Private	2	2	4
Educational Career Paths[c]			
Traditional	5	11	16
Nontraditional	8	5	13
Community college first	3	5	8
K–12 Schooling (type of school attended)			
Predominantly White	4	6	10
Predominantly Latino	4	3	7
Diverse	1	0	1
All-girls/private/Catholic	2	2	4

[a] Many Latinas spoke of having multiple ways of self-identifying, depending on the context, situation, and purpose.

[b] Identifying as *Mexican* did not necessarily mean that the interviewees had Mexican citizenship. Some of the professional students used the term to identify their country of birth, and some of the doctoral students used it to identify their primary cultural identity and heritage.

[c] *Traditional* is defined as having an initial goal of becoming an academic or a professional and pursuing an education without stopping for work, family, or other non-education-related reasons. *Nontraditional* is defined as the opposite: completing or pursuing an education with stops along the way for non-education-related reasons, such as career or family.

voice and being able to write about challenging the dominant Eurocentric ideology and culture.

Centrality of (Multilayered) Oppression

The comments that follow are representative of how these doctoral and professional students experienced their education: marginalization, tokenization, and exclusion based on race/ethnicity, class, gender, and language. There were obvious similarities and differences in the ways in which doctoral and professional students experienced their education. All students felt the cultural dissonance between Latina cultural capital and the social capital that is needed to succeed in American higher education. One notable difference is that the doctoral students were more race conscious and used words like *racism, discrimination,* and *institutional racism* more frequently to describe their experience and condition.

The professional students seemed less race conscious but more gender and language conscious. Their greater consciousness of gender probably had something to do with the fact that the fields of medicine and public health are traditionally more male dominated than the field of education is. Although the professional students lacked the vocabulary to explain the racial discriminatory nuances of their experiences, they still experienced racial/ethnic discrimination at some level. Also, some professional students felt that speaking Spanish was a definite advantage in any field in which they had to work with Spanish-speaking patients.

One doctoral student in sociology spoke about the cultural dissonance between academe and Latina/o culture:

> The socialization process of "they're socializing me to become a faculty member," that's hard. . . . I know [becoming an academic] means conforming, giving up certain things. . . . a lot of people assume that ethnicity is the price you pay for being an academic. You sort of strip yourself of your culture, and you take on the theme culture, and being at the beginning of that process, that's a little frightening.

This socialization occurred in a similar way for professional students, but gender was the primary concern for them. For doctoral students, gender discrimination was also present, but it was not as pervasive as racial/ethnic discrimination. In the following comment, a student finishing her degree in public health explains the existing gender hierarchy:

> Women want to go on to Ph.D. programs, but there's no support to do that. . . . [The status quo is that you end up with] females just kind of

supporting the males who are doing the "top notch research." I don't like that. . . . The women and the Latinas in our field are kind of taught, "you can be a coordinator, you can be a manager, you're really good at being a caring practitioner."

Another area in which discrimination was felt is language, possibly because among the Chicana doctoral and professional students interviewed, a majority of them stated that Spanish was their first language. The doctoral students did not necessarily speak about being discriminated against because they spoke Spanish, but they did speak of being outsiders because they did not know the "language of the academy." Latinas in medicine and nursing in particular saw their Spanish language skills as a definite advantage, but having these skills also meant that they were asked to do more work, without extra pay, to translate documents and conversations between doctors and patients. One nurse explained how she was mistaken by a doctor as a member of the family of the patient merely because she was talking to the patient in Spanish, even though she was wearing her uniform. All in all, the professional students spoke more than doctoral students did about the advantage of knowing Spanish, regardless of the extra work they were asked to do or the discrimination that came with speaking a "foreign" language. A student finishing her master's in nursing explained,

> At the school of nursing you see more of the population that needs more of your help, and it's usually been poorer people and people of color. So that's emphasized in the program for school of nursing. And I can remember in lectures people said, "You're so lucky because you can communicate directly with your clients." And I remember some people in class sharing how they would communicate with people with a "language barrier." That's when I realized, "My gosh, I'm really fortunate that I speak Spanish. I don't have to use an interpreter and it's not gonna take twice as long."

It was these discriminatory experiences that led many Latina students to be less tolerant of their faculty, particularly of any ideas that were perceived as racist, sexist, or Eurocentric. In the educational process, at some point, many of the students began to challenge and critique what they were being taught. Some of these challenges and critiques are presented in the next section.

Challenging Dominant Ideology

The experience of cultural dissonance between Latina/o culture and academic culture caused some Latina doctoral and professional students to react by challenging the dominant ideology that existed in the curriculum, the campus environment, and the discourses of their respective academic fields. The doctoral students used their language (Spanish and colloquialisms) as a form of resistance to the academic language of the academy. They also aggressively asserted themselves vocally against messages that they were receiving from the environment about their academic unworthiness. To challenge the discrimination that they were experiencing, some changed to departments that were more accepting of and receptive to their ideas and culture. Some identified themselves as scholar-activists, to distinguish themselves from scholars who were interested only in living the perceived plush life of people in the ivory tower. Some found mentors outside their department and were involved with the Latina/Chicana communities that existed across the university and in the surrounding community.

The professional-student resistance was not as pronounced, but professional students were very clear about and aware of the pervasiveness of the dominant ideology in their fields. Professional students, more than doctoral students, talked about relying on family support to survive and advance in their professional-school experience. Similarly, the doctoral students talked about connecting with other Latinas/os in their field beyond their department. Staying connected to the language and culture was a challenge, but it was something they felt would enrich not only their personal lives but also their professional lives. It was difficult for the doctoral students to find mentorship from other Latinas in their field since there were so few, and some doctoral students mentioned seeking the mentorship of diverse non-Latina women.

One doctoral student in education talked about her transformation from a practitioner to a scholar-activist. She spoke not only about challenging the dominant ideology of her field, which was primarily Eurocentric, but also about challenging other doctoral students not to passively accept the socialization that they were receiving in the department:

> Before all I ever wanted to do was be a professor and write theory. . . . Now I'm torn because I love theory, but I'm more interested in [figuring out how] I'm going to change the world and help to fight for social justice. . . . And not that I've given up total hope [on becoming an academic], but I just can't figure out how I'm going to do it all. . . . [Now my challenge is to figure out] how I'm going to bring down the theory to a child's level [in my job as a teacher], so that I can teach children without making them so radical that they're outside the system.

In another example of the pervasiveness of the Eurocentric curriculum, a nursing student explains how she diplomatically demanded that her professors teach her something about how to treat Latinas/os and other people of color:

[In my department] they always consider the normal patient to be middle class and Caucasian. So this is a lacking in cultural awareness. . . . Sometimes they say something about minorities, but the focus is on your middle-class White patient with insurance, and that's not the real world as far as all of our patients' care is concerned. . . . In general, there is a lack of the cultural training, and [the result is that] nurses that I work with are struggling to work with a diverse population. . . . I would expect, at the graduate level, that there would be more exposure to cultural diversity [in the curriculum], and that nurses' comfort level with diverse patients would be addressed. . . . I would like to see more exposure to different types of patients and from different types of income levels.

Ultimately, at some point in the resistance process, Latina doctoral and professional students find larger reasons for their existence within an oppressive education system. Some of these reasons are presented in the next section.

Commitment to Social Justice

The challenges faced by doctoral students included the lack of family support after moving to another state or across the country to pursue the doctorate. Once at the institution, these students lacked mentorship, were turned off by the academic politics in their department, and experienced financial difficulties. These challenges were coupled with experiences of racism, isolation, a biased Eurocentric curriculum, tokenism, and hostility from professors and peers.

The professional students had similar experiences, but most mentioned the rigorous curriculum as a challenge, which is not specific to Latinas/os. In addition, some of the most prevalent challenges included the competitive campus and classroom environments in which they were trying to advance professionally and academically. Others spoke of having their culture and language devalued, as well as of racism, discrimination, sexism, and stereotypes. Nearly all the students mentioned the challenges of being away from their family and the comfort of familial support, work-related stress, financial difficulties, and lack of mentorship.

Despite the extensiveness of challenges that these Latina students experienced, many survived, persisted, advanced, and graduated from doctoral and professional programs. One reason for this success is their commitment to social justice and their desire to make a difference in the Latina/o community. The doctoral students spoke of attaining the degree in order to serve the Latina/o community as activist-scholars. Similarly, the professional students explained the need to graduate and begin to serve the health care needs of the Latina/o community.

The following comment from a doctoral student in education explains the relationship between the purpose of her education and the Latina/o community:

> I see myself as part of a community of Latino scholar-activists, and in a sense part of a larger Latino community whom most of us are working to improve. . . . I think as academics we remove ourselves from grassroots activism, but I really feel that my scholarship is still activism, although some people see them as very different. [Scholars can still be activists], and I hope that the research I do is somehow benefiting our community. . . . That's activism, at least that's the way I define it. And I know there's some activists who think we're not doing enough, that we're not out there protesting, but our scholarship is activism, and it is a form of protest and a form of resistance.

Likewise, a public-health student explains how she will use her degree to benefit the Latina/o community:

> I always grew up wanting to be a doctor and being interested in health. . . . My family is also really into health. They grew up in rural Mexico. My mom was trained on how to give vaccinations when the health workers would come [to rural Mexico] to do this, so when I was young I learned how to give shots. . . . Now that I'm older, I'm studying poverty and obesity preventions. . . . And I'm also starting to work more [on] the health and education of recent migrants. . . . My ultimate goal in life is to teach Latinos to bring about change in their own community. . . . I don't like when students who don't have Social Security numbers tell me they can't keep going to school, because I know people who have done it.

The culmination of discrimination, resistance, and commitment to social justice moved many of these Latina students to understand better the social, cultural, and linguistic knowledge that they contributed to academe. This contributory knowledge is further explicated in the next section. It may seem like common sense, but through years of deculturalizing education, many Latinas are made to feel inferior for being different. With a deep understanding of their cultural knowledge, many Latinas focus on serving the Latina/o community as academics and professionals.

Centrality of Experiential Knowledge

In the academy, many of these Latina students found their unique voice and used it to resist the Eurocentric academic socialization that they were receiving and challenge stereotypes directed at their culture. Professional students also used their cultural knowledge and struggled to remain connected (socially and professionally) to other Latinas. Some spoke about using their cultural heritage to get funding from Latina/o-based scholarships. Most mentioned relying on their bilingual knowledge to assist in communication with Spanish-speaking patients. It was because of their cultural knowledge that they believed they were able to understand the health needs and concerns of the Latina/o community. Most of the professional students spoke about remaining close to their family, which nurtured them with the cultural and social support needed to perform well academically.

One doctoral student in sociology talked about the need, desire, and difficulties of doing research of benefit to the Latina/o community:

> Within my department, the few Latinos that are there, we tend to do Latino scholarship. . . . And overall the department has been fairly supportive of what I've been doing, but in the first couple of years when I arrived there was this general attitude [against it], and I actually had one faculty member tell me that focusing on Latino research was going to ghettoize me, . . . that somehow [it] was going to ruin my career. And my reply to him was, "Read my personal statement and letter of interest in this department; that's clearly what I said I wanted to do even before I arrived, and that's what I intend to pursue, and I'm sorry you feel that way." And from that moment I just avoided that faculty member. . . . I'm sure in his view he was trying to be helpful. . . . He was trying to give me good advice, but if anything it was an attack on who I was.

In another example, a public-health student who had just got accepted to medical school talked about using her degree and knowledge for the benefit of the Latina/o community. It was seeing her parents' commitment to serving the Latina/o community throughout their lives that inspired her to pursue medicine and return to her community as a doctor:

> My parents have always made a difference in the [Latino] community. My mom taught at a private school so that we could attend there. It would have been very expensive for my parents if they had to pay all that tuition for five girls. . . . My father could have taught at the university, but he decided to go teach at a community college. For me, I want to practice medicine in an area where I'm needed. Like our parents told us, all of us can go work wherever we want, but how much of a difference are we going to make [is what's important]. . . . And I see that with health care. There are a certain amount of people that no matter what they're gonna get good

care, they're gonna get their prescriptions, but what about those in the low-income rural communities? Are they gonna get it if I'm not there? So that's where I want to go, a place where I can do something about it.

In conclusion, Latina doctoral and professional students had very similar experiences, not only throughout their education but in their careers as well. There are nuanced differences, mostly having to do with the valuing of their social and cultural capital. In addition, other differences are seen in the social, political, and cultural mentality that native and foreign-born Latinas bring to academe.

Discussion

The higher education experiences of Latina doctoral and professional students show that although it is difficult to make generalizations, there are areas of similarity. Namely, Latina cultural devaluation by academia continues to be the norm, although the hostile climate varies department by department, and diverse departments tend to provide the most cultural affirmation. In addition, without the support from family and from the Latina/o community, the educational experiences of the 29 Latina interviewees would have been even more difficult, because it was this external support that helped them face adversity. And even though there is much literature and common knowledge about the benefits and necessities of mentorship for success, few of our interviewees acknowledged having meaningful and positive mentors in the academy. Those who did talk about having mentors, however, were resourceful enough to find them outside their department, in the larger Latina/o community, and within their family, people who might have had some graduate training experiences.

Prior to this attempt to look at the higher education experiences of Latinas in graduate and professional programs, there was little understanding of what might be found. This chapter has tried to shed light on these very different graduate experiences. What do I hope stems from the research presented in this chapter? First, the chapter should add to the dearth of literature on the Latina higher education experience. Second, it should provide higher education researchers and practitioners with an assessment of the present condition of Latina graduate students. And third, it should provide an impetus for higher education to take action to improve the climate conditions for Latinas and other students of color in the interest of social justice and equity. It is time for higher education to take action if it is going to be able to have a positive impact on the largest and fastest growing minority group, which is vital if the United States is to remain globally competitive in the 21st century.

References

Association of American Medical Colleges. (2007a). *Table 5: Applicants by race and ethnicity within sex, 2003–2006*. Retrieved August 1, 2007, from http://www.aamc .org/data/facts/2006/2003to2006det.htm.

Association of American Medical Colleges. (2007b). *Table 7: Matriculants by race and ethnicity within sex, 2003–2006*. Retrieved August 1, 2007, from http:// www.aamc.org/data/facts/2006/2003to2006detmat.htm.

Association of American Medical Colleges. (2007c). *Table 8: Hispanic ethnicity and non-Hispanic race by acceptance status, 2004–2006*. Retrieved August 1, 2007, from http://www.aamc.org/data/facts/2006/2006sumyrs.htm.

Association of American Medical Colleges. (2007d). *Table 21: Total graduates by race/ ethnicity within sex, 2002–2006*. Retrieved August 1, 2007, from http://www.aamc .org/data/facts/2006/grads4table21.htm.

Castellanos, J., Gloria, A. M., & Kamimura, M. (Eds.). (2005). *The Latina/o pathway to the Ph.D.: Abriendo caminos*. Sterling, VA: Stylus.

Chapa, J., & De La Rosa, B. (2006). The problematic pipeline: Demographic trends and Latino participation in graduate science, technology, engineering, and mathematics programs. *Journal of Hispanic Higher Education, 5*(3), 203–221.

Cuádraz, G. (1993). *Meritocracy (un)challenged: The making of a Chicano and Chicana professorate and professional class*. Unpublished doctoral dissertation, University of California, Berkeley.

Delgado, R., & Stefancic, J. (2001). *Critical race theory: An introduction*. New York: NYU Press.

Gándara, P. C. (1995). Over the ivy walls: The educational mobility of Chicanos. Albany: State University of New York Press.

Gay, L. R. (1996). *Educational research: Competencies for analysis and application* (5th ed.). Upper Saddle River, NJ: Prentice-Hall.

González, C. M., & Gándara, P. (2005). Why we like to call ourselves Latinas. *Journal of Hispanic Higher Education, 4*(4), 392–398.

González, J. C. (2005). *Doctoral education experiences of Latinas: A qualitative understanding of the relation of academic socialization to retention and success*. Unpublished doctoral dissertation, Arizona State University, Tempe.

González, J. C. (2006). Academic socialization experiences of Latina doctoral students: A qualitative understanding of support systems that aid and challenges that hinder the process. *Journal of Hispanic Higher Education, 5*(4), 347–365.

González, K., Marin, P., Perez, L. X., Figueroa, M. A., Moreno, J. F., & Navia, C. N. (2001). Understanding the nature and context of Latina/o doctoral student experiences. *Journal of College Student Development, 42*(6), 563–580.

Grijalva, C. A., & Coombs, R. H. (1997). Latinas in medicine: Stressors, survival skills, and strengths. *Aztlan: A Journal of Chicano Studies, 22*(2), 67–88.

Ibarra, R. A. (1996). *Enhancing the minority presence in graduate education VII: Latino experiences in graduate education: Implications for change. A preliminary report.* Washington, DC: Council of Graduate Schools.

Johnson, K. R., & Martínez, G. A. (2000). *Crossover dreams: The roots of LatCrit theory in Chicana/o studies activism and scholarship* [Electronic version]. Retrieved March 28, 2007, from http://ssrn.com/abstract=205210.

Marshall, C., & Rossman, G. B. (1999). *Designing qualitative research* (3rd ed.). Thousand Oaks, CA: Sage.

Maville, J., & Huerta, C. G. (1997). Stress and social support among Hispanic student nurses: Implications for academic achievement. *Journal of Cultural Diversity, 4*(1), 18–25.

Merriam, S. (1998). *Qualitative research and case study applications in education.* San Francisco: Jossey-Bass.

Olivas, M. A. (1988). Latino faculty at the border: Increasing numbers key to more Hispanic access. *Change, 20*(3), 6–9.

QSR International. (2006). N6 application Web page. Retrieved June 20, 2007, from http://www.qsrinternational.com/products/productoverview/product_over view.htm.

Reyes, M., & Halcón, J. J. (1988). Racism in academia: The old wolf revisited. *Harvard Educational Review, 58*(3), 299–314.

Rivera-Goba, M. V., & Nieto, S. (2007). Mentoring Latina nurses: A multicultural perspective. *Journal of Latinos & Education, 6*(1), 35–53.

Rodriguez, A. L., Guido-DiBrito, F., Torres, V., & Talbot, D. (2000). Latina college students: Issues and challenges for the 21st century. *NASPA Journal, 37*(3), 511–527.

Solorzano, D. G. (1993). *The road to the doctorate for California's Chicanas and Chicanos: A study of Ford Foundation minority fellows.* A Report to the California Policy Seminar. A Joint Program of the University of California and State Government.

Solorzano, D. G., & Delgado Bernal, D. (2001). Examining transformational resistance through a critical race and LatCrit theory framework: Chicana and Chicano students in an urban context. *Urban Education, 36*(3), 308–342.

Solorzano, D. G., Rivas, M. A., & Velez, V. N. (2005). *Community college as a pathway to Chicana/o doctorate production* (Latino Policy & Issues Brief No. 11). Los Angeles: UCLA Chicano Studies Research Center.

Taxis, J. C. (2002). The underrepresentation of Hispanics/Latinos in nursing education: A deafening silence. *Research and Theory for Nursing Practice, 16*(4), 249–262.

Taxis, J. C. (2006). Fostering academic success of Mexican Americans in a BSN program: An educational imperative. *International Journal of Nursing Education Scholarship, 3*(1), Article 19. Retrieved June 20, 2007, from http://www.bepress.com/ijnes/vol3/iss1/art19.

Treviño, F. M., Sumaya, C., Miranda, M., Martinez, L., & Saldaña, J. M. (1993, September/October). Increasing the representation of Hispanics in the health professions. *Public Health Reports: Journal of the U.S. Public Health Service, 108,* 551–557.

U.S. Bureau of the Census, Population Division. (2007a). *Annual estimates of the Hispanic or Latino population by age and sex for the United States: April 1, 2000 to July 1, 2006* (NC-EST2006-04-HISP). Retrieved June 20, 2007, from http://www.census.gov/popest/national/asrh/NC-EST2006-asrh.html.

U.S. Bureau of the Census, Current Population Survey. (2007b). *Educational attainment of the population 25 years and over, by citizenship, nativity and period of entry, age, sex, race, and Hispanic origin: 2006.* Retrieved June 20, 2007, from http://www.census.gov/population/www/socdemo/education/cps2006.html.

U.S. Bureau of the Census, Population Projections Branch. (2004). *U.S. interim projections by age, sex, race, and Hispanic origin.* Retrieved June 20, 2007, from http://www.census.gov/ipc/www/usinterimproj/.

Valdes, F. (1996). Latina/o ethnicities, critical race theory and post-identity politics in postmodern legal culture: From practices to possibilities. *La Raza Law Journal, 9,* 1–31.

Villarruel, A., Canales, M., & Torres, S. (2001). Bridges and barriers: Educational mobility of Hispanic nurses. *Journal of Nursing Education, 40*(6), 245–251.

Notes

1. *Hispanic,* as defined by the U.S. Bureau of the Census (2007a), refers to people whose origin is Mexican, Puerto Rican, Cuban, Central or South American, or other Hispanic/Latino, regardless of race. Because of the term's association "with a history of colonialism and continued new-colonist action by the United States government" (Rodriguez, Guido-DiBrito, Torres, & Talbot, 2000, p. 511) toward the people it identifies as Hispanic, I use the term *Latina* (the feminine of the masculine *Latino*) throughout this chapter.

2. The choice to use the term *Latinas/os* throughout this chapter was made because it was the term used by the majority of interviewees who were asked to self-identify their race/ethnicity. González and Gándara (2005) state that the term was "coined by the Mediterranean countries to resist Anglo dominance in the 19th century [and] is currently being used by people of Spanish-speaking ancestry in the United States to express ethnic pride" (p. 392).

3. I have previously (González, 2005) defined *Chicana* as a term to identify women who are of Mexican parentage and descent but who have grown up in the United States, generally in the Southwest. Women who self-identify with the term were born in the United States or Mexico, and a few in other Latin American countries.

7

AFRICAN AMERICAN MALE GRADUATE STUDENTS

Terrell Lamont Strayhorn

Many studies have consistently indicated that the educational outcomes of African American students are not on a par with those of their White and Asian counterparts (Chubb & Loveless, 2002; Fordham & Ogbu, 1986). Educational disparities are even more pronounced with respect to African American men. Recent reports suggest a virtual absence of African American males in college (Cuyjet & Associates, 2006; Roach, 2001) and graduate school (Strayhorn, 2008). The existing literature provides information about the precarious predicament of Black men throughout the educational pipeline (Bailey & Moore, 2004; Bonner & Bailey, 2006); Black male youth are underrepresented in honors courses and college but are overrepresented in special education classrooms (Kunjufu, 1986) and among those suspended (Lane, 2006) or expelled (Meier, Stewart, & England, 1998) from school. Their challenges at the postsecondary level have also been well documented in a number of sources. For example, although we have seen some progress in the enrollment of Black students over the past half century, advances for Black men have been inconsistent. In fact, most reports indicate that there has been little to no progress in increasing the college-going rates among Black men over the past quarter century (Mortenson Research Seminar, 2001). Indeed, the causes of the crisis with which many Black men contend are varied and complex; but surprisingly there appear to be no published studies that describe the status of African American male graduate students.

This chapter seeks to expand on the existing body of research by focusing on the status of African American male graduate students, using nationally representative data from the *Baccalaureate and Beyond Longitudinal Study*

(B&B:1993/2003), sponsored by the U.S. Department of Education, National Center for Educational Statistics (NCES).

Conceptual Framework

Although we know little about the status of African American men in graduate school, we do know some of the individual, institutional, and sociocultural factors that appear to affect students' success in higher education (Tinto, 1993) and graduate student persistence (Strayhorn, 2005). Thus, this chapter employs a blended conceptual framework to establish relationships among the variables studied and to guide the selection of variables to include in the analysis. As in previous work, I have sought to bring together a set of interconnected propositions that provide constructs for talking about Black men in graduate school. Blended frameworks of this sort are useful; they allow researchers to see in new and different ways what seems to be overly complex or unambiguously familiar. Framing this examination of the status of African American men in graduate education are theories of socialization, human and sociocultural capital, and graduate student retention.

A growing body of research has employed socialization theory to understand the "process by which persons acquire the knowledge, skills, and dispositions that make them more or less effective members of their society" (Brim, 1966, p. 3). For instance, using qualitative interviews, Jablin and Miller (1990) have identified four stages[1] in the vocational socialization process: (a) vocational socialization, (b) anticipatory socialization, (c) encounter, and (d) exit. Another school of thought views socialization as a *"learning* process through which the individual acquires the knowledge, skills, the values and attitudes, and the habits and modes of thought of the society to which he belongs" (Bragg, 1976, p. 3). Therefore, in the context of student socialization, the process is often defined by three phases: anticipatory socialization, encounter, and change or acquisition (Feldman, 1981).

Perhaps the most widely cited conceptualization of socialization is the one proposed by Weidman, Twale, and Stein (2001). The authors simplify the socialization process into three phases: (a) knowledge acquisition, (b) investment, and (c) involvement. A three-stage model has several improvements over other conceptualizations. Three-stage models are perhaps more parsimonious and still allow researchers to study the fine nuances that distinguish one phase from others (Strayhorn, 2006). Parsimonious models help to alleviate the paradox of theory, that "workable models are too complex to research and researchable models are too simplified to be useful in practice" (Parker, 1977, p. 420).

Weidman et al.'s (2001) theoretical orientation to socialization has been applied to a number of groups in higher education. Prior research has examined the socialization experiences of working-class students (Wegner, 1973), doctoral students (Austin & McDaniels, 2006), and faculty members (Tierney & Rhoads, 1993). To my knowledge, however, there are no existing scholarly works that apply socialization theory to understanding the status of African American men in graduate school. I settled on this frame because it allowed me to examine the processes (and external influences) by which African American men acquire the knowledge and skills needed to participate successfully in graduate education. Thus, I collected data on a number of variables to operationalize the sources of influence or *preparation* as delineated in the conceptual framework: educational aspirations, time to degree, and characteristics of the undergraduate institution, to name a few.

Other theoretical frameworks have influenced my approach to studying this topic. Human capital theory has informed this discussion (Becker, 1993; Schultz, 1971). Human capital suggests that individuals make investments in education, thereby gaining additional skills that are often associated with increased likelihood of occupational or professional success. In short, the more education that individuals attain, the more human capital they accumulate and, in turn, the more they benefit from their initial investments with respect to the outcomes they achieve. With this idea in mind, I examined the relationship between African American males' participation in graduate education and their academic achievement and degree attainment prior to graduate school.

Like human capital, social and cultural (also referred to as *sociocultural*) capital refers to resources that can be invested to enhance profitability (Bourdieu, 1977), productivity (Coleman, 1988), and upward mobility (DiMaggio & Mohr, 1985; Lamont & Lareau, 1988). Social capital takes the form of information-sharing networks (Coleman, 1988); cultural capital refers to the beliefs, tastes, and preferences derived from one's parents (McDonough, 1997). Drawing on these sociocultural explanations, I study Black males' enrollment in graduate school as a function of their parents' level of education. There is substantial agreement in the literature that parents' encouragement and active involvement in the schooling process facilitate students' achievement (Bandura, 1977; Feuerstein, 2000; Hess, Holloway, Dickson, & Price, 1984; Karraker, 1972; Keith, Reimers, Fehrmann, Pottebaum, & Aubey, 1986) and students' educational aspirations (Hong & Ho, 2005; Hossler, Schmit, & Vesper, 1999; Jun & Colyar, 2002). Often youth acquire some of the skills necessary to succeed in school from their parents, especially racially and ethnically diverse students, whose backgrounds are typically incongruent with dominant cultural perspectives. For example, Freeman (2005) has explained how college-educated African American parents instill a value of higher education in their children, which engenders an internal motivation or drive that makes the decision to attend college virtually automatic.

Finally, graduate student persistence theory justifies the inclusion of several demographic variables that relate to potential external pressures. Although Tinto's (1993) interactionalist theory of undergraduate student retention has reached near-paradigmatic status (Braxton, 2000), his theory of doctoral persistence is far less known. Surprisingly, despite the fact that approximately 50% of all graduate students drop out of college before earning their graduate degree (Bowen & Rudenstein, 1992), the forces that shape graduate student decisions and the way such factors coalesce under *certain* conditions for *certain* students remain unclear. Theoretically, graduate student persistence is a function of students' attributes and external commitments, as well as the nature of the academic and social systems of their department, among other factors (Strayhorn, 2005; Tinto, 1993). Several variables have been included in this study based on these theoretical understandings of the factors that influence graduate student success: age, marital status, graduate field of study, and number of dependents.

An important contribution of this chapter is the embedding of factors in a blended framework that draws on notions from socialization theory, human and sociocultural capital, and student persistence models. In some ways, this approach has allowed me to look at one topic from several vantage points—"to exoticize the ordinary" (Besnier, 1995, p. 560) or, expressed differently, "to make the ordinary strange" (Jakobson, 1987, p. 25). As an African American male (former graduate student turned faculty member) writing about African American males in graduate school, I think this is a potentially fruitful activity.

Review of the Relevant Literature

Since there has been virtually nothing written about Black men in graduate school, I have drawn from other bodies of literature to inform this chapter. Specifically, I have reviewed the literature on African American students in higher education, African American men in college, and graduate students in the United States.

African American Students in Higher Education

One segment of the literature on African Americans in higher education consists of historical accounts that accentuate the long history of unequal educational opportunity for African Americans. For example, even as late as the 1900s, some Southern states, like Virginia, either mandated statutory segregated education or prohibited the education of "colored" persons.[2] In segregated higher education systems, African Americans were accommodated at historically Black colleges and universities (HBCUs), which are largely located in the Southeast region of the country. Despite the fact that predominantly White institutions (PWIs) enroll 75% of all African American students today, historically Black colleges, representing less than 3% of all postsecondary institutions in the United States, still award over 50% of all Black bachelor's degrees (Nettles & Perna, 1997; U.S. Department of Education, 2006). Other historical pieces concentrate on the post–*Brown v. Board of Education* era, recognizing the significance of *Brown*, a court decision that effected changes of monumental proportions with respect to Black education in America (Brown, 1999; Kluger, 1975).

By the 1990s, research started to shift away from discourse on unequal educational opportunity and social stratification of the races and toward purposeful examinations of the experiences of African Americans in college. For example, a long line of research has established that HBCUs foster a nurturing environment that promotes Black students' success (DeSousa & Kuh, 1996; Flowers, 2003; Hirt, Strayhorn, Amelink, & Bennett, 2006; Kimbrough & Harper, 2006). Although most HBCUs have fewer resources than PWIs do, Nettles, Thoeny, and Gosman (1986) argue that Black students who attend HBCUs benefit from a supportive social, cultural, and racial environment that enhances their successful adaptation to the academic demands of college life. Such environments facilitate positive psychosocial adjustments, stronger cultural solidarity, and a commitment to racial uplift (Allen & Haniff, 1991; Fries-Britt & Turner, 2002; Hirt et al., 2006).

Another stream of inquiry focuses on the labor market outcomes of African American students (Allen, 1992; Constantine, 1994, 1995; Ehrenberg & Rothstein, 1994; Fitzgerald, 2000; London, 1998; Sagen, Dallam, & Laverty, 1997; Strayhorn, 2008; Thomas, 2000). The weight of evidence suggests that Black college graduates are at a disadvantage with respect to postbaccalaureate earnings and occupational status. For instance, some studies have shown that African Americans report lower scores on job satisfaction than do their White counterparts (Phelan & Phelan, 1983) and other minority groups

(Mau & Kopischke, 2001). Ehrenberg and Rothstein (1994), along with Thomas (2000), analyzed national data and found that institutional characteristics do not explain disparities in earnings and occupational status, controlling for an array of intervening variables. In contrast, I have found that African Americans who graduate from historically Black colleges report lower post-B.A. earnings and higher occupational status, on average, than do their counterparts at predominantly White institutions.

Despite such studies, socioeconomic disparities persist. A dramatic depiction of the current situation is reflected in national net-worth comparisons: "In 2001, the typical Black household had a net worth of just $19,000 (including home equity) compared with $120,000 for Whites" (Muhammad, Davis, Lui, & Leondar-Wright, 2004). Although the evidence is somewhat clear that African Americans face significant disparities with respect to labor market outcomes, it is less clear just why this is the case. Some scholars point to social pathologies (e.g., racism and discrimination) that systemically disadvantage African Americans, but most scholars agree that the underlying causal mechanism is not completely known. Analysts tend to focus on the decision to attend college, but it may be that what matters most is what happens *in* college (i.e., involvement) and *after* college (i.e., graduate education).

Studies on the *in*-college experiences of Black students form, arguably, the largest single body of research on this population and include experiences such as involvement in clubs and organizations (Sutton & Kimbrough, 2001), mentoring relationships (Strayhorn & Terrell, 2007), and racialized spaces such as Black cultural centers (Patton, 2006; Stennis-Williams, Terrell, & Haynes, 1988), to name a few. For instance, several studies have shown that African American students, especially those who attend PWIs, tend to become involved in ethnocentric or cultural organizations (e.g., Black student unions, gospel choirs, and fraternities) in an attempt to create a strong social enclave on campus that "reflects Black," that is, a "safe space" that affirms their cultural identity and their experiences on campus (Sutton & Kimbrough, 2001; Tatum, 1997). Involvement in ethnic organizations often leads to involvement in the broader campus community.

Most of the research on African American students in college, however, treats Black men and women as a monolithic group whose experiences are more similar than different. So although we know a great deal about African American students in general, we know relatively little about Black male collegians in particular.

African American Men in College

In the most recent comprehensive treatment of the topic of African American men in college, Cuyjet and Associates (2006) provide extensive summaries of extant literature, and several authors provide empirical evidence to describe the status of African American men in college. Throughout the text, authors describe the circumstances from which many African American males emerge and offer suggestions for ways to assist Black men to succeed in college. The volume fills a noticeable gap in the literature, as most monographs focus on African American students collectively. In contrast, Cuyjet and Associates include separate chapters on Black male subgroups including fraternity men, student leaders, athletes, and gay men. Strikingly, however, Cuyjet's encyclopedic treatment of the topic fails to address African American male graduate students.

Indeed, there are other holes in the existing literature. For example, the comparatively few studies that have explored the educational experiences of African American men have used single institutions (Canady, 2007; Stevens, 2007), small samples at multiple institutions (Hamilton, 2005), and qualitative methods (Hamilton, 2005; Harper, 2003), specifically interviews. Without exception, all these studies focus on African American male undergraduates rather than Black men in graduate school. These methodological and sampling choices result in a body of evidence that "present[s] only a partial picture" of Black males' collegiate experiences (Pascarella & Terenzini, 2005, p. 630). The study on which the present chapter is based sought to add a missing component to the existing literature by using large, national data to focus on the status of African American males in graduate school.

Graduate Students in the United States

Over time, a growing body of research has amassed on graduate education (Berelson, 1960; Bowen & Rudenstein, 1992; Golde & Walker, 2006) and on graduate students in general. For instance, some studies highlight aspects of the graduate student socialization process (Gardner, 2005; Golde & Dore, 2001) including students' involvement in campus and professional organizations (Gardner & Barnes, 2007). Other works seek to understand graduate student behaviors and decisions such as program choice (Poock, 1999; Poock & Love, 2001), college choice (Strayhorn & Mertz, 2006), and the decision to leave graduate school (Golde, 1998; Lovitts, 2001; Strayhorn, 2005). Scholars agree that virtually 50% of all students drop out of graduate school (Bowen & Rudenstein, 1992). Although we know a great deal about the state of graduate education and the numbers and types of degrees awarded annually, we know relatively little about the experiences of specific subgroups such as African American males in graduate school. It is out of this context that the need for this chapter grew.

Methodology

The *Baccalaureate and Beyond Longitudinal Study* (B&B:1993/2003) was the primary data source for this chapter. The B&B study followed baccalaureate degree completers over time to provide information on work experiences after college and on their progress and persistence at the graduate level. Using the National Postsecondary Student Aid Study (NPSAS:93) as the base year, the B&B:93/97 fourth-year follow-up provides data on college graduates up to 4–5 years beyond college graduation. The most recent follow-up (B&B:1993/2003) provides information on 1992–1993 B.A. degree completers, 10 years after college graduation. Because the B&B provided information on a nationally representative sample of students and has been used extensively in higher education research (Perna, 2004; Strayhorn, 2005), it was deemed an appropriate database for the present research.

The weighted analytic sample consisted of approximately 25,100 African American males who participated in the B&B study. Of this sample, 60% were married, 27% were single, and the balance were separated, divorced, or widowed. Nearly 50% of the sample aspired to earn a master's degree, and 37% aspired to earn a doctorate. Fifty-seven percent of the sample attended a public, 4-year, bachelor's-degree-granting institution; 42% attended a private, 4-year institution. These data reflect the population of African American males enrolled in the United States (U.S. Department of Education, 2006).

Findings

National data revealed that only 40% of all African American male bachelor's (B.A.) degree recipients had enrolled in a graduate degree program[3] by 2003, that is, 10 years after they had obtained an undergraduate degree. This group included 21% who completed a graduate degree, 14% who were enrolled in graduate school at the time of data collection, and 6% who had enrolled but left without completing the degree (i.e., dropouts).

Considering only those Black men who enrolled in graduate school, about half (52%) had completed a degree, 35% were still enrolled by 2003, and 15% left without earning their degree (percentages do not add to 100 due to rounding). Figure 7.1 depicts these trends.

Parents' level of education was associated with Black males' enrollment in graduate school. African American men who had parents with an advanced degree were more likely to enroll in graduate school than those who had parents with less education (e.g., B.A. degree, some postsecondary education, high school diploma or less). Moreover, Black men whose parents had more education also were more likely to have completed a graduate degree by 2003. For instance, whereas only 16% of Black men who had parents with a high school education had earned a graduate degree within 10 years of college graduation, 34% of those with highly educated parents (i.e., advanced degree) had completed a master's, doctoral, or first professional degree by 2003. These findings suggest the importance of sociocultural capital in explaining the educational pathways of African American men; I return to this point later in the chapter. Table 7.1 presents a summary of these results.

Having higher educational aspirations at the time of college graduation (i.e., 1993) was associated with Black males' enrollment in graduate school. Blacks who aspired to earn a terminal degree (26% of the sample) were more likely than were those who had lower aspirations (19%) to complete a graduate degree within 10 years of college graduation. Generally speaking, Black men who aspired to the doctorate were just as likely as those who desired a

FIGURE 7.1
Percentage distribution of 1992–1993 bachelor's degree recipients' graduate school enrollment and completion, 2003.

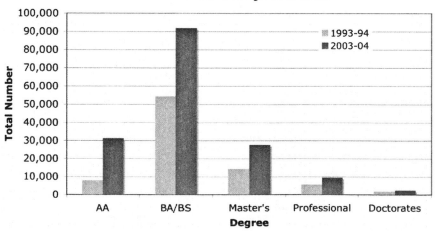

TABLE 7.1
Percentage Distribution of 1992–1993 African American Male Bachelor's Degree Recipients' Graduate School Enrollment Status, by Selected Characteristics, 2003

Characteristic	Completed	Enrolled	Left, no degree	No enrollment
Parents' education				
HS diploma or less	15.5	9.8	10.8	63.9
Advanced degree	33.7	14.9	4.1	47.3
Educational aspirations				
Master's degree	19.7	13.5	6.2	60.6
Doctoral/FP degree	26.2	13.2	7.0	53.7

Note: HS = high school. FP = first professional.

master's degree to be enrolled in graduate school by 2003. Surprisingly, graduate school attrition was a problem for a slightly larger proportion of Black men who aspired to earn a terminal degree than of those who aspired to earn a master's degree, as shown in Table 7.1.

Several demographic variables were related to African American males' enrollment in and completion of graduate school. Age (at B.A. receipt) was such a factor; those who were younger at B.A. receipt (22 years and below) were more likely than those who were older to have completed a graduate degree by 2003. External commitments and extenuating circumstances may explain this finding, as older students tend to be part-time students, commuters, transfer admits, full-time workers, or parents (Pascarella & Terenzini, 2005). Responsibilities off campus may prolong older students' time in graduate school or compromise their graduate degree plans.

There were interesting trends with respect to the time it took for the men to earn a B.A. degree. That is, African American men who took 5–6 years to earn their bachelor's degree were more likely to enroll in graduate school than those who took more than 6 years to complete their B.A. (17% versus 13%). Similar results were found with respect to graduation degree completion (21% versus 19%, respectively). African American men who took more than 6 years to complete their undergraduate degree were much more likely to drop out of graduate school before earning their degree; perhaps this was due to burnout or the imminent need to work to earn a salary.

African American males' marital status also was related to their status in graduate school. For example, more married men had completed a graduate degree than had those who were single and never married (23% versus 18%).

Given the time frame of the B&B study (i.e., 10 years), it is likely that most of those who had completed a graduate degree had earned a master's degree rather than a doctoral or first professional degree. It may be the case that family responsibilities created additional pressures to complete the degree in a relatively short period of time. On the other hand, single Black men were more likely still to be enrolled in graduate school by 2003, and a significantly higher proportion of married men had dropped out of graduate school without earning their degree.

Similar patterns were uncovered with respect to the number of dependents under age 18. Those without dependents were more likely than those with dependents to have completed a graduate degree within 10 years of college graduation (27% versus 17%), and a higher percentage were still enrolled and pursuing their degree (20% versus 9%). This statistic may be explained by the fact that students with dependents often encounter additional stressors (e.g., financial, marital, and child care) that keep them from enrolling in graduate school or create conditions that lead to dropout. That nearly 8% of Black men with dependents had dropped out of graduate school is a cause for alarm. Table 7.2 presents a summary of these findings.

TABLE 7.2
Percentage Distribution of 1992–1993 African American Male Bachelor's Degree Recipients' Graduate School Enrollment Status, by Labor Market Characteristics, 2003

Characteristic	Completed	Enrolled	Left, no degree	No enrollment
Age at B.A. receipt				
22 or younger	24.2	7.1	6.5	62.2
23 + years	17.9	22.4	2.8	56.9
Time to B.A. degree				
5–6 years	21.2	16.6	2.6	58.6
More than 6 years	19.0	13.0	6.4	61.6
Marital status				
Single, never married	17.5	16.8	3.3	62.4
Married	23.2	6.7	8.0	62.2
Dependents under 18				
None	27.2	19.9	2.7	50.2
One or more	16.5	9.3	7.9	66.4

Note: B.A. = bachelor's degree.

In consonance with the underlying theoretical frameworks that guided this national analysis and my own research interests in the labor market outcomes of African American college graduates (Strayhorn, 2008), I studied the status of Black men in graduate education with reference to a number of socioeconomic indices including employment status, occupational field, and salary as of 2003. A larger proportion of African American males who were working full-time had enrolled in or completed graduate school by 2003; most of these were employed in the for-profit sector. Few, if any, unemployed men had even attempted postbaccalaureate education. So graduate education may be one of many ways to reduce, if not eliminate, high unemployment rates among Black men.

Occupational field was related to the distribution of African American males in graduate education. For instance, Black men who worked in research/technical fields were much more likely than were those in business/management fields still to be enrolled in graduate school (22% versus 16%) or to have completed a graduate degree (25% versus 8%) by 2003. That Black men in the highest quartile of annual salaries were more likely than those in lower quartiles to have completed graduate school may reflect the assumptions of human capital theory. That is, individuals make investments in higher education, thereby accumulating additional skills that can be exchanged in the labor market for returns such as salary (Becker, 1993; Schultz, 1971). Consider the fact that the overall average annual salary (in 2003) for African American male college graduates who attempted graduate school was approximately $63,580; the average salary for those in the highest quartile was $103,400. Taken together, results from this national study provide suggestive evidence of the benefits of graduate education for African American males. Table 7.3 presents a summary of these results.

Limitations

As with all research investigations, the study on which this chapter is based was not without limits. First, the analysis was limited by the magnitude of missing data in the data set. Almost without exception, the amount of missing data was related to the relatively small number of Black men who enroll in graduate school. Unfortunately, the missing data limited the number of factors that could be included in the analysis. For instance, I could not disaggregate the sample by graduate major because of the low Ns that would result in some fields such as physical science, computer science, and math; thus, such variables were excluded from the analysis, as recommended by others (Galloway, 2004). Still today, African American graduate students are largely

TABLE 7.3

Percentage Distribution of 1992–1993 African American Male Bachelor's Degree Recipients' Graduate School Enrollment Status, by Selected Characteristics, 2003

Characteristic	Completed	Enrolled	Left, no degree	No enrollment
Employment status				
Full-time	18.7	11.9	7.16	2.3
Part-time/unemployed	—	—	—	—
Occupational field				
Business/management	8.1	15.6	0.0	76.3
Research/technical	25.1	21.5	8.3	45.1
Current salary				
Middle quartiles	18.8	13.9	3.9	63.5
Highest quartile	29.0	9.8	7.1	54.2

concentrated in the social sciences (Hrabowski, Maton, & Greif, 1998). Until more Black men enroll in graduate school and occupy these "empty" spaces, future analyses will be limited in the same fashion. Thus, I advocate for the formulation and implementation of policies and programs that enable their enrollment in post-B.A. education.

Second, the B&B study did not employ a simple random sampling strategy. Instead, a complex sampling design was used to collect data from a nationally representative sample. This design presents analysts with a number of technical issues that require statistical adjustments (Thomas & Heck, 2001). In this case, appropriate weights were applied to the database to account for the stratified, complex sampling design used in the B&B:1993/2003 study.

Finally, another limitation relates to all secondary data analyses. Despite its widespread use in the social sciences, secondary data analysis is rife with measurement issues. That is, measurement decisions are circumscribed by the factors that can be defined, operationalized, and measured by variables available in the database. It is possible that items from the B&B:1993/2003 study may be marginally related to the constructs (e.g., educational aspirations and expectations) that they purport to measure (Pedhazur & Schmelkin, 1991). To the extent that these issues alter the relationships between variables, these results should be interpreted with a degree of caution. Nevertheless, these data paint a bird's-eye view of the status of African American men in graduate school and provide an initial foray into the factors that influence their success.

Discussion of Key Findings

Using data from the *Baccalaureate and Beyond Longitudinal Study*, I found a number of trends that are noteworthy and potentially important for future policy, practice, and research. These findings provide empirical evidence to advance scholarly inquiry about Black men in general and Black men in graduate school in particular. Accordingly, I identify a number of directions for future research. Overall, the results presented here augment and shift our collective understanding of the various factors that relate to graduate student outcomes for African American males. Understanding the intersection of such factors may be instrumental in modeling the situation in which many African American males exist and may provide clues to potential levers over which educators have some control through policy or programmatic intervention.

Generally, my findings coincide with the assumptions of human and sociocultural capital theories. That educational aspirations, age, and salary were associated with enrollment in and completion of a graduate degree program for African American men may reflect, at least in part, the additional knowledge and skills gained from human capital investments in undergraduate and graduate training (Becker, 1993). In addition, African American men who had highly educated parents (i.e., parents with a graduate degree) were more likely to enroll in and to complete graduate school themselves. This finding may reflect the benefits that accrue to individuals whose parents possess the social and cultural capital necessary for success in higher education. For example, highly educated parents are generally well prepared to assist their sons in the "getting ready" activities (e.g., performing well academically and applying to graduate school) that precede enrollment in graduate school (Hossler et al., 1999; Hrabowski et al., 1998).

Previous studies have underscored the importance of educational aspirations as powerful predictors of actual enrollment (Carter, 2001; Hossler et al., 1999). The same holds true for African American male graduate students. Those who had higher educational aspirations at the point of B.A. receipt were more likely to enroll in or complete graduate school by 2003. This is an important finding for at least two reasons: First, it adds to the conclusion that, in general, "people cannot attain what they do not dream (or think possible)" (Carter, 2001, p. 6). Second, to the extent that aspirations reflect an "internalization of objective probabilities" (MacLeod, 1995, p. 15), this finding gives weight to the role of noncognitive variables (e.g., internal locus of control and motivation) in explaining educational outcomes of ethnically and culturally diverse students. Educators may consider these results when designing educational environments that engender Black male success.

In light of the chapter's findings, I make the following recommendations for higher education and student affairs professionals who are interested in fashioning policies that address the concerns of African American males in graduate school:

1. What may be obscured in this descriptive analysis is that some African American male graduate students may face multiple disadvantages (Davies & Guppy, 1997). For instance, we can only assume that the odds of enrolling in or completing a graduate degree would be near zero for African American males whose parents have less than a high school education; who have low aspirations for the future; and who might be married, have dependents, and be working part time. Such men would require an appropriate balance of support to offset these challenges (Sanford, 1966). Thus, educators are encouraged to remember that risk factors rarely exist in isolation but rather come in twos and threes. Some programs and services should be targeted to those who are arguably in greatest need.

2. Federal policies must play a role in increasing the participation rates of African American men in graduate school. Financial aid, precollege intervention (e.g., TRIO), and research and development policies should be fashioned to ameliorate the academic and financial barriers that may constrain the graduate school choices of Black men. For example, aid policies can be redesigned to offer handsome compensation packages to Black men who have spouses and other dependents.

3. We lose a significant number of Black men at critical junctures throughout the educational pipeline. To increase participation among this group at the graduate level, educators must find ways to inhabit the gaps between home and school, high school and college, and undergraduate and graduate education. Graduate departments should create pipeline programs that provide early support and assistance to help young Black men navigate their way to and through graduate school. Indeed, we can no longer afford to study the educational pipeline in individual, segmented units; rather, we must acknowledge the various ways in which each part influences the other (Jackson, 2007).

Concluding Remarks

This chapter may be significant for several campus constituencies. One group that might benefit from this discussion includes those who work in

K–12 schools and precollege outreach programs. Given African American men's lack of representation among the graduate ranks, relative to their White, Asian, and Black female counterparts, more work must be done to assist Black men as they negotiate their transition from high school to college, through college, and from college to graduate school. Precollege outreach, summer bridge, and federal TRIO programs like McNair represent mechanisms through which Black men can gain access to college and prepare for their postbaccalaureate careers (Swail & Perna, 2002).

There are implications for future research as well. For instance, this chapter reports findings from a national, descriptive study of African American male graduate students. Future studies might examine within-group differences (e.g., high versus low achievers) and subtle nuances that may exist between master's and doctoral students. Such studies would expand on the information available about graduate students in general and Black graduate men in particular.

It is also important to note in closing that studies in higher education have focused too little attention on graduate education (Burgess, 1997). As Clark (1993) has said,

> The first degree level has historical primacy, predominates numerically and possesses a deep hold on traditional thought and practice. It comes first in budget determination, public attention and the concerns of governments. Graduate or advanced education is then prone to develop at the margin as an add-on of a few more years of unstructured work for a few students. (p. 356)

The future of graduate education, our successes and losses, rests on our ability to see graduate education as more than "a few more years of unstructured work." And for the future status of African American males in graduate school to be brighter than it has been in the past, we must work to illuminate potential remedies to persistent problems. Findings presented in this chapter provide clues to potential solutions, especially for those standing on the outside looking in.

References

Allen, W. R. (1992). The color of success: African-American college student outcomes at predominantly White and historically Black colleges and universities. *Harvard Educational Review, 62,* 26–44.

Allen, W. R., & Haniff, N. Z. (1991). Race, gender, and academic performance in U.S. higher education. In W. R. Allen, E. G. Epps, & N. Z. Haniff (Eds.), *College in Black and White: African American students in predominantly White and in historically Black public universities* (pp. 95–109). Albany: State University of New York Press.

Austin, A. E., & McDaniels, M. (2006). Preparing the professoriate of the future: Graduate student socialization for faculty roles. In J. C. Smart (Ed.), *Higher education: Handbook for theory and research* (Vol. 21, pp. 397–456). Netherlands: Springer.

Bailey, D. F., & Moore, J. L., III. (2004). Emotional isolation, depression, and suicide among African American men: Reasons for concern. In C. Rabin (Ed.), *Linking lives across borders: Gender-sensitive practice in international perspective* (pp. 186–207). Pacific Grove, CA: Brooks/Cole.

Bandura, A. (1977). *Social learning theory.* Englewood Cliffs, NJ: Prentice Hall.

Becker, G. S. (1993). *Human capital: A theoretical and empirical analysis with special reference to education.* Chicago: University of Chicago Press.

Berelson, B. (1960). *Graduate education in the United States.* New York: Carnegie Corporation.

Besnier, N. (1995). The appeal and pitfalls of cross-disciplinary dialogues. In J. A. Russell, J. M. Fernandez-Dols, A. S. R. Manstead, & J. C. Wellenkamp (Eds.), *Everyday conceptions of emotion: An introduction to the psychology, anthropology, and linguistics of emotion* (pp. 559–570). Netherlands: Kluwer Academic.

Bonner, F. A., II, & Bailey, K. W. (2006). Enhancing the academic climate for African American men. In M. J. Cuyjet & Associates (Eds.), *African American men in college* (pp. 24–46). San Francisco: Jossey-Bass.

Bourdieu, P. (1977). Cultural reproduction and social reproduction. In J. Karabel & A. Halsey (Eds.), *Power and ideology in education* (pp. 487–510). New York: Oxford University Press.

Bowen, W. G., & Rudenstein, N. L. (1992). *In pursuit of the Ph.D.* Princeton, NJ: Princeton University Press.

Bragg, A. K. (1976). *The socialization process in higher education.* Washington, DC: American Association of Higher Education.

Braxton, J. M. (Ed.). (2000). *Reworking the student departure puzzle.* Nashville, TN: Vanderbilt University Press.

Brim, O. G. (1966). Socialization through the life cycle. In O. G. Brim & S. Wheeler (Eds.), *Socialization after childhood* (pp. 3–49). New York: Wiley.

Brown, M. C. (1999). *The quest to define collegiate desegregation: Black colleges, Title VI compliance, and post-Adams litigation.* Westport, CT: Bergin & Garvey.

Burgess, R. G. (Ed.). (1997). *Beyond the first degree: Graduate education, lifelong learning, and careers.* Bristol, UK: Open University Press.

Canady, D. M. (2007). African American male college dropouts: Expectations of and experiences with an historically Black university's customer service delivery and student service provisions and implications for retention. *Dissertation Abstracts International, 68*(1A), 32.

Carter, D. F. (2001). *A dream deferred? Examining the degree aspirations of African American and White college students.* New York: RoutledgeFalmer.

Chubb, J. E., & Loveless, T. (2002). Bridging the achievement gap. In J. E. Chubb & T. Loveless (Eds.), *Bridging the achievement gap* (pp. 1–10). Washington, DC: Brookings Institution Press.

Clark, B. R. (Ed.). (1993). *The research foundations of graduate education.* Berkeley: University of California Press.

Coleman, J. S. (1988). Social capital in the creation of human capital. *American Journal of Sociology, 94*(Suppl.), 95–120.

Constantine, J. M. (1994). The "added value" of historically Black colleges and universities. *Academe, 80,* 12–17.

Constantine, J. M. (1995). The effects of attending historically Black colleges and universities on future wages of Black students. *Industrial and Labor Relations Review, 48*(3), 531–546.

Council of Graduate Schools. (2004). *Organization and administration of graduate education.* Washington, DC: Author.

Cuyjet, M. J., & Associates (Eds.). (2006). *African American men in college.* San Francisco: Jossey-Bass.

Davies, S., & Guppy, N. (1997). Fields of study, college selectivity, and student inequalities in higher education. *Social Forces, 75*(4), 1417–1438.

DeSousa, D. J., & Kuh, G. D. (1996). Does institutional racial composition make a difference in what Black students gain from college? *Journal of College Student Development, 37,* 257–267.

DiMaggio, P., & Mohr, J. (1985). Cultural capital, educational attainment, and marital selection. *American Journal of Sociology, 90,* 1231–1261.

Ehrenberg, R. G., & Rothstein, D. S. (1994). Do historically Black institutions of higher education confer unique advantages on Black students? An initial analysis. In R. G. Ehrenberg (Ed.), *Choices and consequences: Contemporary policy issues in education* (pp. 89–137). Ithaca, NY: ILR Press.

Feldman, D. C. (1981). The multiple socialization of organization members. *Academy of Management Review, 6*(2), 309–318.

Feuerstein, A. (2000). School characteristics and parent involvement: Influences on participation in children's schools. *Journal of Educational Research, 94*(1), 29–39.

Fitzgerald, R. (2000). *College quality and the earnings of recent college graduates* (Research Development Report No. NCES 2000-043). Washington, DC: U.S. Department of Education, National Center for Education Statistics.

Flowers, L. A. (2003). Effects of college racial composition on African American students' interactions with faculty. *College Student Affairs Journal, 23,* 54–63.

Fordham, S., & Ogbu, J. (1986). Black students' school success: Coping with the "burden of acting White." *Urban Review, 18,* 176–206.

Freeman, K. (2005). *African Americans and college choice: The influence of family and school.* Albany: State University of New York Press.

Fries-Britt, S., & Turner, B. (2002). Uneven stories: Successful Black collegians at Black and White campuses. *Review of Higher Education, 25,* 315–330.

Galloway, F. J. (2004). *A methodological primer for conducting quantitative research in postsecondary education at Lumina Foundation for Education.* Retrieved November 27, 2004, from the Lumina Foundation Web site: http://www.luminafoun dation.org/research/researchersgalloway.pdf.

Gardner, S. K. (2005). *"If it were easy, everyone would have a Ph.D.": Doctoral student success: Socialization and disciplinary perspectives.* Unpublished doctoral dissertation, Washington State University, Pullman.

Gardner, S. K., & Barnes, B. J. (2007). Graduate student involvement: Socialization for the professional role. *Journal of College Student Development, 48*(4), 369–387.

Golde, C. M. (1998). Beginning graduate school: Explaining first-year doctoral attrition. In M. S. Anderson (Ed.), *The experience of being in graduate school: An exploration* (pp. 55–64). San Francisco: Jossey-Bass.

Golde, C. M., & Dore, T. M. (2001). *At cross purposes: What the experiences of today's doctoral students reveal about doctoral education* (Pew Charitable Trusts Report). Retrieved June 1, 2005, from http://www.phd-survey.org.

Golde, C. M., & Walker, G. E. (Eds.). (2006). *Envisioning the future of doctoral education: Preparing stewards of the discipline.* San Francisco: Jossey-Bass.

Hamilton, J. P. (2005). Reasons why African American men persist to degree completion in institutions of higher education. *Dissertation Abstracts International, A65*(10), 3717.

Harper, S. R. (2003). Most likely to succeed: The self-perceived impact of involvement on the experiences of high-achieving African American undergraduate men at predominantly White universities. *Dissertation Abstracts International, A64*(6), 1995.

Hess, R. D., Holloway, S. D., Dickson, W. T., & Price, G. G. (1984). Maternal variables as predictors of children's school readiness and later achievement in vocabulary and mathematics in 6th grade. *Child Development, 55*, 1901–1912.

Hirt, J. B., Strayhorn, T. L., Amelink, C. T., & Bennett, B. R. (2006). The nature of student affairs work at historically Black colleges and universities. *Journal of College Student Development, 47*(6), 661–676.

Hong, S., & Ho, H. (2005). Direct and indirect longitudinal effects of parental involvement on student achievement: Second-order latent growth modeling across ethnic groups. *Journal of Educational Psychology, 97*(1), 32–42.

Hossler, D., Schmit, J. L., & Vesper, N. (1999). *Going to college: How social, economic, and educational factors influence the decisions students make.* Baltimore: Johns Hopkins University Press.

Hrabowski, F. A., III, Maton, K. I., & Greif, G. L. (1998). *Beating the odds: Raising academically successful African American males.* New York: Oxford University Press.

Jablin, F. M., & Miller, V. D. (1990). Interviews with applicant questioning behavior in employment interviews. *Management Communication Quarterly, 4*, 51–86.

Jackson, J. F. L. (2007). Introduction: A systematic analysis of the African American educational pipeline to inform research, policy, and practice. In J. F. L. Jackson

(Ed.), *Strengthening the African American educational pipeline: Informing research, policy, and practice* (pp. 1–14). Albany: State University of New York Press.

Jakobson, R. (1987). On realism in art. In K. Pomorska & S. Rudy (Eds.), *Language in literature* (pp. 25–26). Cambridge, MA: Harvard University Press.

Jun, A., & Colyar, J. E. (2002). Parental guidance suggested: Family involvement in college preparation programs. In W. G. Tierney & L. S. Hagedorn (Eds.), *Increasing access to college: Extending possibilities for all students* (pp. 195–215). Albany: State University of New York Press.

Karraker, R. J. (1972). Increasing academic performance through home-managed contingency programs. *Journal of School Psychology, 10*, 173–179.

Keith, T. Z., Reimers, T. M., Fehrmann, P. G., Pottebaum, S., & Aubey, L. (1986). Parental involvement, homework, and TV time: Direct and indirect effects on high school achievement. *Journal of Educational Psychology, 78*, 373–380.

Kimbrough, W. M., & Harper, S. R. (2006). African American men at historically Black colleges and universities: Different environments, similar challenges. In M. J. Cuyjet & Associates (Eds.), *African American men in college* (pp. 189–209). San Francisco: Jossey-Bass.

Kluger, R. (1975). *Simple justice: The history of* Brown v. Board of Education *and Black America's struggle for equality.* New York: Vintage Books.

Kunjufu, J. (1986). *Countering the conspiracy to destroy Black boys.* Chicago: African American Images.

Lamont, M., & Lareau, A. (1988). Cultural capital: Allusions, gaps, and glissandos in recent theoretical developments. *Sociological Theory, 6*, 153–168.

Lane, L. S. B. (2006). Black in the red zone: A study of disproportionate suspension of African American males. *Dissertation Abstracts International, 68*(1A), 55.

London, C. (1998, April). *A pilot study on the career advancement of Black graduates of predominantly Black versus predominantly White colleges.* Paper presented at the annual meeting of the People of Color in Predominantly White Institutions, Lincoln, NE.

Lovitts, B. E. (2001). *Leaving the ivory tower: The causes and consequences of departure from doctoral study.* Lanham, MD: Rowman & Littlefield.

MacLeod, J. (1995). *Ain't no makin' it: Aspirations and attainment in a low-income neighborhood.* Boulder, CO: Westview Press.

Mau, W., & Kopischke, A. (2001). Job search methods, job search outcomes, and job satisfaction of college graduates: A comparison of race and sex. *Journal of Employment Counseling, 38*, 141–149.

McDonough, P. M. (1997). *Choosing colleges: How social class and schools structure opportunity.* Albany: State University of New York Press.

Meier, K., Stewart, J., & England, R. (1998). *Race, class and education: The politics of second generation discrimination.* Madison: University of Wisconsin Press.

Mortenson Research Seminar on Public Policy Analysis of Opportunity for Postsecondary Education. (2001). College participation by gender, age 18 to 24, 1967 to 2000. *Postsecondary Education Opportunity, 109*, 1–16.

Muhammad, D., Davis, A., Lui, M., & Leondar-Wright, B. (2004). *The state of the dream 2004: Enduring disparities in Black and White.* Boston: United for a Fair Economy.

Nettles, M. T., & Perna, L. W. (1997). *The African American education data book: Higher and adult education.* Fairfax, VA: Frederick D. Patterson Research Institute.

Nettles, M. T., Thoeny, A., & Gosman, E. (1986). Comparative and predictive analyses of Black and White students' college achievement and experiences. *Journal of Higher Education, 57,* 289–318.

Parker, C. A. (1977). On modeling reality. *Journal of College Student Personnel, 18*(5), 419–425.

Pascarella, E. T., & Terenzini, P. T. (2005). *How college affects students: A third decade of research* (Vol. 2). San Francisco: Jossey-Bass.

Patton, L. D. (2006). The voice of reason: A qualitative examination of Black student perceptions of Black culture centers. *Journal of College Student Development, 47*(6), 628–646.

Pedhazur, E. J., & Schmelkin, L. P. (1991). *Measurement design and analysis: An integrated approach.* Hillsdale, NJ: Lawrence Erlbaum.

Perna, L. W. (2004). Understanding the decision to enroll in graduate school: Sex and racial/ethnic group differences. *Journal of Higher Education, 75*(5), 487–527.

Phelan, T. J., & Phelan, J. C. (1983). *A comparative study of college impacts on human outcomes.* Paper presented at the annual meeting of the Association for the Study of Higher Education, Washington, DC.

Poock, M. C. (1999). Students of color and doctoral programs: Factors influencing the application decision in higher education administration. *College and University, 74*(3), 2–7.

Poock, M. C., & Love, P. G. (2001). Factors influencing the program choice of doctoral students in higher education administration. *NASPA Journal, 38*(2), 203–223.

Roach, R. (2001). Where are the Black men on campus? *Black Issues in Higher Education, 18*(6), 18–24.

Sagen, H., Dallam, J., & Laverty, J. (1997). *Effects of career preparation experiences on the initial employment success of college graduates.* Unpublished manuscript, University of Iowa, Iowa City.

Sanford, N. (1966). *Self and society: Social change and individual development.* New York: Atherton.

Schultz, T. W. (1971). *Investment in human capital: The role of education and of research.* New York: Macmillan.

Stennis-Williams, S., Terrell, M. C., & Haynes, A. W. (1988). The emergent role of multicultural education centers on predominantly White campuses. In M. C. Terrell & D. J. Wright (Eds.), *From survival to success: Promoting minority student retention* (pp. 73–98). Washington, DC: National Association of Student Personnel Administrators.

Stevens, C. D. (2007). Skating the zones: African American male students at a predominantly White community college. *Dissertation Abstracts International, 68*(1A), 62.

Strayhorn, T. L. (2005). More than money matters: An integrated model of graduate student persistence. *Dissertation Abstracts International, A66*(2), 519.

Strayhorn, T. L. (2006). Factors influencing the academic achievement of first-generation college students. *NASPA Journal, 43*(4), 82–111.

Strayhorn, T. L. (2008). Influences on labor market outcomes of African American college graduates: A national study. *Journal of Higher Education, 79*(1), 28–57.

Strayhorn, T. L., & Mertz, N. T. (2006). *Graduate college choice: Understanding the process.* Paper presented at the 31st annual meeting of the Association for the Study of Higher Education, Anaheim, CA.

Strayhorn, T. L., & Terrell, M. C. (2007). Mentoring and satisfaction with college for Black students. *Negro Educational Review, 58*(1/2), 69–83.

Sutton, E. M., & Kimbrough, W. M. (2001). Trends in Black student involvement. *NASPA Journal, 39*(1), 30–40.

Swail, W. S., & Perna, L. W. (2002). Pre-college outreach programs: A national perspective. In W. G. Tierney & L. S. Hagedorn (Eds.), *Increasing access to college: Extending possibilities for all students* (pp. 15–34). Albany: State University of New York Press.

Tatum, B. D. (1997). *Why are all the Black kids sitting together in the cafeteria? And other conversations about race.* New York: Basic Books.

Thomas, S. L. (2000). Deferred costs and economic returns to college major, quality, and performance. *Research in Higher Education, 41,* 281–313.

Thomas, S. L., & Heck, R. H. (2001). Analysis of large-scale secondary data in higher education research: Potential perils associated with complex sampling designs. *Research in Higher Education, 42*(5), 517–540.

Thornton, R., & Nardi, R. M. (1975). The dynamics of role acquisition. *American Journal of Sociology, 80,* 870–885.

Tierney, W. G., & Rhoads, R. A. (1993). Postmodernism and critical theory in higher education: Implications for research and practice. In J. C. Smart (Ed.), *Higher education: Handbook of theory and research* (pp. 308–343). New York: Agathon.

Tinto, V. (1993). *Leaving college: Rethinking the causes and cures of student attrition* (2nd ed.). Chicago: University of Chicago Press.

U.S. Department of Education, National Center for Education Statistics. (2006). *The condition of education 2006* (NCES 2006-071). Washington, DC: U.S. Government Printing Office.

Wanous, J. P., Reichers, A. E., & Malik, S. D. (1984). Organizational socialization and group development: Toward an integrative perspective. *Academy of Management Review, 4,* 670–683.

Wegner, E. L. (1973). The effects of upward mobility: A study of working-status college students. *Sociology of Education, 46*(3), 263–279.

Weidman, J. C., Twale, D. J., & Stein, E. L. (2001). *Socialization of graduate and professional students in higher education: A perilous passage?* ASHE-ERIC Higher Education Report 28(3) (pp. 25–54). San Francisco: Jossey-Bass.

Notes

1. It is important to note that some scholars discuss socialization in terms of "stages" (Thornton & Nardi, 1975), whereas others refer to "phases" (Wanous, Reichers, & Malik, 1984).

2. According to the Commonwealth of Virginia's Constitution (art. IX, sec. 140).

3. Graduate degree programs include those that award master's, doctoral, and first professional degrees, as defined by the Council of Graduate Schools (2004). Postbaccalaureate certificates are not included.

8

OPPOSITIONAL STANCES OF BLACK FEMALE GRADUATE STUDENTS

Perspectives From Social and Natural Sciences

Venice Thandi Sulé

T he presence of Black women, though minimal, in top-tier institutions is noteworthy given the history of government-sanctioned exploitation of African Americans (Anderson, 1988; Giddings, 1984; Pinkney, 1987). Throughout the enslavement and Jim Crow eras, popularized depictions and socially ascribed roles for Black women represented something far from intellectual competence. Their value was thought to be in their physicality, not their minds. Thus, hypersexualized (Jezebel) and docile servant (Mammy) images prevailed and served to justify Black female subordination (Collins, 2000; Jewell, 1993). Nevertheless, many Black women are now succeeding in didactic spaces that historically excluded them. Their success may be attributed to the enactment of what I label oppositional positions, an awareness of being a part of a socially marginalized group, combined with actions that challenge marginalization.

As a way to explore how Black women engage historically exclusive institutions, this chapter analyzes the experiences of Black female graduate students at a predominantly White university (PWU). The limited research on Black women at PWUs focuses on barriers to social integration, but it places less emphasis on factors that promote the successful negotiation of these barriers. This study, then, aims to examine how Black women navigate through a PWU, with emphasis on manifestations of oppositional positions.

This study is significant for several reasons. First, because access to premier higher education institutions affords the opportunity to influence social attitudes and social policy through service, teaching, and research, an examination of the socialization experiences of Black female graduate students provides insight into how they, as potential faculty, can access resource-rich institutions. Their preentry (prefaculty) experiences may influence their ability both to acquire a faculty position and to meet criteria for tenure and promotion. Second, this study is important because it looks at a group that has been historically overlooked within the empirical and theoretical literature. The literature on underrepresented people in academe emphasizes the experiences of people of color (both men and women) or White women but rarely focuses on the experiences of women of color. As a result, intersectional identities are often not recognized. That is, experiences that reflect the intersection of being a person of color and a female are not reflected in the literature. Crenshaw (1991) states,

> Feminist efforts to politicize experiences of women and antiracist efforts to politicize the experiences of people of color have frequently proceeded as though the issues and experiences they each detail occur on mutually exclusive terrains . . . and so when the practices expound women as woman or person of color as an either/or proposition, they relegate the identity of women of color to a location that resists telling. (p. 1242)

Women's issues, then, are intimately connected to politics of race. For this reason, and because female graduate students of color have a distinctive standpoint, an exploration into their experiences deserves attention. In essence, this study helps determine how race and gender matter in the experiences of Black female graduate students at predominantly White research institutions. Their experiences may add to our understanding of graduate student socialization.

This examination also responds to the need to understand the experiences of underrepresented graduate students during an era when diversity and affirmative action practices are under attack. As such, the experiences of underrepresented students can serve as an indicator of the condition of higher education as it relates to promoting diversity.

In an attempt to gauge the experiences of Black women in fields in which there is a relatively high or low representation of women and/or Blacks, the study focuses on women in social sciences and women in natural sciences and engineering.

Literature Review

The literature on Black female graduate students is very limited. To get a sense of what the key issues might be for this group, I surveyed the sparse literature on Black females in academe: undergraduates, graduate students, and faculty. Combined, empirical studies using these groups as units of analysis elucidate factors that both hinder and enhance their socialization experiences.

Limited research has been conducted on the ways in which race and sex influence Black female experiences in higher education settings (Alfred, 2001; Jackson, 1998; Myers, 2002; Thomas, 2001; Woods, 2001). The extant literature, however, provides some insight into the experiences of Black female students within traditionally White institutions. The research shows that Black women are keenly aware that their sexual and racial identities may be negatively perceived (Johnson-Bailey, 1998; Schwartz, Bower, Rice, & Washington, 2003). Jackson (1998) found that women equate being Black and female with struggle—working harder than others and fighting negative stereotypes. Struggle is a common thread in the literature. For instance, O'Connor's (2002) cohort study of Black women's experiences at PWUs before and after the civil rights era revealed a pattern of social isolation triggered by discriminatory practices perpetrated by White faculty and students. These alienating practices ranged from withholding course materials, grading unfairly, making racist comments in class, and restricting Blacks from study groups. Although the women in these studies remained determined to complete their education, their social environment was a reminder that they were not totally welcome.

The theme of isolation and invisibility persists among Black female graduate students and faculty. In Ellis's (2001) study, Black female graduate students viewed their experiences differently than their Black male and White peers did. These women expressed feeling more isolated and less satisfied with their graduate experiences. Another recurring theme is that Black female graduate students and faculty feel intellectually devalued and hindered from developing professionally (Allen, 1995; Gregory, 1999; Holmes, 2001; Myers, 2002; Woods, 2001). Consequently, Black women may not have access to networking opportunities such as presenting papers at professional conferences, coauthoring papers with faculty, and serving as research assistants (Turner & Thompson, 1993).

Despite the challenges, what resonates from the few qualitative studies on Black female faculty is that marginality and invisibility can be used as a tool to transcend boundaries. Because Black women are on the margins, they are not bounded by arbitrary expectations. Their marginality forces them to acquire skills to maneuver diverse settings. This skill set allows them to negotiate multiple communities (Alfred, 2001; Johnson-Bailey, 1998; Thomas & Hollenshead, 2001). It is within the context of intersectionality that this chapter seeks to explore the experiences of Black female graduate students.

Most of the studies on Black women and Blacks in general accentuate impediments to social integration and persistence at PWUs but place less emphasis on factors that promote transcendence of barriers. This study, then, intends to examine how participants maneuver through their programs.

Theoretical Framework

The primary interpretive lenses for this study are Black feminist thought (BFT) and critical race feminism (CRF), because both are concerned with power and justice and the ways that race, class, gender, and other identities matter in society. BFT emphasizes interconnecting identities and the idea of a collective standpoint based on social location. As a critical social theory, BFT rearticulates Black women's everyday experiences and promotes equity (Collins, 2000). From the perspective of BFT, oppositional position is manifested when one is both aware of one's social location and resisting oppressive forces. Thus, resistance is a central feature of BFT. Collins (2000) states,

> As a collectivity, U.S. Black women participate in a *dialectical* relationship linking African-American women's oppression and activism. Dialectical relationships of this sort mean that two parties are opposed and opposite. As long as Black women's subordination within intersecting oppressions of race, class, gender, sexuality, and nation persists, Black feminism as an activist response to that oppression will remain needed. (p. 22)

Similarly, critical race feminism asserts that racism and sexism are endemic and permanent. Thus, the experiences of women of color can be explained with a race and gender analysis. Storytelling is advocated as a way to promulgate the experiences of nondominant groups and to challenge dominant narratives. For women of color, it allows for discussion and analysis that takes into consideration intersections of identity, particularly race and gender (Crenshaw, 1991; Wing, 1997). Self-affirmation and dialogue is the impetus for the Black female standpoint. King (1995) elaborates:

> A Black feminist ideology, first and foremost, thus declares the visibility of Black women. It acknowledges the fact that two innate and inerasable traits, Black and female, constitute our special status in American society.

Second, Black feminism asserts self-determination as essential. Black women are empowered with the right to interpret our reality and define our objectives. While drawing on a rich tradition of struggle as Blacks and as women, we continually establish and reestablish our own priorities. (p. 312)

Thus, utilizing BFT and CRF to analyze Black female engagement with higher education appropriately places Black women's interpretation of their experience at the forefront. These theoretical perspectives also allow one to frame the pursuit of a doctorate at historically White institutions as an oppositional action in a society still plagued by discrimination. Essentially, BFT and CRF are interpretive tools that add depth to Black women's stories and validate their subjective experiences.

Research Methods

Strategy of Inquiry

Qualitative methods were employed for this study because the study explores how Black females experience and respond to their graduate programs at a PWU, and qualitative methods are the best way to glean information about what experiences mean to individuals (Creswell, 1998; Patton, 2001). Specifically, the analysis is informed by some aspects of grounded theory (Strauss & Corbin, 1998). First, the grounded method emphasizes building theory through the inductive approach. Second, grounded theory involves a systemic process of verifying assertions through a detailed process of categorization, coding, member checks, and searching for disconfirming evidence. Third, the theory supports theoretical sampling, a method of selecting appropriate informants based on the phenomenon of interest. Finally, the grounded approach fits well with this study because it promotes situated theorizing based on data collected within a particular context. In this way, this study interrogates the navigational experiences of Black female doctoral students at PWUs.

Sampling Procedure

I used theoretical sampling to ensure that the study included the necessary participants to address the orienting question (Creswell, 1998).[1] I recruited nine Black female doctoral students with at least 1 year of course work from a public university. I contacted participants through professional and support organizations that target graduate students of color, and I made contact with participants via email or in person.

Data Collection

Interviews were the primary form of data collection. Using open-ended questions, I interviewed the women once for an average of 2 hours over the course of 5 months. I used a semistructured interview schedule, and I constructed questions to elicit information about participants' experiences prior to and during graduate school by delving into three areas: (a) family and education background, (b) higher education experiences, and (c) collective experiences with the Black community (see Appendix A). During the interview, I took notes in a journal to record my thoughts and observations of the participants. I tape-recorded and transcribed all the interviews. My journal notes were also incorporated into the analysis of the data.

Data Analysis

The study sought to discover the essential meanings that the respondents applied to their experiences (Creswell, 1998; Strauss & Corbin, 1998; Weiss, 1994).[2] Utilizing comparative methods, emerging themes were defined. I began with what Weiss (1994) calls "local integration," which means that I summarized the interviews by focusing on what was articulated and on what I thought it meant. I then used open coding, which involves examining the data to identify categories and dimensions of each category. The language of the participants guided the development of the coding process. Once the initial codes were developed, they were compared and contrasted to bring forth more complex and inclusive categories (Strauss & Corbin, 1998).[3] The categories represent themes that emerged from the way respondents described their experiences.

Some measures were taken to enhance the validity of the outcomes. For instance, the themes were referenced back to the participants' narratives to ensure close alignment with the interpretative outcome. Furthermore, member checks were conducted by returning transcribed interviews to participants in order to determine if the transcriptions adequately captured their experiences. To assist in transferability—ability of the study to be replicated in a similar environment—I attempted to provide ample contextual information without jeopardizing the confidentiality of the respondents (Guba & Lincoln, 1982).

The analysis adheres to the belief that meaning is coconstructed and constitutive. Coconstruction of meaning is essentially the coauthoring of meaning through human interaction (Heyl, 2001; Taylor, 2001). It is a reflection of the principle of reflexivity, which states that it is impossible for the researcher to be objective and separate from the research. Everything from the selection of research topic to the way in which the researcher analyzes data is a product of the researcher's experiences (Taylor, 2001). Constitutive interpretations view discourse as the "site where meanings are created and changed" (Taylor, 2001, p. 6). Therefore, I am aware of my influence on the construction of knowledge.

As an African American female graduate student at a predominantly White institution (PWI), I have intimate knowledge of the issue in question. The respondent selects information to share with me on the basis of my identity, her level of familiarity with me, and the types of questions she is asked. Furthermore, I realize that the construction of questions, though informed by my orienting question, is partly driven by my desire to understand issues of intersectionality and professional socialization within a higher education setting. From this perspective, I believe that I can bring forth information that may be useful for Black female graduate students, as well as for other nondominant groups, by explaining how women in this study negotiate higher education.

According to the principles of BFT, my experience with the topic of research may be an asset. BFT is designed to concretize the standpoints and reflect the interests of Black women. Black female scholars, then, are encouraged to rearticulate the taken-for-granted knowledge of Black women as a means to challenge hegemony and to awaken the critical consciousness of Black women (Collins, 2000). bell hooks (1989) has observed:

> The struggle to end domination, the individual struggle to resist colonization, to move from object to subject, is expressed in the effort to establish the liberatory voice—the way of speaking that is no longer determined by one's status as object—as oppressed being. That way of speaking is characterized by opposition, by resistance. (p. 15)

Accordingly, Black female scholars who use BFT as a theoretical framework are furthering the empowerment of Black women for the following reasons: (a) Black women have critical insights based on personal experiences, (b) Black female scholars are not as likely as others may be to abandon BFT research when it is not expedient, (c) Black female scholars are needed to articulate Black female self-definition because empowerment is derived from self-authorship, and (d) Black female scholars are needed to help forge coalitions among Black women and other groups as a means to enhance consciousness about experiences of subjugation (Collins, 2000). Therefore, my identity can be viewed as a constructive resource for data collection and analysis.

Despite the benefits of having shared experiences with the participants in my study, being a "native" researcher does have challenges. First, both parties (researcher and participant) may assume that there is a mutual understanding of what they tacitly believe to be cultural knowledge. Thus, there is a risk of making inappropriate interpretations of verbal and nonverbal cues. Second, there is the expectation that a native researcher provide an authentic, "really real" view of the marginalized group, when, in fact, many notions of authenticity are context driven and subjective.

Interview Findings

Although there was diversity within the women's backgrounds, there was a clear similarity of experiences (see Appendix B). Most of the women grew up in two-parent, self-described middle-class households. Furthermore, they all discussed how their parents had high educational expectations for them and structured their lives to ensure that they received a good education. Also, three of the four science and engineering students participated in pipeline science and engineering summer programs.[4] In all, the experiences of the participants in this study support the research that shows a relationship among parental education, social class, and educational achievement. In other words, middle-class students with educated parents have easier access to higher education than lower-resourced students do (Cabrera & Nasa, 2000; Pascarella & Terenzini, 1991). The women also talked about the multigenerational appreciation for education within their families, a fact that supports the historical work that speaks to the high regard that Blacks have for education (Anderson, 1988).

Although the emphasis of this chapter is on how participants navigate through their programs, it must be noted that they all described elements of their learning environment as hostile. Narratives from the women both in the social sciences and in science and engineering revealed evidence of a chilly climate or of behaviors and attitudes that made the women feel marginal (Hall & Sandler, 1982). In essence, the women discussed subtle yet ever-present incidents of bias or neglect such as the heralding of research that disparages African Americans, feeling socially isolated, or lacking faculty and peer support. Nevertheless, these women persisted. So how and why have these women navigated an educational terrain that is sometimes precarious? What kind of behaviors or beliefs have they employed that allow them to stay in graduate school and transcend barriers? How is their oppositional position evidenced, if at all? What follows is an examination of some of the attitudes and behaviors that may help explain how these women navigate through their respective programs. The navigational factors are divided into three groups: (a) Black female leadership images, (b) self-efficacy, and (c) uplifting the race.

Black Female Leadership Images: Bathed in Black Womanhood

The most pervasive theme among the women was a deep sense of their capability and potential as Black women. Most of the women shared stories of determined and successful women in their family. Images of Black women as leaders—assertive, determined, loving, reliable, and hardworking—primarily derived from mothers or mother figures. Francine explained,

> There is my mom and my grandmom. . . . I mean, my grandmother, . . . she's very independent, very strong willed and strong minded. Just that whole, "if I can do this without someone, you should be able to handle whatever on your own." She raised two daughters by herself because her husband died. . . . My mom is a very strong-minded individual—speaks her mind. That's really what I think of. It's just them and how they are, but there really was no set things they did that made me feel like, "Okay this is a woman." I just know if I emulate my mom and my grandmother, then that's what I would be. I would [be] independent. I would be strong willed. I will [be] strong minded. I will be self-sufficient.

MeMe added, "I think just growing up in the inner city, it's just so common to see women in the leadership role." She later stated, "I had no White dolls. My mother did not allow such things. I think I always felt Black women were strong and that they were beautiful and that they were something to be desired. . . . I don't think it was until college that I realized Black women weren't the ideal beauty type." The cues that MeMe picked up from her mother helped to insulate her from cultural images of African American womanhood that are designed to sustain inequitable treatment. Jewell (1993) says that these images "portray African American women as the antithesis of the American conception of beauty, femininity and womanhood" (p. 36). That MeMe's mother took action to filter out these images is a testament to her mother's determination to instill self-love through self-affirming images of beauty.

Kendra's mother, a nurse, factored into her image of Black womanhood:

> I always looked up to her. Even those days when you had to dress like your role model, I would dress up like a nurse. Embarrass myself because she worked right there. . . . I never realized until you asked me that question that I really just looked up to her. I think my mom is a very strong woman.

The thing I like about her most is that she lets me know the mistakes she's made in my life.

Bett said in reference to her neighborhood growing up,

There's a bunch of Clair Huxtables all over the place. And it was like she will tell you off but then she'll give you a cookie. . . . it was like they were always very strict with their kids, very giving and loving but very focused and determined and very career oriented and like they won't take what they are given—It's just like I am not just going to be in the community but I am going to be the head of my community and do things that are positive for the girls in this group. A lot of good role models, a lot of women that I still keep in contact with now.

There are two things that are notable in these responses. First, the participants discussed how they witnessed Black women juggling multiple career and family responsibilities. This characteristic is reflective of Black women's contributions to sustaining the Black family throughout the slave and Jim Crow economies. Black women, as a collective, have always had to work to support their families within a racially stratified society that relegates Blacks to the bottom of the economic caste structure (Brown, 1989; Giddings, 1984). Second, the narratives depict Black women as dignified, self-loving, and nurturing. The positive image of Black womanhood is noteworthy because it is in opposition to the mainstream images of Black women as lazy welfare queens, domineering matriarchs, and the "bad Black mother" (Collins, 2004; Jewell, 1993). The counterimages serve as examples of oppositional position. The narratives reveal that the participants were influenced by Black women in their lives. They grew up in environments in which Black women exhibited self-determination and defiance despite overarching race and gender constraints. This modeling of womanhood equipped participants with tacit knowledge about the resiliency of Black women. Through the experiences of their mothers, they learned that Black women are equipped with the attributes to empower and sustain a community. It was an early lesson in self-efficacy.

Self-Efficacy: "I Need to Reinvent Some Things"

The narratives are replete with examples of perseverance in the face of marginalization. The women expressed a belief that they could overcome challenges through creativity, hard work, and faith. For instance, Dorothy acknowledged that she periodically doubts her ability to succeed in her program, but she added, "If this is what I want to do, . . . I think there is always some road and window or something that's going to open so I can finish. I think as long as I keep wanting to do it, I don't doubt that I will finish." Bett explained,

> This road is being blocked, so you need to go around it and take it from a different perspective. As an African American, that is real stuff. There are many times when you are not going to be able to go straight through. . . . So it's like I might need to get a little bit more creative. I need to reinvent some things, change the way the other people look at things.

Bett provided the following example of a road blockage:

> There are established knowns that African American students are unaware of. When they do become aware, they have to work around that situation without knowledge of the most successful solution. Situations may not be conducive to the African American perspective of education and success. For example, White students may go to the bar to socialize. . . . However, African American students may not have that same perspective. . . . Therefore, they may try to be present at other functions to obtain the same social visibility.

Francine discussed how she deals with her frustration and self-doubt:

> Even though I've done all of the things that I needed to do, I feel like I am starting from the bottom again. . . . It's not like I don't think I can do this, but there are some days that I am like, "Why am I here?" So I seek counseling, and I talk to my mom. I mean, that's what I have to do because I don't like to internalize, "You're not able. You did get in here from affirmative action. You really are not that smart," that type of stuff. So I try to study that much harder. I try to do whatever I can.

Self-efficacy has been defined as "people's judgments of their capabilities to organize and execute courses of action required to attain designated types of performances" (Bandura, 1986, p. 391). Bandura argues that people make choices based on personal efficacy. Unless people believe that their efforts will produce desirable outcomes, they have little reason to persevere. The narratives speak to the presence of self-efficacy, which may stem from leadership images of Black womanhood in childhood. The women may have derived another source of confidence from their precollege experiences. For instance, all the women shared stories of academic success in primary and secondary schools. Their achievements were recognized and encouraged by teachers and family members. As a result, they believed that they were capable of academic success. This knowledge, even up against great odds, may have instilled faith and determination. As the next section illustrates, having faith and determination, combined with an understanding of racial injustice, fosters a commitment to racial uplift.

Uplifting the Race

A factor that motivates women to persist in their graduate programs is allegiance to the Black community. The women talked about the need to serve as role models for Black students. Several believed that their mere presence in a doctoral program was a way to give back to the community and the family that nurtured them. Also, some participants felt that demonstrating competence was an opportunity to challenge those who believe Black students cannot withstand the rigors of graduate school. Kendra's narrative is an example of the responsibility that comes with being a Black graduate student:

> I had to go [to graduate school] in a way, . . . as far as the whole theory that you are on the shoulders of those who came before you. They paved the way. I felt like I had to really achieve the highest I could get to. I felt like that was my motivation. I had the weight of the Black community on my back. They really needed me to get this degree to show the future generations that it can be done. . . . I really felt that burden. . . . I have a poster of all of the Black scientists on my wall.

Here, Kendra expresses her gratitude for the achievements of those who preceded her in her field. The success of other Blacks, however, appears to serve as both a source of motivation and a source of angst, because she describes her sense of responsibility as a burden. Nonetheless, her burden may be what motivates her to excel. Despite the negative connotation, Kendra uses "burden" to convey the pressure that she puts on herself to live up to the standards of her predecessors and to make a difference. She elaborated: "For a while, I thought it [giving back] was something I couldn't really do, that whole weight on my shoulders. Even with me getting a Ph.D., that is a good thing, but you really have to do something with that." What can be discerned from Kendra's comments is that the very factors that inspire participants may also be a source of stress. The role of educated Black women in fostering Black empowerment through the establishment of mutual-aid societies, schools, and advocacy organizations is well documented (Giddings, 1984; Hine & Thompson, 1998). Historically, success among this group was measured by their ability to assist those with the least opportunity. Thus, feeling compelled to be a community servant may emanate from shared cultural values resulting from group-based subjugation. So the notion of service may be a calling, albeit a stressful one, that is unique to Black graduate students.

Some participants expressed that simply attaining a Ph.D. and becoming a professor is an important contribution to the Black community because it challenges negative conceptions of Blackness. MeMe said,

> Just my being a professor, me as a Black woman, would change America just because I would be one more to that number, and the numbers are small, so it will change America somehow. I can guarantee that based on statistics, I would be the first African American professor for someone.

Acquisition of a Ph.D. was also viewed as a way to challenge racism and sexism. Brenda stated,

> You don't want them to say, "You see what happens when you let them in." . . . I think that's one of the things that made me self-conscious of my depression. You never want anyone saying, "She can't handle it because she's Black" or "because she's a woman."

Brenda's comments reveal that some women deliberately put on a public face of strength or neutrality regardless of inner turmoil because emotional vulnerability has negative race and gender connotations. It would not merely be viewed as a sign of weakness. It would buttress negative beliefs about the intellectual capacity and commitment of Blacks and women. Brenda's comments are indicative of what Hines (1989) calls a *culture of dissemblance.* Hines argues that Black women created "the appearance of openness and disclosure, but actually shielded the truth of their inner lives and selves from their oppressors" (p. 380). The culture emanated from the constant threat of sexual exploitation, and a key characteristic of this culture is the maintenance of emotional distance as a self-protective measure.

Although acquiring a Ph.D. was viewed as a means to challenge negative assumptions about race and gender, some of the women made it clear that the Ph.D. is not enough to demonstrate commitment to Blacks. The real work comes after getting the Ph.D., and it is indicated by direct engagement and responsiveness to Black students. Thus, graduate school is a vehicle to help the Black community. For instance, Angela weighed the significance of teaching at a predominantly White institution: "I think that being in a nonminority school and trying to encourage the students all the way through—they need that. I'm sure there are tons of students that fall through the cracks." Similarly, Bett reflected on the importance of working at a historically Black college and university (HBCU) or a predominantly White university (PWU). She believes her presence at a large PWU is important because "there are Black students here who will probably never have a Black professor." However, she also feels that she is needed at an HBCU:

> If I go to an HBCU, I want to open a research lab and give Black students a chance to do research at a certain level. . . . You know, it's great if Bob Smith is doing research on African American adolescents, but what if Kareem Johnson was doing work on adolescents, because that's where he grew up and he understands the community?

Similarly, Amerie's comment is reminiscent of the service imperative among participants:

> If you think by virtue of you becoming a professor that you did something for Black America, then hat's off to you. I'm not going to comfort myself with that because you know you could still be doing more. You could always be doing more. It's nice that Condoleezza is a Black secretary of state, but . . . do you think that's a good example of what a Black woman can become? She pretty much de-races herself. I know people are walking around telling themselves, "I'm doing something good for Black America because I am here and I am going to be a professor." So what? I want to make sure that in my life that every Black kid, every Latino kid, every Asian kid that comes my way, I take special care for them, because that's the best that I can do. But I am not going to comfort myself saying, "I'm an associate, full professor, and I am just doing something good for Black America because I'm here" or "I can't really help the Black students because I really have to work on this book." No.

So getting the Ph.D. is not enough to demonstrate gratitude and commitment. Utilizing the credential to empower Blacks and other people of color is a genuine expression of solidarity and appreciation. Essentially, in order for the degree to have true value, it must be transformative. It must be employed to alter the status quo by helping Blacks navigate higher education.

What distinguishes social science and science and engineering participants is that all the social science respondents discussed how their research will help Black people or further understanding of diversity. MeMe emphasized that her interest in social theories is based on how they can help her understand "race and racialized organizations." Similarly, Missy asserted,

> I want it [research] to be used to improve our understanding of Black women and other women of color too, I think, to sort of advance our understanding of racialized gender and to really unpack that. So I really

kind of plan to balance my work in doing, like, empirical research which would have to be published in sociological journals. . . . I would like to write books. I mean, like, reading bell hooks and Patricia Hill Collins, that, like, changed my life. So, I would love to at some point write something along those lines . . . and generally help people understand things.

In regard to racial uplift, all the women discussed their desire to empower Blacks through education and resources or to serve as a role model for the race. Thus, career success is not simply measured by individual accomplishments but by collective responsibility. Their beliefs reflect oppositional position because not only do the women appear to have an understanding of the disempowering aspects of academe and society in general, but they also recognize what role they can play to foster empowerment. Critical consciousness and resistance are the mainstays of oppositional position.

Another pattern of response involved the ability of women to withstand obstacles and find ways to counterbalance inhospitable climates by relying on personal determination and maintaining a commitment to service. This line of reasoning may be attributed to the concept of *creative marginality* (Alfred, 2001; Johnson-Bailey, 1998; Thomas & Hollenshead, 2001). As noted in the literature review, marginality encourages Black women to be resourceful because they are given little support and few resources. It is the resourcefulness of Black women that encourages them to create and take advantage of opportunities.

Summary

The women in this study responded to their environment in ways that are indicative of oppositional position, which may derive from several factors. First, the women had female role models who exhibited both nurturing and leadership qualities. Second, their childhood experience with resourceful and vocal women may have contributed to their self-confidence. Third, the women felt that their achievements were due in part to the sacrifices and advocacy of other Black people. Therefore, they believed it was their responsibility to continue the tradition of racial uplift by helping Black people. These experiences, attitudes, and aspirations point to the willingness to defy group-based marginalization.

This study is the first step to developing a theory on the way Black female doctoral students navigate predominantly White institutions. For instance, oppositional position is encouraged through childhood experiences with influential Black women. Within the context of PWUs, oppositional position is manifested in response to an unwelcoming departmental environment. Once a critical consciousness is developed, it is manifested in navigational techniques, career goals, and community service. I do not want to suggest that this model applies to all Black female graduate students at a PWU. The framework is distinctly based on the women in this study, yet it may be applicable to other Black women within similar contexts.

Implications

This study affirms that Black women have distinct experiences that may place them on the periphery of the graduate community. More important, it shows how and possibly why they endure climates that have an undercurrent of racism and/or sexism. PWUs can support the successful negotiation of graduate school, however, through practices that address hostile climate issues.

First, a major part of universities' retention effort should be the installation of peer and faculty mentoring programs designed to assist women with negotiating their environment. Retention efforts can also be aided by workshops geared toward first-generation graduate students, women, or Black women specifically. Second, there should be an explicit recognition that the majority of the policies, behaviors, and values in place are contextually bound and designed to support the matriculation and graduation of Whites, particularly White males. With this understanding, departments should be encouraged to promote a climate that is supportive of students' varied life experiences. Such support may include selecting diverse readings, supporting nontraditional research, and scheduling social events that promote diversity. Furthermore, there should be recognition that the very life experiences that may promote one's persistence in graduate school may also hinder one's ability to function in an environment that is perceived as unwelcoming. One way to address hostile climate issues is to actively recruit students, faculty, and staff of color in order to reduce their isolation.

Future Research

To garner more information about Black women in higher education, this study can be extended to look at intragroup differences. For instance, Black females who are parenting young children or Black women from varied class backgrounds may have different navigational experiences. Also, one wonders if the reasons for pursuing a graduate degree are overwhelmingly different for other nondominant identity groups (e.g., Latinas or Native American women). Furthermore, it would be useful to study Black women after their completion of graduate school to determine if service-oriented plans were implemented.

In any event, the narratives in this study reveal that many women are not pursuing knowledge for the sake of knowledge. Applicability of knowledge for the benefit of the larger community is paramount. It is unfortunate that some of the personal experiences of Black women in graduate school affirm the need for the type of oppositional position that counters institutional bias and neglect. Oppositional behaviors and attitudes, however, appear to be an important navigational strategy.

Appendix A: Excerpt of Interview Guide

The questions represent components of themes that are central to the research.

Development/Family Background/Educational Experiences

1. Describe your childhood community.
2. Describe your school experiences.
3. How was education viewed in your family?
4. What images did you have of Black women growing up?

Higher Education

Undergrad/general

1. How would you describe your ability to access college?
2. What kind of impact has higher education had on your life?

Graduate

1. How did you decide to go to graduate school?
2. How would you describe your ability to succeed in graduate school?
3. What kind of support system do you have?
4. Describe your relationship with your advisor. Other faculty?
5. How do you want your research to be used?

Collective

1. Discuss your community service activities.
2. In what ways, if any, does your education reflect the African American experience?
3. Do you believe that racism and/or sexism have had an impact on you?

Science and Engineering	Age	Childhood community	Childhood schools	Household	Parental Education	Childhood SES
Dorothy	20s	Black neighborhood	Predominantly White; science prep programs	Two-parent	Both parents have a master's degree	"middle class"
Kendra	20s	Black neighborhood	Predominantly Black; science prep programs	Two-parent	Mother has associate in nursing; father has a bachelor's degree	"had enough to get by"
Angela	20s	Black neighborhood	Predominantly Black	Two-parent	Mother has a high school diploma; father has a bachelor's degree	"lower middle class because middle class went to the mall every weekend"
Bianca	20s	Black neighborhood	Predominantly Black; science prep programs	Two-parent	Grandparents completed college; Both parents have a master's degree	"upper middle class" because of education and income

Social Science	Age	Childhood community	Childhood schools	Household	Parental Education	Childhood SES
Francine	20s	Black neighborhood	Predominantly Black	Two-parent	Both parents completed high school	"lower middle class"
Bett	20s	Racially diverse neighborhood	Racially diverse	Two-parent	Both parents have a bachelor's degree	"middle class"
MeMe	30s	Predominantly Black	Predominantly Black	Two-parent	Mother has a master's degree; father has a primary school education	"middle class" because her parents could afford to send her to private school
Missy	30s	Predominantly White	Predominantly White	Two-parent	Mother has a master's degree; father has a high school diploma	no label given
Amerie	20s	Racially diverse neighborhood	Racially diverse	Two-parent	Parents have a high school education	mother was homemaker and father worked several blue-color jobs

References

Alfred, M. V. (2001). Reconceptualizing marginality from the margins: Perspectives of African American tenured female faculty at a White research university. *Western Journal of Black Studies, 25*(1), 1–11.

Allen, B. J. (1995). *Twice blessed, doubly oppressed: Women of color in academe.* Paper presented at the Speech Communication Association, San Antonio, TX.

Anderson, J. (1988). *The education of Blacks in the South, 1860–1935.* Chapel Hill: University of North Carolina Press.

Bandura, A. (1986). *Social foundations of thought and action.* Englewood Cliffs, NJ: Prentice Hall.

Brown, E. B. (1989). Womanist consciousness: Maggie Lena Walker and the Independent Order of Saint Luke. *Signs, 14*(3), 610–633.

Cabrera, A., & Nasa, S. L. (Eds.). (2000). *Understanding the college choice of disadvantaged students.* San Francisco: Jossey-Bass.

Collins, P. H. (2000). *Black feminist thought.* New York: Routledge.

Collins, P. H. (2004). *Black sexual politics.* New York: Routledge.

Crenshaw, K. (1991). Mapping the margins: Intersectionality, identity politics, and violence against women of color. *Stanford Law Review, 43*(6), 1241–1299.

Creswell, J. (1998). *Qualitative inquiry and research design.* Thousand Oaks, CA: Sage.

Ellis, E. M. (2001). The impact of race and gender on graduate school socialization, satisfaction with doctoral study and commitment to degree completion. *Western Journal of Black Studies, 25,* 30–45.

Giddings, P. (1984). *When and where I enter.* New York: William Morrow.

Gregory, S. T. (1999). *Black women in the academy: The secrets to success and achievement.* Lanham, MD: University Press of America.

Guba, E. G., & Lincoln, Y. S. (1982). Epistemological and methodological bases of naturalist inquiry. *Educational Communications and Technology Journal, 4,* 311–333.

Hall, R., & Sandler, B. (1982). *The classroom climate: A chilly one for women?* Washington, DC: Association of American Colleges.

Heyl, B. S. (2001). Ethnographic interviewing. In P. Atkinson, A. Coffey, S. Delamont, J. Lofland, & L. Lofland (Eds.), *Handbook of ethnography.* London: Sage.

Hine, D. C. (1989). Rape and the inner lives of black women in the Middle West: Preliminary thoughts on the culture of dissemblance. *Signs, 14*(4), 383–385.

Hine, D. C., & Thompson, K. (1998). *A shining thread of hope.* New York: Broadway Books.

Holmes, S. L. (2001). *Narrated voices of African American women in academe.* Paper presented at the Association for the Study of Higher Education, Alabama.

hooks, b. (1989). *Talking back: Thinking feminist, thinking black.* Boston: South End Press.

Jackson, L. (1998). The influence of both race and gender on the experiences of African American college women. *Review of Higher Education, 21*(4), 359–375.

Jewell, K. S. (1993). *From Mammy to Miss America and beyond.* New York: Routledge.

Johnson-Bailey, J. (1998). Black reentry women in the academy: Making a way out of no way. *Initiatives, 58*(4), 37–48.

King, J. E. (1995). Culture-centered knowledge: Black studies, curriculum transformation, and social action. In J. Banks & C. A. McGee Banks (Eds.), *Handbook of research on multicultural education* (pp. 265–290). New York: Macmillan.

Myers, L. W. (2002). *A broken silence: Voices of African American women in the academy.* Westport, CT: Bergin & Garvey.

O'Connor, C. (2002). Black women beating the odds from one generation to the next: How the changing dynamics of constraint and opportunity affect the process of educational resilience. *American Educational Research Journal, 39*(4), 855–903.

Pascarella, E., & Terenzini, P. (1991). *How college affects students.* San Francisco: Jossey-Bass.

Patton, M. Q. (2001). *Qualitative research and evaluation methods.* Thousand Oaks, CA: Sage.

Pinkney, A. (1987). *Black Americans* (2nd ed.). Englewood Cliffs, NJ: Prentice Hall.

Schwartz, R. A., Bower, B. L., Rice, D. C., & Washington, C. M. (2003). "Ain't I a woman, too?": Tracing the experiences of African American women in graduate school. *Journal of Negro Education, 72*(3), 252–268.

Strauss, A., & Corbin, J. (1998). *Basics of qualitative methods.* Thousand Oaks, CA: Sage.

Taylor, S. (2001). Locating and conducting discourse analytic research. In M. Wetherell, S. Taylor, & S. Yates (Eds.), *Discourse as data: A guide for analysis* (pp. 5–48). Thousand Oaks, CA: Sage.

Thomas, G. (2001). The dual role of scholar and social change agent: Reflections from tenured African American and Latina faculty. In R. Mabokela & A. L. Green (Eds.), *Sisters of the academy.* Sterling, VA: Stylus.

Thomas, G., & Hollenshead, C. (2001). Resisting from the margins: The coping strategies of Black women and other women of color faculty members at a research university. *Journal of Negro Education, 70*(3), 166–175.

Turner, C. V., & Thompson, J. R. (1993). Socializing women doctoral students: Minority and majority experiences. *Review of Higher Education, 16*(3), 355–370.

Weiss, R. (1994). *Learning from strangers: The art and method of qualitative interview studies.* New York: Free Press.

Wing, A. K. (Ed.). (1997). *Critical race feminism.* New York: NYU Press.

Woods, R. L. (2001). Invisible women: The experiences of Black female doctoral students at the University of Michigan. In R. Mabokela & A. L. Green (Eds.), *Sisters of the academy* (pp. 105–116). Sterling, VA: Stylus.

Notes

1. Theoretical sampling is selecting individuals who can contribute to an evolving theory. All participants must meet a stated criteria such as being a Black female doctoral student.

2. Specifically, grounded research is theory that is derived from the data. It entails systemic data gathering, analysis, and eventual theory development (Strauss & Corbin, 1998).

3. The themes derived from this exploratory study will inform subsequent interview probes and possibly sampling of respondents (Strauss & Corbin, 1998).

4. *Pipeline* programs are precollege programs designed to prepare students for higher education through tutoring, academic enrichment, and financial assistance.

9

"GOD HAS A PURPOSE AND I LANDED SOMEWHERE"

Understanding the Spiritual Journey
of Racially Diverse Graduate Students

Mary F. Howard-Hamilton, Kandace G. Hinton,
and Ted N. Ingram

raduate students of color have employed various coping strategies and methods to persevere and persist while attempting to obtain advanced degrees. One such coping strategy is to be connected consistently and constantly with a spiritual awareness or belief that provides the internal or cognitive dialogue needed to counteract the negative or self-debilitating actions that may occur inside and outside the classroom environment. This spiritual connectedness has been a coping mechanism used by oppressed groups throughout history in order to resist the negative messages sent overtly and covertly by dominant groups. Oppressed communities use spirituality as a means to "prevail against the odds with moral integrity" (Cannon, 1988, p. 2). Fried (2007) states that "faith traditions provide all-encompassing frameworks of belief for the people who adopt them" (p. 1). These faith traditions help underrepresented groups develop positive and purposeful methods to counteract detrimental events. Overwhelming discriminatory practices such as sexism, racism, and classism require underrepresented groups to shape and interpret their own world from a higher moral and spiritual plane, one that is not repressive but respectful and accepting. The purpose of this research study is to elucidate the little-known factors

The authors would like to thank Dwyane Smith for his thorough search of spirituality literature.

that affect graduate school transitions for students of color. Therefore, this chapter focuses on the use of a spiritual framework as a coping strategy by graduate students of color.

Religion, Faith Development, and Spirituality

Until recently, spirituality is a topic that has not often been addressed in higher education research. The differentiation among the terms *religion, faith,* and *spirituality,* however, has provided a broader perspective on individuals' faith development and identity formation as well as added depth and breadth to research in these areas.

Religion is defined as "encompassing an affiliation with and practice of an established denominational tradition" (Stamm, 2006a, p. 38). Love (2001) characterizes religion as a shared system of values, principles, or doctrines related to a belief in and worship of a supernatural power or powers regarded as creator(s) and governor(s) of the universe. In this chapter, we share statements from graduate students of color. We did not ask the students about a specific religious affiliation such as Christian, Muslim, or Judaism, but they did talk about their experiences in graduate school from a spiritual or faith framework.

According to Stamm (2006a), faith, in contrast to religion, "is more personal and existential. Faith is not always religious in its content or context" (p. 39). Love (2001) defines faith as "a process of meaning making, which is the process of making sense out of the activities of life and seeking patterns, order, coherence, and relation among the disparate elements of human living" (p. 8). Faith development, as described by Parks (2000), encompasses three interactive components: (a) knowing (cognitive aspects of faith development), (b) forms of dependence (an affective aspect of faith development), and (c) forms of community (social aspects of faith development). Furthermore, there are four stages within this framework: (1) adolescent or conventional faith, (2) young adult faith, (3) tested adult faith, and (4) mature adult faith. Parks has found most graduate students, postgraduates, or beyond to be in Stage 3—tested adult faith—because "as an individual's faith develops, he or she begins to associate with others who share similar meanings and have similar socioeconomic, political, religious, and philosophical views (self-selected groups)" (Stamm, 2006a, p. 61).

Fowler's (1981) faith development theory involves six stages and a pre-stage of Undifferentiated or Primal Faith that occurs during infancy. Following Primal Faith, in Stage 1, Intuitive Projective Faith (early childhood), the child's conceptualization of faith is influenced by examples and stories provided by adults. In Stage 2, Mythic Literal Faith (childhood and beyond), the person begins to interpret stories, drama, and myth from a concrete and literal perspective rather than an abstract and symbolic one. In Stage 3, Synthetic Conventional Faith (adolescence and beyond), the person is establishing a self-identity and creating a life story. "To provide stability, deeply held beliefs and values may be sought, often by identifying with authority figures or peer role models" (Stamm, 2006a, p. 55). Stage 4, Individuative Reflective Faith (young adulthood and beyond), involves critical personal reflection analysis of one's worldview about faith. Stage 5, Conjunctive Faith (early midlife and beyond), connects the individual in spiritual fellowship with all human beings, and there is a commitment to justice that transcends social class, religion, race, and ethnicity. Stage 6, Universalizing Faith (midlife and beyond), is a sense of communal humanism in which the person seeks to liberate others from social, political, and systemic injustices. Fowler's (1981) and Parks's (2000) faith developmental theories provide the psychosocial and cognitive road maps for understanding the coping strategies used by graduate students of color to navigate the obstacles encountered when proceeding through their graduate programs.

There is some overlap among the definitions of *religion, faith,* and *spirituality*. The defining difference, however, is that religion is organized and has specific doctrines, codes, and governing policies (Tisdell, 2003). *Spirituality,* according to Love (2001), is a search for meaning, transcendence, wholeness, and purpose, a search more for personal growth and affirmation than for public influence. Tisdell states that "spirituality is more about how people make meaning through experience with wholeness, a perceived higher power, or higher purpose" (p. 47).

Literature Review

The study of college-student transitions helps provide insight into issues of student persistence and success (Perna, 2004; Strayhorn, 2008). The literature on student transitions, which focuses on the undergraduate experience, indicates that students of color in predominantly White institutions (PWIs) face unique transitioning challenges such as financial issues (St. John, 1991), lack of college-preparatory course work or academic preparation (Flowers, 2002; Terenzini, Pascarella, & Blimling, 1996), and racial discrimination and alienation (Brown, Hinton, & Howard-Hamilton, 2007; Howard-Hamilton, 2003; Patton, McEwen, Rendon, & Howard-Hamilton, 2007; Torres, Howard-Hamilton, & Cooper, 2003). These challenges leave some students without a support system, but alternative coping mechanisms such as finding a spiritual, religious, or faith connection may fill a void and lead to persistence and academic success.

Students struggle with spirituality, values, and purpose in life during their college years (Chickering & Reisser, 1993; Fowler, 1981; Parks, 2000; Stamm, 2006b). Bryant and Astin (2008) hypothesize that a higher incidence of spiritual struggle would be evident among marginalized undergraduate students who face discrimination and maltreatment on college campuses. In addition, these researchers have "tested the extent to which individuals with compassionate self-perceptions and orientations toward social activism and charitable involvement struggle spiritually" (p. 7). The students who engage in social justice activities typically personally experience or observe oppressive acts, and these researchers hypothesize that such experiences cause enough dissonance that "they might struggle to make sense of the stark contrasts between goodness and malevolence in the world" (p. 7). Bryant and Astin's analysis of the first hypothesis finds that women, as a marginalized group, struggle with spirituality more than men do. Conversely, the students who were involved in social justice concerns, engaged in volunteer or service endeavors, and had a compassionate self-concept did not struggle with their spiritual beliefs.

Several researchers have begun exploring the spiritual development of students of color on college campuses (Constantine, Wilton, Gainor, & Lewis, 2002; Herndon, 2003; Sanchez & Carter, 2005; Stewart, 2002; Walker & Dixon, 2002; Watt, 2003). Students of color, and more specifically African American students, have encountered numerous challenges on predominantly White campuses. Often, these students "turn to spiritual beliefs to cope with the everyday struggles that come with living in a socially and politically oppressive system" (Watt, 2003, p. 29). African American students who have attended predominantly White colleges have reported higher levels of faith and spiritual development than have majority students (Walker & Dixon, 2002). African American males have found comfort in their spiritual beliefs, which in turn has provided them with the strength to remain in school (Herndon, 2003). Three themes emerged from Herndon's research: (a) resilience is sustained by spirituality, (b) purpose is linked with spirituality, and (c) African American institutions with a religious affiliation support the faith development of their students. The African American men in Herndon's study who received spiritual support from family and who believed in God had a higher likelihood of successfully navigating through school.

Watt (2003) uncovered several spiritual coping themes when she interviewed 48 African American women who were attending predominantly White colleges. The themes capture the process of psychological resistance through the use of symbols, rituals, and affirmations that connected the women to a relationship with God or a deeper sense of spirituality. Stewart (2002) explored the role of faith and spirituality in the development of five African American upper-level undergraduate men and women. She reports that "four out of the five students indicated that spirituality was a central component of their identity makeup" (p. 592). More important, the students defined spirituality differently and had different ideas of the way their identity and beliefs intersected.

Constantine et al. (2002) investigated the role of spirituality and religious participation in relation to Africultural coping approaches and religious-dilemma-driven resolution styles among 144 African American college students. They found that higher levels of spirituality were interrelated with a greater use of Africultural coping strategies as well as a belief that the Creator will provide solutions to a problem or that the individual with help from the Creator can resolve an issue. Overall, spirituality among students of color is clearly an essential element to their racial identity development as well as the key to coping or to maintaining a positive self-concept and developing healthy resistance to negative influences on college campuses.

Racial identity attitudes were predictive of religious orientation in Sanchez and Carter's (2005) research with African American college students attending a predominantly White college. In these researchers' comparison of religious belief to Cross's (1991) Nigrescence model, African American men who adopted a strong internalized racial identity reported a stronger religious orientation. African American women, however, held stronger faith and religious beliefs when they were immersed in a more intense and reflective phase of racial identity development, one stage lower than the men in this study.

The purpose of the research study reported in this chapter was to elucidate the little-known factors that affect graduate school transitions for students of color. A theme that emerged from the transcribed data is a sense of spiritual identity development among the participants in the study. Their comments were analyzed and compared to Fowler's (1981) and Parks's (2000) stages of faith development as well as to the findings of researchers who have studied the spiritual development of students of color (Constantine et al., 2002; Stewart, 2002; Watt, 2003). The findings have ramifications for the recruitment, support, and retention of underrepresented students in graduate-degree programs.

Methodology

Employing convenience and purposeful sampling techniques, we contacted administrators at two universities. At Midwest University (MU), a predominantly White, public, midwestern, research-extensive institution, we contacted a graduate administration office for two schools. Similarly, a graduate administration office at Northeast University (NU), a predominantly White, private, northeastern, elite institution, provided permission and access to students. The two institutions were polar opposites in their academic focus and surrounding environment. There were a total of 26 participants involved in the study.

At Midwest University, the participants consisted of 12 first-year doctoral students of color in education, law, and sociology. The demographics of the MU participants were as follows: 5 doctoral students in education, 3 doctoral students in sociology, and 4 law students; 2 Latina, 1 Dominican, and 9 African American; 3 men and 9 women.

The Northeast University interviewees consisted of 14 first-year doctoral participants from the following fields: computer science (2), urban studies and planning (2), technology and policy (2), chemistry (4), business (2), political science (1), and electrical engineering (1). The racial demographics of the participants at NU were as follows: 6 Latino/a, 1 Arab American, 1 Chinese American, and 6 African American. At NU, we interviewed 8 men and 6 women.

Focus groups were assembled at each of these institutions to collect data. At least two members of the eight-member research team were present at each focus group. As one team member directed questions to the students, another recorded field notes and observed the interview process. Focus group sessions were audio-tape-recorded and transcribed verbatim.

The data were analyzed using the Constant Comparative Method, an inductive process for forming a categorical model to describe the data collected in a study (Glaser & Strauss, 1967; Guba & Lincoln, 1989). This method of data analysis continuously develops a process from explaining individual units of information to the construction of a descriptive model. Following transcription, we examined interviews line by line as part of the open coding process used to identify potential themes and meaningful categories from actual text examples (Denzin & Lincoln, 2003; Strauss & Corbin, 1990). In addition, we used coding software to process the data electronically. Once the data were processed, we shared an initial draft of the interview transcriptions and findings with focus group participants as part of a member check. Each participant was asked to provide feedback on his or her focus group session, thus ensuring the correct interpretation of participant comments and responses. Our analysis of the transcripts from each institution found that spirituality or faith and God were common themes but were discussed in a variety of contexts.

Findings and Discussion

Spirituality at Midwest University

The two themes that emerged from the interviews with MU graduate students were their search for a purpose and their coping strategies. All the women participants remarked on their faith, religion, or spirituality and on how important it was to have a purpose and vision when away from family and loved ones. One student found solace and peace from the fact that there was more than one Black church to choose from in MU's surrounding community:

> I know that another important thing for me in this program and also in life is my faith. And that is what keeps me going. At times when I feel overwhelmed or something like that, it is just like, it is going to be all right. And I pray about it. And . . . this kind of goes back to the question we talked about that when I came here was the churches. And finding that they had churches . . . not just one Black church, but more than one Black church. So that is really important. Because you know, no matter what, that is what gets me through everything. And that is what I am so thankful for. Because when times get hard . . . and having people I can talk to. I talk to my family and I know they're praying for me. You know, praying for me. And that is just . . . it is just necessary.

The interviews with the MU students show that they have reached Fowler's Stages 4 and 5: they engage in deep personal reflection about faith and are passionate about social justice and changing the world. As one participant stated,

> I wanted to be able to give back. That's when I found out that international education was my field. I had so many opportunities and I know how it has impacted me, and I wanted to give that opportunity to other students. To whom much is given, much is required. And that was it, that sense of social responsibility. We have been so blessed to have the opportunity to go to school and have people to support you. There is no way in the world you can get where you are and not look back . . . pull somebody up and bring somebody with you. We got here because of being blessed by God.

This response connects with Bryant and Astin's (2008) findings: the participant is thankful and optimistic about her educational endeavors and about

her goal after receiving her degree to empower those who are disenfran-
chised. Because of her faith in God, her faith in her mission has not been
disrupted and tainted by the obstacles she faced but has been strengthened.

Individuals in Fowler's Stage 5 exhibit humanistic faith values, and one
respondent made a statement that parallels Fowler's definition:

> There are a lot of reasons for being here and for staying in school and
> getting this degree. Like you, I am doing it for God, for myself, for my
> family. I'm not here by myself. You have your entire family here in college,
> your entire family's in college.

All the participants at MU indicated a sense of purpose and spiritual ground-
ing as they proceeded through their doctoral programs. Furthermore, their
faith became stronger when they were faced with challenging situations or
obstacles that may have hindered their progress.

One student found her journey to be more challenging because there
were not enough role models to help with the day-to-day challenges in and
out of the classroom. Her perspective of the situation was that there seemed
to be an unfair advantage given to majority students:

> We don't really get the support that we see other students getting, but I
> am determined to finish the program no matter what they do, what they
> don't do, no matter what happens. This is not for them; I see it as some-
> thing I have to do for myself, for my family, and for God. I'm not here by
> myself. You have your entire family here in college. God, I feel like there's
> a reason why I'm here. I don't think it is just by my own nature or my
> own abilities. I feel like God put me here for a reason. My GRE scores
> were terrible. I mean, they really suck! That's why when I do my research
> and the things that I do, I focus it around spirituality and things like that
> because I feel like there's a purpose. I'm not here for myself. I'm not just
> here by myself.

Another student concurred regarding test scores and the way the tests
seem not only to weed out students of color but also, if they are admitted,
to cause the faculty to assume they are not capable or qualified to handle the
course work. She also felt that standardized tests are biased:

> The GRE, SAT, none of those tests are set up for us. They're not; English
> is not my first language. That test is not set up for me. There was no way.
> So, for me . . . I am here because God has a purpose and I landed
> somewhere.

The students at MU found moral and ethical strength in their religious and spiritual beliefs. This strength helped them persevere in an environment that continued to devalue their intellect and academic prowess.

Spirituality at Northeast University

The study participants at Northeast University (NU) followed a more intellectual and analytical path to understanding their purpose in pursuing a terminal degree. Only 5 out of the 14 participants talked about faith, spirituality, or religion as the reason they were in graduate school or about using faith, spirituality, or religion as the foundation for their perseverance. One student commented that it was his academic abilities, test scores, and recommendations from top scholars in the field that were the critical elements in gaining admittance to NU. Furthermore, the participants shared how their intrinsic abilities such as determination; keeping their eyes on the prize, or focus; and self-motivation were the attributes that kept them from letting obstacles hinder their progress. The students who were involved with community service did so in order to make a connection with people who "looked like them." This community engagement, however, was not "a calling" or spiritually framed (Bryant & Astin, 2008; Constantine et al., 2002; Watt, 2003).

The five graduate students at NU who recognized a spiritual presence that was instrumental in their day-to-day perseverance on campus and overall academic experience verbalized a belief in God, having a Christian philosophy, and the need for prayer at all times.

An African American woman talked about the importance of going to church in order to forget about her hectic schedule of going to classes and working throughout the week:

> My husband has two jobs and goes to school. We make sure to have dates on weekends and go to church. We are both in Bible study. Mine are tonight, so I can't wait to go tonight and hang out with my friends. I try to do things like that. I was volunteering at my church. I cook on Wednesday nights for the homeless. This really helps, going to church and things like that.

This woman's statements suggest that going to church and morning prayers gave her the energy to handle the pressures of being a newlywed, starting graduate school, and living far away from her family:

> I feel like if I start in the morning just praying to God and acknowledging dependence on Him, He gives me strength to go through the day. When

I don't pray, life gets too overwhelming, and I begin to break down. Having God as a focus helps. I know it's His will for me to be here.

An African American male participant echoed similar sentiments about prayer. He said that going to church and spirituality have a tremendous impact on how successful a person will be in graduate school:

There are times when I feel like I can't make it and "how can I possibly work these things out?" and feel like if I start my morning out praying to God and getting things worked out. When I don't pray or recognize God on a daily basis that is when things get a little crazy and everything gets a little hectic. It's overwhelming, and I feel like having God as my focus really helps me to work out everything that is around me. So it's crucial—in my case I would be drowning.

Echoing the sentiments of the graduate students who shared their personal experiences regarding faith, another African American male participant said,

I'm also a spiritual person, so I get a lot from that. . . . I think it changes my outlook on everything because that is the reason I am here is because God wants me to be here. I believe if you're in God's will . . . like, in the mornings I try to do this [pray] faithfully. I try to read the Bible and pray and focus on God because He is the most important thing. Like even tomorrow if something happened and I didn't get a Ph.D. I'd be fine. A lot of people think chemistry is all I have. You see a lot of people just throwing all of their everything into chemistry. This is not all I have. It doesn't define me. I have a source. I go to church every Sunday and hang out with those people and center myself.

A Mexican American male indicated that he is "semispiritual" because his wife prays for the family and because his involvement in church has shifted from being very active to very little involvement now that he is in school:

Last night my wife was trying to read the Bible to me and I had to go study. I am probably pretty bad about it. I guess it's not where I get a lot of my foundation. I get it from my wife and little girl. My wife is very spiritual, but . . . before I came here, there was a time when I went all the time. Now I put it to the side. That's not good.

One respondent's engagement in a Christian community outside church and throughout the week was important for him, and he found the perfect environment living in a house with five people:

I'm a Christian and wanted to live with Christians. I found a listing that said "willing to form a Christian house." So my house is in some ways a social center. I try to incorporate my faith in God into all decisions. It is a way to react to challenges. In general I believe God provided what I have to be here. Who I believe God is and what I believe is for me how I choose my future path.

The graduate students at NU have a strong and positive racial/ethnic self-concept, which is connected with the internalization stage of Cross's (1991) Nigrescence model. At this stage there is a sustained commitment to the community and to "paying forward" their time and talents to others who may not have the gifts that they do. Overall, the Africultural beliefs espoused by the students are directly related to the findings of Constantine et al. (2002), Stewart (2002), and Watt (2003), who have found that religion and faith help students of color fight oppressive acts, concentrate on their studies, and connect with a community that shares similar beliefs. The church or a spiritual community that has a similar atmosphere, as noted by the student who lives in a Christian house, is a primary location for psychological and social support (Constantine et al., 2002). All the students have the attributes of a mature adult faith that connects them to others in spiritual fellowship (Fowler, 1981; Parks, 2000).

Implications

According to developmental theorists (Chickering & Reisser, 1993; Erikson, 1968; Evans, Forney, & Guido-DiBrito, 1998; Perry, 1999; Sanford, 1966), in order for intellectual and psychosocial growth to occur, students need to encounter some optimal dissonance in their lives. This dissonance does not necessarily need to be negative, but it should be challenging. Furthermore, there needs to be a support system available to help students negotiate the dissonance that occurs. The graduate student participants in this study have encountered challenging situations that created that optimal level of dissonance as they made their way through college. They found support and solace in their faith and spirituality, which gave them a clear understanding of why they landed at their respective institutions. The findings of this study parallel those of Watt (2003), who reports that African American women use spirituality in multifaceted ways: to cope with difficulty, to resist negative images, and to develop identity.

The graduate students in this study used strategies derived from faith development to cope with the "chilly" environment that they associated with a predominantly White institution. In addition, faith development allowed students to navigate through the rigors of obtaining an advanced degree. Given the dearth of literature concerning access for graduate students of color, this research can widen the lens of access inquiry and add to the body of knowledge on this topic. Moreover, this research may be particularly useful to graduate schools, administrators, and faculty, as well as to those directly responsible for the recruitment of students of color into graduate programs, because it might provide insight and lay the foundation for additional research in understanding the complexities of access.

Both policy-related and practical implications emerged from this study. According to the results of this study, having a spiritual identity can be a support structure for graduate students of color. The extent to which graduate students of color expressed the need for spirituality was pervasive. If there is to be an increase in the number of graduate students of color in the academy, policy makers, faculty, and administrators need to give serious consideration to the support offered to this population. Understanding spirituality and providing opportunities for this subset of students to demonstrate their beliefs can aid in their persistence in advanced-degree programs. From this study, we offer the following strategies for professionals who work with graduate students of color:

1. *Bring in speakers.* It is important for informed individuals to come to campuses to speak on diversity issues, including spirituality, with the intent of creating a more inclusive environment. Particularly at a large predominantly White university, it is critical to have diverse conversations to create a multiculturally competent environment.

2. *Have midday meditation sessions.* At a research-extensive institution, it is easy for students and professionals to become consumed with the daily, demanding work schedule. Therefore, providing a designated time period in the workday for students and professionals to reflect or meditate is encouraged. Creating this opportunity in the workday may provide for healthier and more productive individuals.

3. *Arrange trips to organized religious events.* MU, like most PWIs, is characterized by having few churches with small congregations in the immediate area. Based on the data generated from the focus groups, being part of a small congregation was atypical for most students. Student affairs practitioners may want to consider providing transportation to neighboring churches in larger cities so students can broaden their networks.

4. *Organize spiritual support groups.* Because spirituality is a significant part of the identity of graduate students of color, students should have regular discussion about this subject. It is important for them to engage in conversation with other like-minded individuals so they can grow and share experiences.

5. *Identify religious spaces on campus.* Having a space on campus where students can come together and openly practice their spirituality is essential. Having such a space may be extremely beneficial for students who reside on campus and cannot easily access off-campus resources.

This study suggests that spirituality can help equalize the opportunity for graduate students of color to persist in graduate education. We know that spirituality is important for many undergraduate students (Stewart, 2002; Watt, 2003), but what helps balance opportunities for graduate students? This study merely begins to answer that question; there is clearly room for additional research in this area. Further investigation is necessary to address the multitude of variables that potentially affect retention for graduate students of color. Perhaps a better understanding of this issue will inform optimal ways to increase the number and retention of graduate students of color.

References

Brown, O. G., Hinton, K. G., & Howard-Hamilton, M. F. (2007). Unleashing suppressed voices at colleges and universities: The role of case studies in understanding diversity in higher education. In O. G. Brown, K. G. Hinton, & M. F. Howard (Eds.), *Unleashing suppressed voices on college campuses: Diversity issues in higher education* (pp. 1–14). New York: Lang.

Bryant, A. N., & Astin, H. S. (2008). The correlates of spiritual struggle during the college years. *Journal of Higher Education, 79*(1), 1–27.

Cannon, K. G. (1988). *Black womanist ethics.* Atlanta: Scholars Press.

Chickering, A. W., & Reisser, L. (1993). *Education and identity* (2nd ed.). San Francisco: Jossey-Bass.

Constantine, M. G., Wilton, L., Gainor, K. A., & Lewis, E. L. (2002). Religious participation, spirituality, and coping among African American college students. *Journal of College Student Development, 43*, 605–613.

Cross, W. E. (1991). *Shades of black: Diversity in African American identity.* Philadelphia: Temple University Press.

Denzin, N. K., & Lincoln, Y. S. (2003). *Collecting and interpreting qualitative material.* Thousand Oaks, CA: Sage.

Erikson, E. H. (1968). *Identity: Youth and crisis.* New York: Norton.

Evans, N. J., Forney, D. S., & Guido-DiBrito, F. (1998). *Student development in college: Theory, research, and practice.* San Francisco: Jossey-Bass.

Flowers, L. (2002). The impact of college racial composition on African American students' academic and social gains: Additional evidence. *Journal of College Student Development, 43,* 403–410.

Fowler, J. W. (1981). *Stages of faith: The psychology of human development and the quest for meaning.* San Francisco: HarperCollins.

Fried, J. (2007). Thinking skillfully and respecting differences: Understanding religious privilege on campus. *Journal of College and Character, 9*(1), 1–7.

Glaser, B. G., & Strauss, A. L. (1967). *The discovery of grounded theory: Strategies for qualitative research.* New York: Aldine.

Guba, E. G., & Lincoln, Y. S. (1989). *Fourth generation evaluation.* Newbury Park, CA: Sage.

Herndon, M. K. (2003). Expressions of spirituality among African-American college males. *Journal of Men's Studies, 12,* 75–84.

Howard-Hamilton, M. F. (Ed.). (2003). *New Directions for Student Services, Vol. 104: Meeting the needs of African American women.* San Francisco: Jossey-Bass.

Love, P. G. (2001). Spirituality and student development: Theoretical connections. In M. A. Jablonski (Ed.), *New Directions for Student Services, Vol. 95: The implications of student spirituality for student affairs practice* (pp. 7–16). San Francisco: Jossey-Bass.

Parks, S. D. (2000). *Big questions, worthy dreams: Mentoring young adults in their search for meaning, purpose, and faith.* San Francisco: Jossey-Bass.

Patton, L. D., McEwen, M., Rendon, L., & Howard-Hamilton, M. F. (2007). Critical race perspectives on theory in student affairs. In S. R. Harper & L. D. Patton (Eds.), *New Directions for Student Services, Vol. 120: Responding to the realities of race on campus* (pp. 39–54). San Francisco: Jossey-Bass.

Perna, L. W. (2004). Understanding the decision to enroll in graduate school: Sex and racial/ethnic group differences. *Journal of Higher Education, 75*(5), 487–527.

Perry, W. G. (1999). *Forms of ethical and intellectual development in the college years: A scheme.* San Francisco: Jossey-Bass.

Sanchez, D., & Carter, C. T. (2005). Exploring the relationship between racial identity and religious orientation among African American college students. *Journal of College Student Development, 46,* 280–295.

Sanford, N. (1966). *Self and society.* New York: Atherton Press.

Stamm, L. (2006a). The dynamics of spirituality and the religious experience. In A. W. Chickering, J. C. Dalton, & L. Stamm (Eds.), *Encouraging authenticity and spirituality in higher education* (pp. 37–65). San Francisco: Jossey-Bass.

Stamm, L. (2006b). The influence of religion and spirituality in shaping American higher education. In A. W. Chickering, J. C. Dalton, & L. Stamm (Eds.), *Encouraging authenticity and spirituality in higher education* (pp. 66–91). San Francisco: Jossey-Bass.

Stewart, D. L. (2002). The role of faith in the development of an integrated identity: A qualitative study of Black students at a White college. *Journal of College Student Development, 43,* 579–596.

St. John, E. (1991). The impact of student financial aid: A review of recent research. *Journal of Student Financial Aid, 21,* 18–32.

Strauss, A., & Corbin, J. (1990). Basics of qualitative research: Grounded theory procedures and techniques. Newbury Park, CA: Sage.

Strayhorn, T. L. (2008). Influences on labor market outcomes of African American college graduates: A national study. *Journal of Higher Education, 79*(1), 28–57.

Terenzini, P., Pascarella, E., & Blimling, G. (1996). Students' out-of-class experiences and their influence on learning and cognitive development: A literature review. *Journal of College Student Development, 37,* 149–162.

Tisdell, E. J. (2003). *Exploring spirituality and culture in adult and higher education.* San Francisco: Jossey-Bass.

Torres, V., Howard-Hamilton, M. F., & Cooper, D. L. (2003). *Identity development of diverse populations: Implications for teaching and administration in higher education.* ASHE-ERIC Higher Education Report, 29(6). San Francisco: Jossey-Bass.

Walker, K. L., & Dixon, V. (2002). Spirituality and academic performance among African American college students. *Journal of Black Psychology, 28,* 107–121.

Watt, S. K. (2003). Come to the river: Using spirituality to cope, resist, and develop identity. In M. F. Howard-Hamilton (Ed.), *New Directions for Student Services, Vol. 104: Meeting the needs of African American women* (pp. 29–40). San Francisco: Jossey-Bass.

10

OUR STORIES OF MENTORING AND GUIDANCE IN A HIGHER EDUCATION AND STUDENT AFFAIRS PROGRAM

Kandace G. Hinton, Valerie Grim,
and Mary F. Howard-Hamilton

Arican American women have significantly empowered one another, their families, and their communities while struggling to achieve education at all levels. Their difficulties and hardships have often stemmed from the disengaged academic cultures in higher education that have made and continue to make the social and intellectual climates chilly environments for people of color, specifically for African American women. African American women account for 7.15% of all students (*Chronicle of Higher Education Almanac,* 2003–2004), 2.14% of tenure-track faculty at 2- and 4-year institutions, and 6% of senior-level administrators (National Center for Education Statistics, 2002). Because the environment is frequently convoluted by race and gender discrimination, African American women, more than most, have been the victims of inequality, having to confront on a daily basis the lack of equity in higher education. Consequently, the treatment that African American women in the academy have received has made it essential for them to create support systems to survive, cope, and persist (Harry, 1994; Hinton, 2001; Moses, 1997; Patitu & Hinton, 2003). Since emancipation, Black women have pursued education and consequently have involved themselves with the establishment of schools; with the development of educational outreach through strong teaching, service, and research; and with the creation of "sister circles" to move beyond just having a "voice" to the self-defined standpoint that resists and "talks back" to the power structure (Collins, 1998; hooks, 1989).

The purpose of this chapter is to connect research on African American women in higher education with the experiences of the authors as doctoral students, junior faculty, and mentors in a higher education and student affairs program. Utilizing a research framework that emphasizes Black feminist and critical race theoretical perspectives, this chapter also gives voice to three African American women who are mentors and faculty at predominantly White institutions (PWIs) of higher learning.

Critical Race Theory

There are very few theories that can effectively provide a context for the varying situations experienced by African American women (Howard-Hamilton, 2003). Many traditional theories are very general, and there is an inherent assumption that most people have similar personal, professional, and developmental issues; as a result, some scholars involved in the creation of models related to race and mentoring have operated from the perspective that "one size fits all." One theory that takes into consideration the multifaceted and dynamic identities, roles, and experiences of African American women is critical race theory (CRT) (Delgado & Stefancic, 2001).

CRT "emphasizes the importance of viewing policies and policymaking in the proper historical and cultural context to deconstruct their racialized content" (Villalpando & Bernal, 2002, pp. 244–245). Critical race theorists understand that laws and legal policies subjugate oppressed people in our society (Delgado & Stefancic, 2001). The reason for this is that the dominant culture designed laws that were supposed to be race neutral but still perpetuated racial and ethnic oppression. Thus, CRT

- Recognizes that racism is prevalent in our society
- Expresses skepticism toward dominant claims of neutrality, objectivity, color blindness, and meritocracy
- Challenges ahistoricism and insists on a contextual and historical analysis of institutional policies
- Insists on recognizing the experiential knowledge of people of color and our communities of origin in analyzing society
- Is interdisciplinary and crosses epistemological and methodological boundaries
- Works toward eliminating racial oppression as part of the broader goal of ending all forms of oppression (Villalpando & Bernal, 2002, p. 245)

For people of color and in particular for African American women, CRT is a liberating frame of reference because it speaks to the complexity of their multiple identities and the personal issues that they face on a daily basis. Methods used to heighten the sensitivity and consciousness of people of color are exposure to microaggressions, creation of counterstories, and development of counterspaces (Delgado & Stefancic, 2001; Howard-Hamilton, 2003). Microaggressions are the covert and overt verbal, nonverbal, and visual forms of insults directed toward people of color, and they are a form of racist psychological battering. In order to minimize the impact of these micro insults, the use of counterstories is employed. Counterstorytelling is used to reframe and dispel the myths being told by those casting aspersions on people of color. A safe and comfortable counterspace should be provided for marginalized groups to share their counterstories, so they can be open and honest about living in an unsupportive environment and about communicating what that means for their daily survival.

When the ideology of racism is examined and racist injuries are named, victims of racism can find their voice. Further, those injured by racism discover that they are not alone in their marginality. They become empowered participants, hearing their own stories and those of others, as they listen to the way the arguments are framed. These interactions provide the intellectual foundations to help those victimized by racism make arguments themselves (Solorzano, Ceja, & Yosso, 2000, p. 64).

Black Feminism

African American women's lives and careers are placed at the intersections of race, class, gender, and orientation, which shape their experiences (Collins, 1998). According to Collins (1998), this perspective supports the "weaving together of personal narratives, stories, and critical social theory" (p. 119). Black feminist research, or a Black women's standpoint, is primarily aimed at "maintaining dialogues among Black women that are both attentive to heterogeneity among African American women and shared concerns arising from a common social location in the U.S. market and power relations" (p. 73). In contrast, mainstream research published by the dominant culture tends to ignore the experiences and voices of women, ethnic minorities, and those speaking from lower socioeconomic backgrounds.

According to Black feminists, the metaphor of voice breaks the silence for oppressed persons, develops self-reflexive speech, and confronts elite discourses. Collins (1998) writes,

Self-reflexive speech refers to dialogues among individual women who share their individual angles of vision. In a sense, it emphasizes the process of crafting a group-based point of view. In contrast, I prefer the term self-defined standpoint, because it ties Black women's speech communities much more closely to institutionalized power. (p. 47)

Although African American women have race and gender in common, they are not part of a monolithic culture. Unlike most theories, the Afrocentric perspective and Black feminism support the notion that each group member of the race is unique but shares core values and philosophical assumptions that have their origins in African history (Alfred, 2001; Asante, 1987; Collins, 1998). In developing their own unique characteristics, Black women have also developed a sense of belonging to the cultural and ethnic group. Because of racism and sexism, African American women see themselves as both racialized and sexualized individuals, and they perceive that they are treated differently because of their group status (Scheurich, 1993). Alfred asserts that African American women are situated at the bottom of academe's White-male-dominated hierarchy, which results in the belief that this dominance is the socially accepted way to think, act, speak, and behave in the academy. Promotion and tenure, as well as academic standards and activities, are historical designs emanating from White male dominance. Therefore, African American women pursuing graduate degrees, tenure, and promotion through the ranks of administration have to learn and "reproduce the ways of the dominant group" (Alfred, 2001, p. 115).

Speech that defines a standpoint in higher education environments is often difficult for Black women to establish because of the lack of a critical mass of Black women on most campuses. However, as Black women get opportunities to "talk" to one another away from the dominant space—in their homes, community organizations, and religious institutions—they share the challenges that they face as either the only person of color or one of few on predominantly White campuses working as students, faculty, or administrators. In their private spaces, Black women's speech and testimonials have empowered one another because they are able to "disrupt public truths about them" that have been developed by the "elite discourses" (Collins, 1998, p. 49). Elite discourses are those that occur when African Americans are in positions without power and the power structure views them as incompetent when failure seems apparent. These offstage opportunities to share are referred to as "safe spaces" or "home places" (Alfred, 2001, p. 118), and they allow African American women to move from the margins to the center, from object to subject. African American women who are pursuing graduate degrees or who are junior faculty use the strength of other African American women and men as safe places that provide support, advice, encouragement, and collaborative scholarship opportunities (Alfred, 2001; Hinton, 2001; Patitu & Hinton, 2003). Mentoring and support networks, then, can assist African American women as they persist through undergraduate schools, graduate schools, and the tenure and promotion process.

Mentoring

The traditional concept of mentoring, according to Williams and Schwiebert (2000), involves an older individual who has years of professional experience tapping a younger and inexperienced individual to follow in the footsteps of the mentor. This privilege has been maintained as a pipeline for White men to maintain a position of power within existing institutions. The traditional model of mentoring has left many women and people of color on the organizational periphery, leaving them with few opportunities for an upgrade in their positions, salary increases, and learning the skills to train others. Groups that have traditionally been excluded from having a role model could benefit from multiculturally inclusive mentoring processes.

An inclusive multicultural mentoring model emphasizes "dialogue between mentors and protégés regarding their unique experiences, personalities, interests, and backgrounds" (Williams & Schwiebert, 2000, p. 60). In addition, this mentoring process encourages and allows the celebration of differences. Thus, the central concept of multicultural mentoring is learning, which is described as "an active process that is deeply conceptualized and developmental" (Williams & Schwiebert, p. 60). In other words, it is important to respect the cultural background and experiences of each individual and tailor the mentoring experience according to the needs of the protégé. "When mentor and protégé view each other as individuals in the process of development rather than as superiors or subordinates, the power and hierarchy are diminished and may be replaced by collaboration and openness" (Williams & Schwiebert, p. 61).

Narratives, personal stories, autoethnographies, and oral histories are consistent with Afrocentrism, Black feminism, and critical race theory, all of which encourage oppressed persons to verbalize and resist domination by offering counterstories, personal narratives, and opportunities to break the silence. In this chapter, we use an autoethnographic methodological approach to break the silence, to provide counterstories, and to address issues of mentoring for graduate students at Indiana University. Indiana University is a predominantly White research-extensive institution. African Americans represent approximately 3% of the student graduate and undergraduate population. The higher education student affairs program is consistently ranked in the top ten among comparable institutions and programs (*U.S. News & World Report*, 2008). Furthermore, faculty of the higher education administration program are predominantly White, are renowned in the field, and have historically had access to an abundance of resources.

Indiana University's social, cultural, and academic environments are very similar to those of most predominantly White research-extensive institutions. These environments provide a context for understanding why some students of color struggle to identify mentors and to receive the kind of mentoring needed to help them appreciate the benefits associated with attending a majority-White institution. Moreover, the academic cultures at predominantly White institutions may also provide a context for understanding the difficulties that faculty and staff of color encounter as they attempt to become an integral part of the decision-making apparatus within the upper administration. And yet, as the evidence suggests, it is within these manufactured, exclusive, White academic cultures that we may find answers as to why faculty of color, along with staff and administrators representing minority populations, find themselves largely responsible for mentoring an overwhelming majority of minority students who seem unable to find White mentors who feel comfortable establishing mentoring relationships with minority students.

A 2006 study entitled *Report on the Status of Minorities at Indiana University* revealed that this institution of higher learning has put forth considerable efforts to address its diversity and multicultural needs for more faculty, staff, and students of color to help improve the academic culture and to encourage retention among students (many of whom are first-generation students struggling to graduate). The report revealed that students from underrepresented minority groups graduate at a lower rate than do students of other racial/ethnic backgrounds (University Reporting and Research, 2006). According to the report, "between the fall of 2002 and the fall of 2005, 11% of all [Indiana University] graduate students were students of color, and 9% were specifically from underrepresented minorities" (p. iii). During this same period, "14% of all first-professional [i.e., graduate] students at Indiana University were students of color [and] students from underrepresented minorities constituted 8% of all Indiana University's first-professional students" (p. iii). With this limited number of students, there is a tacit concern about students' ability to build community and develop networks among themselves, which are critical for coping with marginalization, while at the same time amassing a strong portfolio, which is essential for career planning and development.

The statistics concerning faculty are as disheartening as those associated with underrepresented undergraduate and graduate students. Across all the Indiana University campuses, faculty members of color represented 9% of full professors (two thirds of whom are Asian American), 16% of associate professors (half of whom are Asian American), and 27% of assistant professors (approximately two thirds of whom are Asian American). Persons of color also constituted 15% of non-tenure-track faculty (more than half of whom are Asian American) at Indiana University. Comparatively, faculty members from underrepresented racial/ethnic groups made up 3% of full professors, 8% of associate professors, 10% of assistant professors, and 7% of non-tenure-track faculty (University Reporting and Research, 2006). Despite an increasingly diverse applicant pool at the assistant and associate ranks, underrepresented minority faculty members are disproportionately represented at lower ranks.

Staff demographics at Indiana University reflect a similar trend. Persons of color represented "8% of executive-level staff, 16% of other professional staff, and 18% of all new professional staff hires" (University Reporting and Research, 2006, p. iii). Among nonprofessional and new nonprofessional staff hires, staff members of color constituted 17% and 23%, respectively.

Given the lack of underrepresented faculty, administrators, and staff at Indiana University, it is not surprising that many people assume that the university's social and academic climates contribute a great deal of stress and tension, as people of color attempt to educate themselves and feel connected to the academic cultures produced by the majority. Because of a lack of presence and the limited number of minorities in powerful positions due to racial marginalization, it is likely that many minorities—especially African American students—would experience difficulties adjusting. The evidence suggests that students of color, especially African Americans, find it difficult to build social and cultural networks that affirm who they are. Even more disconcerting are the potential hardships that these students face as they struggle to identify mentors who are willing to invest in them and serve as guides in their transition from college to professional life.

This was the environment in which Kandace Hinton was attempting to acquire a graduate education and the type that shaped her perspective and belief concerning the likelihood that African American students, in general, could succeed at predominantly White institutions that offered graduate education. It is within this context that we discuss how important mentoring was in preparing Kandace Hinton for a career in higher education and the way meaningful mentoring relationships continue to facilitate educational success and attainment for students of color.

Struggling in the Valley to Get to the Mountaintop: Kandace Hinton's Story

Pursuing graduate education for some is a daunting experience. Often the encounter can be made richer when there is an assurance that there will be at least one person serving as a supporter, mentor, guide, or friend. When I entered Indiana University as a master's student in the higher education and student affairs program, there were four other African American women and one Latino also enrolled, which made the time spent in the 2-year program endurable. Subsequently, upon completion of the master's degree, I was encouraged to apply to the doctoral program by a number of faculty members, including a White male full professor with whom I had one graduate course, a Latina junior faculty member, and an adjunct instructor. Initially, I was denied admission to the doctoral program because of substandard Graduate Record Examination (GRE) scores. It was only after I met with the program chair, shared my goals, and stressed my ambition to complete the degree, despite the predictive nature of the GRE, that I was admitted. Furthermore, I was aided by the fact no African Americans were admitted to the doctoral program that academic year. Ultimately, the program chair overrode the decision of the faculty not to admit me and warned that I would have difficulty in the classes taught by faculty who voted to deny my admission. He then offered to be my program adviser, and I accepted. As the only African American woman in the program, I experienced a very lonely existence. I also felt alienated because no opportunities were presented to collaborate with faculty, submit proposals for conferences, and write for publication. I noticed that my peers in the program, who included two or three African American men, were continually involved in these academic activities. In hindsight, and as I have observed cohorts that have followed, faculty seem to offer a limited amount of mentoring activities to one "golden child" at a time. These opportunities were unavailable to me primarily because faculty did not value or approve my probationary admit status, which I obtained against their will.

Although I had been encouraged to pursue the higher educational degree, the faculty who encouraged me to apply were somewhat distant during the years of my doctoral course work. The Latina faculty member, Dr. Guadalupe Anaya, would send out a search-and-rescue team to find me periodically via a phone call or email to see how I was doing when I was in retreat mode. And the adjunct faculty member did not work on campus and completely disappeared. These realities caused me to wonder if I would persist through the program's course work and the dissertation. The Latina professor apparently recognized the alienation that I suffered and offered to serve as my dissertation chair.

In an effort to address the fact that students of color were not receiving mentoring and to address their need for professional development, Professor Anaya created a research focus group composed of her dissertation students. This effort provided the opportunity for us to address our need for collaboration. As a result, five students and I met biweekly with Professor Anaya to discuss our research. The objectives were (a) to help us become comfortable discussing relevant literature and the way our perspectives were similar to and differed from the established points of view, (b) to provide support for one another through the varying stages of the dissertation process, (c) to assist and encourage us to collaborate with one another, and (d) to help us create frameworks that emphasized the relationship of our research to future studies.

Participating in this process helped me mature. With Professor Anaya's help and direction, I slowly came to understand the process of transitioning from a graduate student to researcher-scholar. Along the way, I learned that active learning and mentoring involves sharing information, engaging intellectual discourse, and developing collegial relationships. I began to view myself as an evolving scholar equipped with the language that the discipline uses to define the significance of one's work. In addition, Professor Anaya's mentoring became the initial support that I needed to persist toward the completion of my degree and to create relationships with other students to build research groups for scholarly activities.

One additional way that I sought support and a "safe place" was to look for African American women in other departments or schools on campus. In doing so, I landed a teaching assistant position with an African American woman, Dr. Valerie Grim, who was a historian in the African American Studies Department. Eventually, she became a member of my dissertation committee, after reading early iterations of my work, especially the literature review and sections that attempted to historicize the experiences of Black women in the larger American society. Professor Grim immediately became a sister-mentor who understood my experiences as a doctoral student. She shared similar stories and provided offstage testimonials about her experiences of persisting against the odds.

The Mentoring Plan of Professors Valerie Grim and Guadalupe Anaya

In the summer of 1999, I (Valerie Grim) met Kandace Hinton, who at that time seemed disconnected and somewhat confused about the direction of her graduate training and where she would land, even if she pressed through to the completion of her doctoral studies. Later, in the fall semester of 1999, Kandace introduced me to her faculty mentor, Guadalupe Anaya. After hearing from Kandace and me concerning how African American studies programs have a national reputation regarding the mentoring of their students, Professor Anaya invited me for a conversation. Of course, this ended up as a meeting to discuss how to move Kandace through the higher education student affairs (HESA) doctoral program. I agreed to work with Professor Anaya, and we immediately became busy establishing an effective and efficient work pace to get the work done.

Initially, we surveyed the academic landscape and began to assess its impact. In doing so, we identified several issues that were making it difficult for Kandace to complete her work. At this time, she was one of few students of color and was among an even smaller percentage of African American students in HESA. Kandace was isolated from mainstream academia, in the sense that she was not a part of the majority-White student support networks; she was not being included in the aggressive research plans of any of the professors; she was not being asked to collaborate on conference papers with peers and faculty; she was not involved with collaborative pedagogy essential to learning how to teach in the higher education field; and she was not given any assistantships from the HESA program during her 4 years of doctoral training, even though in the end, she was awarded a fellowship to help her conduct fieldwork.

As an African American female doctoral candidate, Kandace was, in essence, spending her years of graduate training alienated and ill mentored. To address this problem, Professor Anaya and I began reconstructing Kandace's thinking. We wanted her to hear the invaluable voice that she brought to discourses concerning minority students' experiences in higher education. We used a case study approach with her. This meant that we studied what her experiences were as a student at the time and also devised a plan to minimize the impact of the negative cognitive messages that she internalized. Concomitantly, we developed a mentoring program designed specifically to motivate and help Kandace complete the doctorate.

The dimensions of our approach included several phases. The first involved racial affirmation; the second included professional development;

the third consisted of practical training. Since Kandace was writing a dissertation concerning the experiences of African American women administrators at predominantly White universities, I was invited to be a dissertation committee member because of my training as a historian. I have taught African American history courses that deal with the history of Blacks in higher education, the history of African American women, and African American studies theoretical and methodological approaches. Professor Anaya and I believed my expertise would be useful in helping Kandace understand her graduate training experiences as well as useful in the critical analysis of the qualitative data that she would collect from her dissertation participants.

Professor Anaya and I implemented our mentoring plan with Kandace in three ways during the 1999–2000 academic year. In the first phase, weekly meetings were established with Kandace. In these meetings, we helped her understand how the intersections of race and gender in higher education continued to affect students and faculty of color negatively. Professor Anaya approached her conversations from a contemporary point of view, and I addressed the issue from historical perspectives.

Throughout the academic year we met as a group once a month to assess Kandace's development. We wanted to determine whether the conversations were helping her feel more connected to academia and to her study of African American women in higher education. Within 2 months, we could see radical changes. Specifically, Kandace was less reserved and was becoming more confident in expressing her views concerning our approach and concerning the way her research interest could help the academy better understand avenues to address critically race and gender discrimination.

As we continued with our mentoring plan, there was an understanding that Kandace's psychosocial racial identity needed to be affirmed. We wanted her to understand that success in higher education depended, to a significant degree, on exposure and networking with faculty who understood how racialized environments affect scholarly and intellectual productions and who, in spite of their marginalization, are willing to speak truth to this struggle and offer insights concerning coping strategies. For us, it was important that Kandace understood how the invisibility of faculty of color had more to do with the lack of exposure than with intellectual inability or some notion of racial and gender inferiority. We elected not to allow Kandace to focus on what could have been perceived as the existence of racial and gender insensitivity in higher education but instead to persuade her to focus more on the coping strategies that students and faculty of color must learn and internalize in order to succeed.

Consequently, Professor Anaya and I spent considerable time using our professional interactions and experiences as texts for Kandace to analyze and to compare and contrast how she perceived and internalized her own experiences. We were simply attempting to help Kandace understand how her experiences influence the interpretation of the voices of her research participants. We wanted Kandace to understand that faculty and students of color learn to cope by building networks and by constructing conversation houses, where students experiencing similar realities meet outside the "perceived hostile" environment and have meaningful and critical conversations among themselves to help one another persist toward the degree.

The second phase of the mentoring plan provided Kandace with an opportunity to work directly with African American faculty members to learn how they approach their subject matter and the academy as a whole, in addition to learning how collaboration in teaching and research worked. As a result, I asked that she be hired as a graduate teaching assistant in the Department of African American and African Diaspora Studies. She assisted with an upper-level course on African American history, which was taught during the fall and spring semesters. While I primarily handled the course content, Kandace integrated the educational experiences of Blacks in different sections of the lectures. She was able to teach the students about the progressive strides of African Americans toward education within every decade of the country's history since the 1700s. This experience elevated Kandace's confidence and provided a collaborative interdisciplinary approach that can help students of color in majority-White programs build networks with faculty in more diverse units, while utilizing materials acquired in the majority-White classroom settings.

Working as a graduate teaching assistant in the Department of African American and African Diaspora Studies gave Kandace many opportunities. She could observe the work of African American administrators and Black faculty at every rank. She could experience working with a more diverse student body whose experiences and questions could help Kandace shape her thinking about race, gender, and culture in higher education. Conversing with different groups of people would provide the opportunity for Kandace to critique the importance of having an inclusive mission statement in higher education that emphasized a programmatic thrust encouraging students to become multiculturally competent. The social and intellectual interactions provided by the Department of African American and African Diaspora Studies improved Kandace's skills, and she became excellent in her capacity to work with students and help them understand coping strategies essential for surviving academic and social life in predominantly White environments.

The professional development aspect of our mentoring plan for Kandace bridged two important areas of training. Recognizing her lack of experience in teaching and in collaborating on research projects and panel proposals, Professor Anaya and I assigned Kandace a co-professor of record in two courses. She worked with me in a graduate course entitled Research Methods and Theoretical Issues in African American Studies; she assisted Professor Anaya in the Diverse College Student course. These classes provided invaluable content concerning qualitative research, Black feminism, and other approaches that Kandace used to broaden students' thinking in the areas of critical observation techniques and ethnographical approaches. Teaching also helped Kandace hone her skills as an evolving junior colleague, one who had learned to connect her lived experiences to research in order to better understand minority experiences and issues of diversity at predominantly White institutions.

The third and final phase of our mentoring plan for Kandace involved creating situations in which Kandace would serve as a mentor. We matched Kandace with students in the M.A. program in African American and African Diaspora Studies as well as the HESA master's program. She had to develop her own plan, which included monthly dinner meetings with two students whom she selected. She was responsible for discussing with these students how they could build a sense of community for themselves and how to develop strategies to achieve their academic and career objectives. Included also in Kandace's plan was the opportunity for the students to have her critique their papers and thesis proposals. In her review of their work, Kandace agreed to focus primarily on their theoretical and methodological approaches. Kandace also supported them by attending their research presentations at the African American Studies Department's Graduate Student Brown Bag Paper Series. She also attended some students' thesis defenses and introduced many of them to students and faculty of color in other graduate programs. Observing Kandace, Professor Anaya and I realized that our mentoring approach was sometimes intrusive, though successful, and we recognized that our strategies were the catalysts that were helping Kandace complete the HESA doctoral degree. We were determined to move her on to an academic life as a college professor.

Although Kandace could see her professional growth, she was not overly enthusiastic or even remotely excited by each interaction or plan of action. She remained primarily concerned with completing the dissertation. For example, after completing her course work in the fall of 1999, she still needed time to conduct fieldwork related to the dissertation, analyze the data, write the results, and prepare for a dissertation defense. The issue for her, therefore, became balancing the activities required in our mentoring plan with completing the dissertation. Because of the demands, there were times when we experienced synchrony with the activities, and then there were other moments when it all seemed too much, when Kandace's desire to write was seemingly compromised by the demands of her mentoring team and the three jobs she held in order to pay for her education and rent. There were a few times when Kandace struggled to believe that Professor Anaya and I were really considering her best interest, because her only objective, during this phase of the process, was to graduate.

But we understood that she had not been close enough to the process to determine whether "graduation only" was her career objective or whether she really wanted to be in the academy. Thus, we continued to train her as if she had decided to pursue an academic career as a researcher, scholar, and teacher. For us, this was a long-term investment, and Kandace was thinking short term—that is, getting the degree completed, period. Ultimately, we knew the task was to guide her, to believe that her work would be completed, and to provide the appropriate support and challenge during this process. When Kandace seemed overwhelmed or simply exhausted, Professor Anaya and I changed our technique but not our goal. Instead of meeting in our offices, for example, we went to dinner, to a concert, or to a movie or had her in our homes for lunch. We wanted to assure Kandace that success was the ultimate goal and that preparation with clear and strong objectives was the only way to accomplish every task.

Through these efforts, we finally reached the goal. In 2001, Kandace completed her doctoral degree. Her confidence soared because she realized that at least two people in the academy cared and were willing to support and encourage her with consistent high-quality mentoring. But Professor Anaya and I recognized that more was needed and that we also needed help to guide Kandace through the next phase, which was getting a job and performing well in a tenure-track assistant professor position. Kandace completed the doctorate without any publications, significant conference presentations, or valued individual teaching opportunities, which placed her at serious risk during the job-search process.

Dr. Mary Howard-Hamilton arrived at Indiana University as I (Kandace) was working as a 1-year visiting lecturer and graduate recruiter for the HESA program at Indiana University–Purdue University in Indianapolis. I was also in the process of accepting a visiting assistant professor position at a nearby institution. From that time to the present, Professor Howard-Hamilton has continued to mentor me by critiquing my work, inviting me to collaborate on writing and research projects, co-presenting with her at national professional conferences, and including me in her professional network of scholars and sister circles. With Professor Howard-Hamilton's support, I landed my first tenure-track position at Indiana State University. Consistent communication with Drs. Grim, Anaya, and Howard-Hamilton about all matters that concern junior faculty—teaching, research, service activities, and professional development—has been a blessed assurance that this journey to tenure and beyond will be successful.

Postdoctorate Mentoring: Mary Howard-Hamilton

I arrived at Indiana University at the beginning of the 2001 fall semester as an associate professor in the Educational Leadership and Policy Studies Department's Higher Education and Student Affairs Program. Mentoring has always been important to me because our new scholars of color need to understand how the unwritten policies and procedures can impede their progress as it pertains to upward mobility in the administrative structure of promotion and tenure as a faculty member. These nebulous policies and procedures magically become apparent during the tenure and promotion process: expectations regarding the number of publications; the importance of teaching evaluations, of being collegial and a good citizen (i.e., service) in the department; and of finding the support systems that could help the protégé move from one institution to another. When I met Kandace she was a newly minted Ph.D. and was hired to teach an overload of graduate courses and coordinate the student affairs program at Indiana University–Purdue University Indianapolis. I was excited to meet and connect with another African American woman in the same department and knew that she would need a tremendous amount of support in order to succeed in her daunting position as a visiting lecturer.

The mentoring relationship that evolved was synergetic and developed through many different activities and into different forms. First, we had lengthy and substantive conversations about our goals, visions, and purposes for ourselves in the field of higher education and student affairs. Second, there were several mutually agreed-on goals, which included Kandace's editing the dissertation for publication, submitting proposals for presentations, and establishing a strong teaching portfolio. Third, we created a plan for publishing and agreed that this path would involve each of us rotating the lead role in publishing articles, book chapters, and other works, so one person would not carry the overwhelming burden of bearing all the microaggressions involved with collaborative research and working with presses, journal editors, and conference committees. Finally, we agreed to develop counter-stories to offset the communications we heard that emphasized our deficiencies rather than our strengths.

Furthermore, it was important that I modeled for Kandace the persistent efforts in which one must engage to build support continuously within the academy, especially among colleagues whose critiques have helped determine the value of our work. Toward this end, I arranged many meetings in which Kandace and I could speak with other scholars of color in a common space, such as in our homes, in restaurants, or in hotels during our conference travels. We laughed, cried, and found our strength in the voices and energies supplied by the belief that we were not alone and that we can succeed in a disempowering environment. The collaboration between us was successful, and the mentoring relationship helped Kandace advance from lecturer to visiting assistant professor at The Ohio State University for 1 year and, later, to Indiana State University as a tenure-track assistant professor.

The first 2 years of this mentoring relationship were very engaging and yielded some very good academic fruit. Kandace is publishing at a level commensurate with a tenure-track faculty member and is presenting at national conferences each year. She is playing a critical role as a mentor and program coordinator for the doctoral program in higher education leadership at Indiana State. Moreover, Kandace is actively engaged with recruiting students, especially reaching out to students of color. From these experiences and interactions, it has become quite evident that a traditional mentoring relationship may not have produced the same results. Working together, we realized that our relationship was forged mainly because of the connection we felt as African American women with similar experiences in higher education at predominantly White institutions. While we have similar stories to share about our struggles in the academy, we now have counterstories that reveal how students and faculty of color can succeed if individual and institutional support is made available to them.

Talking Back and Moving Forward

For us, this chapter symbolizes breaking the silence and sharing counterstories that many African Americans offer to teach and support "each other around the kitchen table, in church, at the hairdresser, or at those all Black women's tables in student dining halls" (Collins, 1998, p. 50). This act of resistance to the hierarchical power structure represents what Collins calls "a moment of insubordination" (p. 50). The increase in research by and about Black women continues to grow and strengthen the legitimacy of our voices in the ivory tower. These mentoring and protégé experiences have proven to be invaluable in environments that are typically not conducive to natural growth and professional development processes.

Further, our work in this particular case has shown that there is no one-size-fits-all mentoring approach for graduate students. Faculty's and students' backgrounds and experiences have to be considered when trying to make all feel valuable and valued (i.e., that their voices, ideas, and presence matter). We encourage those already empowered to lend their power and visibility to help students of color feel connected, despite being contiually and systemically marginalized in the classroom and in other university environments.

Institutions of higher education must embrace the notion of success for all students, particularly those who struggle to fit academically and socially. Given the fact that the discipline is the locus of instruction and socialization, it is also incumbent on academic departments to identify strategies for acclimating graduate students of color and then to provide appropriate resources to ensure their success. This effort would require a university to commit resources and respect equity and also to encourage faculty, administrators, staff, and students from the majority culture to invest time and interest in getting to know minority students and working together with them to ensure that they are no longer marginalized. Graduate programs, then, must become an academic community, and the academy must become an open, broad neighborhood of researchers, students, and teachers utilizing many different paths to achieve academic success with students who elected to give their time and service to be trained and mentored.

Consequently, those involved with the training of graduate students must become more diligent in acknowledging that race, culture, gender, sexual orientation, and other differences have a tremendous impact on the type of academic culture that revolves around graduate studies. Our experience clearly indicates that only through the kind of close association that good mentoring provides can we really know how to teach and serve graduate students of color. This is why it is important that we enable oppressed voices to be released and that we encourage different peoples to speak their truth, using their realities to help the academy provide better educational products and services to all graduate students. Indeed, Hinton's experience has shown that with students' persistence to succeed and with investment by faculty (and not always faculty of color left to mentor the students of color), the recruitment, retention, and graduation rates of minority students will increase significantly.

We hope that, as we have discussed our step-by-step mentoring activities, the approaches and strategies discussed in this chapter will serve as a framework for developing a mentoring model, creating programs designed to foster success for graduate students of color, and implementing strategies as a measurement of our good will toward others. The results will be a great harvest of students of color who will become faculty and administrators poised to continue the struggle as others attempt to press their way through the academy.

References

Alfred, M. V. (2001). Expanding theories of career development: Adding the voices of African American women in the White academy. *Adult Education Quarterly, 51*(2), 108–127.

Asante, M. K. (1987). *The Afrocentric idea.* Philadelphia: Temple University Press.

Chronicle of Higher Education Almanac. (2003, 2004). Washington, DC: Chronicle of Higher Education.

Collins, P. (1998). *Fighting words: Black women and the search for justice.* Minneapolis: University of Minnesota Press.

Delgado, R., & Stefancic, J. (2001). *Critical race theory: An introduction.* New York: NYU Press.

Harry, L. (1994). *Stressors, beliefs and coping behaviors of African American women entrepreneurs.* New York: Garland.

Hinton, K. (2001). The experiences of African American women administrators in predominantly White institutions of higher education. *Dissertation Abstracts International, 62,* 485.

hooks, b. (1989). *Talking back: Thinking feminist, thinking black.* Boston: South End Press.

Howard-Hamilton, M. F. (Ed.). (2003). *New Directions for Student Services, Vol. 104: Meeting the needs of African American women.* San Francisco: Jossey-Bass.

Moses, Y. (1997). African American women in academe: Issues and strategies. In L. Benjamin (Ed.), *African American women in the academy: Promises and perils* (pp. 23–38). Gainesville: University Press of Florida.

National Center for Education Statistics. (2002). *Digest of education statistics.* Washington, DC: U.S. Department of Education.

Patitu, C. L., & Hinton, K. G. (2003). The experiences of African American women faculty and administrators in higher education: Has anything changed? In M. F. Howard-Hamilton (Ed.), *New Directions for Student Services, Vol. 104: Meeting the needs of African American women* (pp. 79–93). San Francisco: Jossey-Bass.

Scheurich, J. J. (1993). Toward a White discourse of White racism. *Educational Researcher, 22,* 5–10.

Solorzano, D., Ceja, M., & Yosso, T. (2000). Critical race theory, racial microagressions, and campus racial climate: The experiences of African American college students. *Journal of Negro Education, 69*(1/2), 60–73.

University Reporting and Research. (2006). *Report on the status of minorities at Indiana University.* Bloomington, IN: Author.

U.S. News & World Report. (2008). *America's Best Colleges.* Retrieved July 30, 2008, from the U.S. News & World Report Web site, http://grad-schools.usnews.rankingsandreviews.com/grad/edu/higher_educ_admin.

Villalpando, O., & Bernal, D. D. (2002). A critical race theory analysis of barriers that impede the success of faculty of color. In W. A. Smith, P. G. Altbach, & K. Lomotey (Eds.), *The racial crisis in American higher education: Continuing challenges for the twenty-first century.* Albany: State University of New York Press.

Williams, J., & Schwiebert, V. L. (2000). Multicultural aspects of the mentoring process. In V. Schwiebert (Ed.), *Mentoring: Creating connected, empowered relationships* (pp. 57–70). Alexandria, VA: American Counseling Association.

II

SUMMARY

Frank Tuitt

T he chapters in this volume serve as a critical reminder that although access to a graduate education has increased for students of color, many of these students remain standing on the outside looking in. The unfortunate reality is that although diversity has become a priority within the discourse of graduate schools throughout the country, these institutions have not been able to become more comprehensive in their approach to creating inclusive educational environments that maximize the rich talents and skills that students of color bring to the learning context. In response to this dilemma, the Association of American Colleges and Universities (AAC&U) has called for higher education institutions to relocate diversity from its role as an additional strategic objective to an integrated priority embedded into all aspects of the organization (Williams, Berger, & McClendon, 2005).

Inclusive Excellence in Graduate Education

In 2005, the AAC&U released a three-article series that called for higher education institutions to move away from a fragmented focus on diversity and begin to think about how to promote inclusive excellence into predominantly White institutions (PWIs). Specifically, the organization challenged leaders to move from rhetoric to action by involving the entire campus community in the work of infusing diversity and excellence (Milem, Chang, & Antonio, 2005). The introduction to this series defines *inclusive excellence* as a purposeful embodiment of inclusive practices toward multiple student identity groups. Inclusive excellence involves the following:

The author thanks graduate students Bridget Coble and Rahul Choudaha for their support in working with the data and preparation of this chapter.

- A focus on student intellectual and social development. Academically, it means offering the best possible course of study for the context in which the education is offered.
- A purposeful development and utilization of organizational resources to enhance student learning. Organizationally, it means establishing an environment that challenges and supports each student to achieve academically at high levels and each member of the campus to contribute to learning and knowledge development.
- Attention to the cultural differences that learners bring to the educational experience and that enhance the enterprise.
- Creating a welcoming community that engages all of its diversity in the service of student and organizational learning. (AAC&U, 2005)

To help institutions guide and assess their efforts to promote and achieve inclusive excellence Williams et al. (2005) propose the Inclusive Excellence Scorecard, which consists of four dimensions: access and equity, campus climate, diversity in the curriculum, and student learning and development. In the case of graduate education, *access and equity* refers to the compositional representation and success of students of color; *campus climate* involves the development of a supporting psychological and behavioral climate; *diversity in the curriculum* encompasses the inclusion of diversity across courses, programs, and experiences; and *student learning and development* focuses on knowledge and learning about diverse groups and cultures (Williams et al., 2005).

This chapter discusses the implications that the important work in this volume has for improving the educational experiences of students of color in graduate school. The discussion begins with a focus on access and equity and then moves the focus to campus climate, diversity in the curriculum, and student learning and development. The chapter concludes with some future considerations.

Access and Equity

There is no debating the facts: today students of color have more access to graduate education than ever before. For example, as outlined in Table 11.1, Cook and Cordova (2007) report that in 2004–2005, students of color made up 19.1% and 14.2% of students seeking master's and doctoral degrees, respectively, to account for 32.5% of the students in graduate education.

Moreover, from 1996 to 2006 about 28% of all graduate students who were U.S. citizens or permanent residents were students of color: African

TABLE 11.1
Graduate School Demographics for Students of Color

2004–2005	Master's degree		Doctoral degree		Population[a] %
Total	578,812		52,705		
Total minority	110,744	19.10%	7,489	14.20%	32.50%
African American	49,415	8.50%	2,873	5.50%	12.80%
Hispanic	28,574	4.90%	1,693	3.20%	14.40%
Asian American/Pacific Islanders	29,777	5.10%	2,699	5.10%	4.30%
American Indian/Alaska Natives	2,978	0.50%	224	0.40%	1.00%

Source: Cook & Cordova (2007).
[a] Population estimates for July 1, 2005, from U.S. Census Bureau, National Population Estimates, retrieved from Infoplease Web site: http://www
.infoplease.com/ipa/A0762156.html.

Americans accounted for 13% of total enrollment; Latinos, 8%; and Asian/ Pacific Islanders, 6% (Redd, 2007). Although on the face of it these statistics suggest that there is indeed something to celebrate, upon a closer examination the outlook may not be as bright.

One of the realities of the increase in access to graduate education is that the doors have been open to some but not all degrees and disciplines. For example, between 1996 and 2006, the two disciplines most often studied by students of color were education and business. Engineering, physical sciences, and biological sciences accounted for small percentages of students of color (8% of African Americans and 13% of Latinos, as compared to 29% of Asian Americans) (Redd, 2007). Moreover, a look at Tables 11.2 and 11.3 shows that in 2004 over 80% of all earned doctorates went to Whites, and 85.4% and 85.0% of earned doctorates in the humanities and physical sciences, respectively, went to Whites.

The foregoing statistics remind those of us concerned with increasing access to graduate education that there is still work to be done and that we need to continue our efforts to find additional ways to open doors not only to graduate school but to all disciplines and degrees. For example, in chapter 4 in this volume, Gasman et al. discuss four primary institutional strategies for addressing the underrepresentation of the students of color in STEM graduate programs and argue that the traditional approaches to STEM education have assumed that the underrepresentation of the students of color is attributable to students' characteristics. This deficit approach assumes that institutions have no responsibility in contributing to persistent problems.

TABLE 11.2
Characteristics of Recipients of Earned Doctorates
in the United States, by Race/Ethnicity

	Year			
Race/Ethnicity	*1989*	*1994*	*1999*	*2004*
Total (known race/ethnicity)	23,028	26,901	27,527	25,811
Asian	626	937	1,404	1,449
Black	822	1,099	1,630	1,869
Hispanic	582	884	1,184	1,177
American Indian	94	143	214	129
White	20,892	23,796	23,093	20,745
Other	12	42	102	442

Source: Hoffer et al. (2005).

TABLE 11.3

Characteristics of Recipients of Earned Doctorates, 2003

	All fields	Business	Education	Engineering	Humanities	Life sciences	Physical sciences	Professional fields	Social sciences
American Indian	0.5	0.2	0.7	0.5	0.4	0.3	0.3	0.9	0.7
Asian	5.3	6.1	2	11.1	3.4	8.5	6.5	3.5	4
Black	6.6	10.8	13.8	3.7	3.8	3.6	3.2	11.7	6.4
Hispanic	4.9	5	6.1	4.9	5.4	4	3.2	3.2	5.7
White	81	76.9	76	78.8	85.4	81.7	85	78.9	81.2
Other	1.7	1.1	1.4	1	1.6	1.9	1.8	1.8	2

Source: Chronicle of Higher Education Almanac (2005–2006), p. 19.

Note: All figures in percentages.

Gasman and her coauthors shed light on the reality that the underrepresentation of students of color in the STEM discipline has more to do with the multiple challenges that these students face at the undergraduate level related to traditional pedagogical practices employed in the academy.

Gasman et al. attribute the underrepresentation of students of color in STEM graduate programs to the failure of undergraduate institutions to (a) develop integrated support systems, (b) ensure inclusive curricula, (c) promote interactive classrooms, and (d) increase the availability of mentoring. In chapter 2 in this volume, DeAngelo provides an additional hypothesis to account for why some students of color may choose not to attend graduate school. Specifically, DeAngelo contends that the aspirations of students of color to seek advanced degrees may be influenced by the type of undergraduate institution that these students attended. The findings of DeAngelo's study indicate that students of color perceive that instead of supporting their future aspirations to pursue an advanced degree, the institution's social structure, environment, and mission aim to ensure they are educated in a manner to make them suitable for the employment marketplace and not for the scholarly marketplace. According to DeAngelo, "this tendency was evidenced not only by the practical orientation of the academic programs at the CSU [California State University system] but also by the overall lack of discussion of graduate study and the limited exposure to the scholarly environment and rigorous course work, as well as by the administrative and other roadblocks to aspirations and preparation that these students experienced" (this volume, p. 42).

The idea that institutional type might influence the way students of color view the possibility of attending graduate school is also supported by the Morelon-Quainoo et al. study, reported in chapter 1 of this volume, which found that reputation trumps type and amount of aid for students attending the elite private institution, whereas students at the highly ranked public institution were much more concerned about affordability or perceptions of affordability. The results of this study suggest that students weigh the amount of return that they will acquire by balancing overall cost associated with attending a particular institution against the value or reputation of the degree. Morelon-Quainoo et al.'s findings call for a deeper understanding of the factors that influence the experience of graduate and professional students of color as it relates to access and choice. One thing that is made clear in this volume is that the cost of attending graduate or professional school definitely influences the choices that students of color make.

In chapter 3, Johnson, Kuykendall, and Winkle-Wagner find that both the amount and source of aid were potential determinants for students of color in pursuing a graduate degree. Finances work as a gatekeeper, in that the decision to attend or not to attend graduate or professional school was based on students' access to financial aid (not including loans), regardless of their future aspirations. The findings of Morelon-Quainoo et al. and Johnson et al. suggest that graduate programs interested in promoting inclusive excellence as it relates to access can use financial assistance as a recruitment tool.

Overall, regarding access and equity in graduate education, the contributions to this volume of DeAngelo, Gasman et al., Johnson et al., and Morelon-Quainoo et al. reinforce the notion that instead of taking a deficit approach to understand why students of color still remain underrepresented in the academy, especially in the STEM disciplines, more research is needed that is grounded in theory that critically examines the unique characteristics of the college environment in which students of color participate and the way this environment affects their ability to navigate, persist, and acquire the Ph.D.

It is important to keep in mind that although compositional diversity is one of the critical components of promoting inclusive excellence in graduate school (Milem et al., 2005; Williams et al., 2005), PWIs must move beyond a sole focus on numbers toward a comprehensive application of diversity that is embedded throughout every aspect of the organization (Milem et al., 2005). In particular, an open and welcoming environment is critical to ensuring that every member in the doctoral program feels authentically included as part of the community (Milem et al., 2005).

Campus Climate

According to Gay (2004), graduate students of color have to function in an alien and often hostile environment in which they are frequently taught by culturally insensitive and uncaring instructors. Gay states that "most graduate students of color exist on the periphery of the academy, and their career trajectories are not as unencumbered as many think" (p. 266). Specifically, in graduate education, students of color confront a range of challenges including but not limited to (a) culture shock (Granados & Lopez, 1999), (b) isolation and alienation (Gay, 2004; Herrera, 2003), (c) marginalization (Gay, 2004), (d) the lack of faculty role models and mentors (Robinson, 1996), and (e) minimal access to social and professional networks (Herrera, 2003). Failure to understand and respond to these challenges can have a tremendous impact on a student's ability to persist in graduate school and can result in a leaky pipeline such that students enter but do not finish (Gutmann et al., 2006).

Several chapters in this volume speak to the importance of creating an optimal campus climate that supports the psychosocial and cultural development of students of color. For example, in chapter 10, Hinton, Grim, and Howard-Hamilton use a Black feminist and critical race theory lens to discuss the experiences of three African American women involved in a mentoring and support relationship at a PWI. The experience of an African American female master's student who transitions to a doctorate program is shared as an example of the isolation and loneliness that can be experienced by students of color. The student's journey from the master's program through her pre-tenure-track faculty position is wrought with isolation, exclusion, and criticism that are countered only by her relationship with her African American female mentors, whose compassion and care support her to develop self-confidence and scholarly contributions. Higher education graduate programs can benefit from the stories shared in this chapter because they encourage an examination of the inclusivity of academic environments. Improvements to programs can alleviate the isolation that students of color may experience and can provide a more nurturing training ground for future scholars.

Similarly, in chapter 5, Poon and Hune use the critical race theory framework to unmask the racialized experiences of Asian American doctoral students. In particular, Poon and Hune challenge the notion that the perceived numerical parity of Asian Americans in higher education has solved the problem of marginalization and racial isolation. They contend that Asian American doctoral students bear "hidden injuries of race," because despite being a racial minority, their injuries of racial microaggressions remain invalidated and hidden. Poon and Hune identify four major themes of hidden injuries of race: racial isolation because of low representation of both Asian American students and faculty in several disciplines like education and social sciences; mistaken identity of being a "perpetual foreigner" and lumping together the needs and experiences of U.S.-born Asian American citizens with those of international students; neglect of ethnic differences within Asian Americans and hence underestimation of the implications of socioeconomic and educational disparities among Asian Americans; and finally, characterization as a "model minority" that dismisses the experiences of Asian Americans as racialized and oppressed. Poon and Hune identify invisibility as the overarching theme that interrelates with invalidation and silencing of the racialized experiences of Asian American doctoral students.

The chapter has significant implications for understanding and improving the experiences and advancement of Asian American doctoral students. Poon and Hune state that racialized and sexualized stereotyping of Asian American women has restricted their advancement in academia. Understanding the challenges faced by Asian American women may aid in developing appropriate strategies for their advancement. Likewise, the authors highlight that lumping together international students and U.S.-born students by geographic or ethnic origins does a disservice to all groups because their experiences are not given an opportunity to be expressed. A deeper understanding of the individual groups and their experiences is needed so that objectives of diversity in academia can be achieved. In addition, the authors note that there are differences in the representation of Asian American students by disciplines, and hence the experiences of Asian American doctorate students in social science and education departments may be further racialized because these students may be the only Asian American in the department. This situation calls for more sensitivity from administrators and faculty in empathizing with the experiences of Asian American doctoral students. Finally, if academia truly values and aspires for diversity, then there is a need to heal the "hidden injuries" of Asian American doctoral students by putting to rest the master narratives of "model minority" and "perpetual foreigner" that were created to maintain White supremacy.

Like the students in Poon and Hune's study, the Latina doctoral and professional students in González's study, reported in chapter 6 of this volume, experienced educational marginalization, tokenization, and exclusion based on race/ethnicity, class, gender, and language. González contends that, rather than overt forms of discrimination, the students in his study discussed subtle yet ever-present incidents of bias or neglect. These incidents were also experienced by the African American women in Sulé's study, reported in chapter 8 of this volume. Sulé found that the types of hostility experienced by the women fell into three categories: (a) redirected or inappropriate research, (b) lack of faculty support and peer neglect, and (c) tokenism.

Collectively, the work of Hinton et al.; Poon and Hune; Sulé; and Howard-Hamilton, Hinton, and Ingram aligns with previous research that suggests that the educational experiences of students of color in PWIs are uniquely affected by the social-psychological climate found on campus. In addition to cultural and social isolation, students of color may find themselves on the receiving end of racial microaggressions (Pierce, Carew, Pierce-Gonzalez, & Wills, 1978; Solórzano, Ceja, & Yosso, 2000) and stereotype threat (Steele, 1997), which contribute to their invisibility in the learning environment (Franklin, 1999). Though the literature tends to treat these phenomena as separate constructs, they represent related forms of racism that collectively work to impede the academic performance of many students of color in PWIs (Carter & Tuitt, 2006). The combination of students' fear that they will be judged and negatively stereotyped based on their skin color and having those fears confirmed creates a racially hostile learning environment. Thus, racial microaggressions can be understood as the actual subtle and not-so-subtle racial assaults that confirm and/or reinforce the threats that graduate students of color anticipate in PWIs (Carter & Tuitt, 2006). It is critical to explore the way graduate programs promote inclusive excellence and at the same time help students of color heal the "hidden injuries" of racism, discrimination, and neglect.

One groundbreaking approach seeking to help address the "hidden injuries" of graduate students of color relates to the role of spirituality, discussed in chapter 9 by Howard-Hamilton et al. In an effort to develop a better understanding of the spiritual journey of racially diverse students, Howard-Hamilton et al. learned that some students rely on their spiritual beliefs, practices, and faith as a coping mechanism to find connection in an environment in which it is often difficult to meet other racially diverse graduate students. In addition, for many students spirituality provides a balance to the often conflicting rigorous workloads of graduate school and their personal lives. According to Howard-Hamilton et al., the students who rely on their spirituality have achieved the fifth and sixth stages of Fowler's faith development theory, which allows them to understand their connection to all human beings regardless of "social class, religion, race, and ethnicity" and to use their strong faith to liberate others through social justice actions. Howard-Hamilton et al. suggest that supporting students who rely on their faith provides an important element to the overall challenge of ensuring that racially diverse students are able to feel welcome in a predominantly White community. In theory, the personal strength of character that is required of a strong spiritual person allows that person to feel connected to others through faith, despite any economic, social, or cultural differences. The idea that spirituality plays a role in whether a student has the developmental and social strengths required to survive and achieve a higher level of learning is truly groundbreaking. In essence, it provides students the opportunity to authentically bring parts of their personal identity to a larger social structure, to feel a sense of belonging, a sense of having an internal source of support and ritual that no one can judge or take away.

Howard-Hamilton et al.'s findings related to the role of spirituality as a strong coping strategy for many graduate students of color supports previous studies by Constantine, Willon, Gainor, and Lewis (2002); Mattis (2002);

Stewart (2002); and Watt (2003). The implications of these findings provide opportunities for higher education institutions that seek to diversify and retain racially diverse graduate students within their communities to implement elements for spiritual recognition and practice through inclusive campus enhancements and curricular innovations. Thus, promoting inclusive excellence in graduate education calls for connecting students' spiritual practice within the institutional environment, as well as with the larger surrounding community.

Diversity in the Curriculum and Student Learning and Development

Inclusive excellence in graduate education embraces the notion that the subjects that students study, the content of the courses they take, and the manner in which those courses are taught all have significant implications for students' learning and development. For example, diversifying the curriculum assists students in further developing their cultural competencies in order to work more effectively in a global society (Williams et al., 2005). This need for a curriculum that supports students' development of cultural competencies is echoed in chapter 6, in which one of González's participants stated,

> In general, there is a lack of the cultural training, and [the result is that] nurses that I work with are struggling to work with a diverse population. I don't know if they've just never been exposed or they just feel uncomfortable, but I would expect, at the graduate level, that there would be more exposure to cultural diversity [in the curriculum], and that nurses' comfort level with diverse patients would be addressed.

This comment speaks to the importance of having a diverse curriculum that helps students focus on knowledge and learning about multicultural groups and cultures (Williams et al., 2005). In this increasingly diverse environment, multicultural competence is critical. Pope, Reynolds, and Mueller (2004) highlight the need for developing multicultural competence among student affairs professionals. This multicultural competence "entails the awareness of one's own assumptions, biases, and values; an understanding of the worldview of others; information about various cultural groups; and developing appropriate intervention strategies and techniques" (p. 9). In this context, the experiences of students of color can be integrated into the curriculum to create opportunities for professional socialization and development of broader multicultural competencies.

In addition to helping students develop their cultural competencies, diversifying the curriculum contributes to the transformation of graduate and professional schools into more inclusive environments (Williams et al., 2005). For instance, using diverse content and perspectives lets students know that their perspectives may also be welcomed, especially if the content aligns with students' interests (Tuitt, in press). This sentiment is expressed in González's study of Latino doctoral students, in which he found that due to the cultural dissonance existing between Latina/o culture and academic culture, some Latina doctoral and professional students challenged the dominant ideology found in the curriculum. In theory, the content of a class can give students insight into their professor's political orientations. For example, Castenell and Pinar (1993) argue that the curriculum can and ought to be regarded as a racial text that is symbolic of the way professors value or do not value diverse perspectives. When professors value and include diverse content and perspectives, they relieve students of the burden of having to be the only ones challenging the dominant ideologies and discourses, which take a deficit approach to the cultural backgrounds of students of color (Tuitt, in press).

The contribution to this volume of Gasman et al. sheds light on the importance of a diverse curriculum. The authors contend that the reason that students of color find STEM courses alienating is the absence of clear social relevance. In addition to wanting to see themselves in the curriculum, students of color are looking for a curriculum that shows the impact of science on the larger world (Busch-Vishniac & Jarosz, 2004). Citing Busch-Vishniac and Jarosz, Gasman et al. argue that students of color and women tend to choose majors that have an apparent benefit to society and that they think involve a high level of interaction with other people. Students of color are also interested in exploring issues that are relevant to their own racial or ethnic subgroup (Busch-Vishniac & Jarosz, 2004).

Gasman et al. contend that to make the curriculum more diverse, relevant, and engaging, STEM programs must retool the curriculum from the ground up. According to Busch-Vishniac and Jarosz (2004), "There has been a strong tendency to use minor changes and additions rather than wholesale revamping [of the curriculum] to achieve diversity. The result is not surprising. Gains are modest at best and cannot be sustained without constant diligence" (p. 256). The authors suggest revamping STEM curricula to emphasize the many examples of the way STEM course content can be used to help humanity.

Though diversifying the curriculum can help graduate students of color feel more included in the learning environment, transforming the curriculum is only the first step. Even in cases in which the curriculum is diverse (Banks, 1991), educators often continue to use traditional modes of instruction that create unwelcoming learning environments, places where graduate students of color are silenced and where diversity issues are ignored or poorly handled when addressed (Feagin & Imani, 1993). Consequently, it is not only what is taught in graduate education that matters to students of color but how it is taught.

Gasman et al. suggest that educators use pedagogical approaches that engage students of color in learning. They cite Seymour and Hewitt (1997), who stress the need to use teaching styles that are inclusive and that foster learning for diverse populations, stating, "The most effective way to improve retention among students of color, and to build their numbers over the longer term, is to improve the quality of the learning experience for all students—including non-science majors who wish to study science and mathematics as part of their overall education" (p. 394). Gasman et al. recommend several approaches that have implications for promoting inclusive excellence as it relates to the learning and development of graduate students of color. Specifically, they propose (a) developing integrated support systems, (b) ensuring inclusive curricula, and (c) promoting interactive classrooms. These three approaches align with principles of inclusive excellence as areas in which to enact and assess change (Williams et al., 2005). The integrated support system encompasses curriculum design, kinds of assignments and exams given, group learning, and university services like financial aid and housing. Inclusive curricula attempt to integrate the connectivity, engagement, and inclusivity in the STEM program by using diverse perspectives, social relevance, and engaged pedagogies. Interactive classrooms encourage collaborative learning as opposed to competitive learning.

Promoting Inclusive Excellence in Graduate Education: Implications and Recommendations

Even though diversity efforts have been widespread within higher education, the AAC&U points to four dilemmas threatening its ability to address issues of diversity successfully (Williams et al., 2005). These dilemmas are (a) islands of innovation: diversity efforts are fragmented and disregard institutional structures; (b) disconnect between diversity and educational excellence: academic excellence and diversity initiatives are considered separate issues; (c) disparities in academic success across groups: achievement gaps across racial and ethnic groups and socioeconomic difference persist, with evidence that some gaps are widening (Bauman, Bustillos, Bensimon, Brown, & Bartee, 2005); and (d) the "post-Michigan" environment: U.S. Supreme Court decisions regarding affirmative action programs require higher education to make a case for the interdependent relationship of diversity and educational quality. These four dilemmas are especially problematic within institutions of higher education, in which loosely coupled systems, multiple goal structures, and complex campus functions exist and operate both independently and interdependently (Williams et al., 2005). In this context, the contributions in this volume have significant implications for those concerned with improving the success of students of color and promoting inclusive excellence in graduate education.

To begin, although access to a graduate education has increased, students of color are still underrepresented compared to their White counterparts. As reasons for this underparticipation, contributions in this volume point to the underpreparation of students of color at the high school and undergraduate levels (Gasman et al., Strayhorn, DeAngelo, and González); the lack of mentors and role models who provide students of color guidance, support, and encouragement to pursue advanced degrees (Gasman et al., DeAngelo, Hinton et al., Sulé, and González); and the manner in which the types of institutions that students of color attend thwarts their aspirations for a graduate education, thus channeling them out of the pipeline (Gasman et al., DeAngelo, and Strayhorn). Strayhorn reminds us that students of color cannot attain what they do not think of as possible. It is vital to create more opportunities for prospective graduate students to consider all disciplines for graduate study as real possibilities, as opposed to considering only business and education. Until all students have that opportunity, we will not be able to achieve full access and equity, a goal that will be attained when the students of color in the overflowing educational pipeline are not standing on the outside looking in but are contemplating which one of the many institutions to call their graduate home.

Unfortunately, although getting more students of color into graduate programs would help, the chapters in this volume suggest that the pipeline in and of itself is not the problem. Many of the authors in this book confirm what previous research has already shown: even if the pipeline were filled with many students of color, "a fundamental challenge would remain: the pipeline empties . . . [some students of color] forgo graduate school altogether, others withdraw midstream" (Trower & Chait, 2002, p. 34). The reality is that PWIs fail to graduate many of the students of color whom they admit (Myers & Turner, 2001; Trower & Chait, 2002). Thus, the issue is not merely limited access to graduate school but also the inability of graduate and professional schools to retain and advance students of color.

The results of several studies in this volume (González, Sulé, Hinton et al., and Poon and Hune) reinforce previous research that shows how many graduate programs continue to use models of professional socialization that do not take into consideration the unique cultural characteristics of graduate students of color (Bensimon & Marshall, 2000; Daresh & Playko, 1995; Kerckhoff, 1976; Weidman, Twale, & Stein, 2001). The reality is that these socialization models do not work very well for students of color, whose personal characteristics do not fit the often dominant White male organizational ethos that exists in the academy (Kerckhoff, 1976; Tierney & Rhoads, 1993). Consequently, many of the graduate students' voices captured in this volume exemplify these students' struggle to find their place in institutions that know very little about how to address their needs. Caldwell and Stewart (2001) suggest that the conflict that some students of color experience in graduate and professional school stems from participation in a system of formal higher education that promotes the uncritical adoption of Western values and negates the knowledge base of students of color. Because, as González contends, this cultural devaluation by institutions of higher education continues to be the norm, graduate programs must keep in mind that the decision of students of color to matriculate into their programs will be shaped by these students' perception of their fit in the institution (Morelon-Quainoo et al., this volume).

In order to promote inclusive excellence in graduate education, scholars and practitioners must heed Gasman et al.'s call to develop greater understanding of the educational experiences of graduate students of color in general and of graduate students of color in STEM fields in particular. Although the questions asked by Gasman et al. focus primarily on the STEM disciplines, they are relevant for all fields. For instance, how does the transition from bachelor's degree programs to graduate programs vary based on characteristics of the undergraduate and graduate institution? What mechanisms most effectively ease the transition from undergraduate to graduate programs for students of color? Why are students of color leaving the pipeline between the master's and Ph.D. except in business and education? How do experiences in various disciplines vary among graduate students of color? Finding answers to these and other questions is essential if graduate programs are to provide institutional climates that welcome and support students of color.

One of the important questions addressed in this volume speaks to the similarities and differences among students of color with varying racial and ethnic backgrounds. Although experiences of marginalization, isolation, and discrimination cut across all groups, the work of González, Sulé, and Poon and Hune reminds us that though their may be some similarities, students of color have multiple complex identities in which race intersects with gender, language, and class to provide unique experiences that are worthy of individual attention. Therefore, promoting inclusive excellence requires that graduate programs examine the experiences of students of color collectively and individually. Although collectively students of color may suffer with what Poon and Hune call "hidden injuries of racism," how institutions choose to respond may vary depending on the specific racial/ethnic group in question.

Another area of concern for scholars and practitioners who want to promote inclusive excellence and improve the educational experiences of graduate students of color relates to the curriculum and pedagogy employed in PWIs. Several studies in this volume (González, Sulé, and Hinton et al.) speak to the overwhelming amount of course content that promotes ideologies and discourse that negatively portray the communities of students of color as deficient. Ultimately, the challenge of diversifying content is that graduate professors must work hard to balance examples of racial group struggles with racial group accomplishments so that all students and students of color in particular see more than just negative images of communities of color represented in course content. Moreover, graduate programs must work to ensure that their curriculum content is culturally responsive to the needs of a racially diverse community of learners. This means that instead of viewing graduate students of color through a deficient lens, educators need to learn to embrace the cultural knowledge that these students bring with them to the learning environment. For example, graduate students of color should be encouraged to do, rather than discouraged from doing, research on issues that directly relate to their communities.

In addition to having a diverse curriculum, graduate and professional school instructors need to become aware of the types of pedagogical techniques that are most effective for ensuring the academic success of graduate students of color. The unfortunate reality is that graduate faculty continue to operate on the misguided notion that one pedagogy fits all students and still use traditional modes of instruction that create inhospitable and potentially harmful learning environments for students of all races (Feagin & Imani, 1993). These traditional pedagogical practices do not serve well some of today's racially diverse graduate students (Tuitt, 2003b). Several of the graduate student voices captured in this volume share experiences of being marginalized, discriminated against, and made to feel invisible in the classroom through overt and subtle acts of racial microaggressions and stereotype threat.

Promoting inclusive excellence in graduate classrooms necessitates that instructors learn how to create identity-safe learning environments by working to reduce overt and subtle acts of racism in the classroom. To this end, graduate educators must anticipate and plan for how their content and instructional methods may position students of color in the classroom. Questions to ask include, How does the content of my lesson plan potentially racialize students of color? Overall, instructors must ensure that the strategies they employ do not further marginalize the very students whom they are trying to serve. The greater the extent to which instructors can build classroom environments grounded in cooperation and not competition, in fairness, in high expectations, and in trust, the more likely that these settings will be inclusive and safe for students. The conclusions drawn by Gasman et al., Sulé, and González align with previous research that shows that creating cooperative learning environments can enhance the academic engagement of students of color because such environments reduce competition, distrust, and stereotyping among students (Aronson & Patnoe, 1997; Marx, Brown, & Steele, 1999).

Overall, using a more inclusive curriculum and content can have a significant impact on the learning and development of all students but especially of students of color. In order to promote inclusive excellence in graduate classrooms, however, faculty members need to transform their teaching. Some key questions for scholars and faculty to consider are the following: (a) How can PWIs improve faculty training to ameliorate or reduce the acts of intolerance in the classroom? (b) What exactly should this training entail? and (c) What are the most effective means for creating buy-in from the majority of professors?

The most significant conclusion reinforced throughout this volume is that in order for students of color to succeed in graduate school they need access to mentors. Each of the contributions in this volume speak to the importance of mentoring relationships. A mentoring relationship between a more knowledgeable individual (faculty) and a less experienced individual (graduate student) provides a means for professional socialization and identity transformation (Galbraith & Cohen, 1995; Tillman, 2001). Both Gasman et al. and DeAngelo conclude that mentoring is especially important to the aspirations of students of color, who are much more likely to enter college without advanced-degree aspirations and much more dependent on faculty recognition, support, and guidance. According to Gasman et al., establishing formal mentoring relationships at the undergraduate level is likely to (a) foster the self-confidence and support that students need to enter and complete graduate study, (b) provide students of color with opportunities to observe research approaches and skills that they can later emulate in graduate school, and (c) acclimate students of color to the culture of graduate and professional education. DeAngelo posits that it is through mentoring relationships that prospective graduate students of color acquire the social capital needed to aspire to a chosen career path. In this context, mentoring relationships may significantly influence the access of students of color to graduate education.

Not only do mentoring relationships affect access, but they also affect the participation of students of color once they enroll in graduate and professional programs. The results from González's study indicate that students of color who do not receive mentorship will not be as successful as students who do receive good mentorship. However, the infrastructure for good mentorship did not exist in the institution in González's study due to the lack of Latina/o academics and other individuals willing to mentor them. Although empirical evidence supports the benefits of mentoring relationships at the graduate level, emerging research suggests that students of color in graduate and professional schools struggle to identify faculty mentors with whom they can connect (Guido-DiBrito & Batchelor, 1988; Hughes, 1988; Locke, 1997; Patton & Harper, 2003; Tillman, 2001). Because 80% of faculty members in the academy are White and mentoring relationships are likely to occur between two individuals of the same racial background, opportunities for mentoring relationships are severely limited for students of color (Kalbfleisch & Davies, 1991; McCormick, 1997; Thomas, 1990; Tillman, 2001). Consequently, graduate students of color may find themselves with no other choice than to try to seek out White faculty members, whom they believe are not as likely to be accepting, trusting, and supportive (McCormick, 1997; Tillman, 2001; Welch, 1997). This inability to establish faculty-student relationships that matter places students of color at a disadvantage (Brown, Davis, & McClendon, 1999; Tuitt, 2003a) and may account for why they fail to graduate at the same rate as their White counterparts (Weidman et al., 2001).

Gasman et al. raise an important question by asking whether graduate students of color can benefit from mentoring relationships with White professors. The reality is that graduate students of color can ill afford to wait for PWIs to solve the problem of diversifying their faculty. Even though establishing mentoring relationships in which individuals have to cross racial boundaries is significantly more difficult than establishing same-race mentoring relationships (Bowman, Kite, Branscombe, & Williams, 1999; Brinson & Kottler, 1993; Johnson-Bailey & Cervero, 2004; Thomas, 1990), graduate institutions need to figure out how to establish formal and informal mentoring opportunities so that students of color can get the proper support and guidance. Hinton et al. suggest that graduate programs need to identify mentors who can come into the student's life and approach the relationship with thoughtful attention to racial affirmation, professional development, and practical training. They use the term *intrusive mentoring* to reflect the very active involvement of mentors as they ensure the student's success.

It is also imperative that graduate and professional programs diversify their faculty so that the responsibility of mentoring graduate students of color is not left to the few faculty of color in the program. As role models, faculty of color have a unique opportunity to help students of color manage and overcome the anxiety and discrimination they experience by providing inspiration and support (Gasman et al., this volume). Moreover, faculty of color may be in the best position to help graduate students of color understand the nuances of collecting data, writing for publication, and presenting the research. In some cases diverse mentors are not available; González notes that the students in his study were able to find people outside their departments, across the university, and within their families and communities whom they could lean on during difficult times. Though this solution is not ideal, graduate students of color must be proactive in seeking out mentors who can provide relevant support, and they cannot wait for individuals to find them. A good place for students to start is to find scholars who are interested in conducting research on issues pertaining to marginalized groups. Whether it is "intrusive mentors" (Hinton et al.) or "talent-seeking mentors" (DeAngelo), these individuals can have a tremendous impact on access, persistence, and success as they embrace the responsibility of caring for the souls of graduate students of color.

In conclusion, it is imperative that those of us concerned with increasing access to high-quality graduation education figure out how to signal to students of color that they constitute the quality of America's future workforce (Long, 2003). It is clear from the work in this volume that students of color are getting mixed signals (Spence, 1973, 2002) about how welcome they are at PWIs. Promoting inclusive excellence in graduate education requires that we develop new models for recruiting graduate students of color, models that align and balance national, institutional, and individual signals (Tuitt, Danowitz, & Sotello-Turner, 2007). In theory, this goal can be accomplished by engaging in inclusive recruitment and retention activities that signal to graduate students that

- Their unique cultural characteristics and not only their skin color will be an asset to the institution. They will be appreciated and respected as intellectually competent.

- The graduate program is aware of the unique experiences and challenges that graduate students of color face in the academy.
- The graduate program is invested in their development and success by ensuring that support and resources will be made available to them.
- The graduate program is committed to diversity and excellence.
- The graduate program will pay attention to the climate and conditions under which they will be studying.
- There are colleagues available who can serve as potential allies and mentors—someone in the institution will "have their back" and look out for them.

Graduate and professional programs that are able to meet the challenge of achieving inclusive excellence will be in the best position to ensure that students of color no longer remain marginalized and on the periphery—no longer standing on the outside looking in.

References

Aronson, E., & Patnoe, S. (1997). *The jigsaw classroom: Building cooperation in the classroom* (2nd ed.). New York: Addison Wesley Longman.

Association of American Colleges and Universities. (2005). *Making excellence inclusive: Diversity, inclusion, and institutional renewal.* Retrieved February 10, 2008, from http://aacu-secure.nisgroup.com/inclusive_excellence/index.cfm.

Banks, J. (1991). Multicultural literacy and curriculum reform. *Education Horizons Quarterly, 69,* 135–140.

Bauman, G. L., Bustillos, L. T., Bensimon, E. M., Brown, M. C., & Bartee, R. D. (2005). *Achieving equitable educational outcomes with all students: The institution's roles and responsibilities.* Washington, DC: Association of American Colleges and Universities.

Bensimon, E. M., & Marshall, C. (2000). Policy analysis for postsecondary education: Feminist and critical perspectives. In J. Glazer-Raymo, B. K. Townsend, & B. Ropers-Huliman (Eds.), *Women in American higher education: A feminist perspective* (2nd ed., pp. 133–147). Needham Heights, MA: Pearson.

Bowman, S. R., Kite, M. E., Branscombe, N. R., Williams, S. (1999). Developmental relationships of Black Americans in the academy. In A. J. Murrell, F. J. Crosby, & R. J. Ely (Eds.), *Mentoring dilemmas: Developmental relationships within multicultural organizations* (pp. 21–46). Mahwah, NJ: Lawrence Erlbaum.

Brinson, J., & Kottler, J. (1993). Cross-cultural mentoring in counselor education: A strategy for retaining minority faculty. *Counselor Education and Supervision, 32,* 241–253.

Brown, C., II, Davis, G., & McClendon, S. (1999). Mentoring graduate students of color: Myths, models, and modes. *Peabody Journal, 74*(2), 105–118.

Busch-Vishniac, I. J., & Jarosz, J. P. (2004). Can diversity in the undergraduate engineering population be enhanced through curricular change? *Journal of Women and Minorities in Science and Engineering, 10,* 255–281.

Caldwell, L., & Stewart, J. (2001). Rethinking W. E. B. Dubois, "double consciousness": Implications for retention and self-preservation in the academy. In L. Jones (Ed.), *Retaining African Americans in higher education* (pp. 225–234). Sterling, VA: Stylus.

Carter, D., & Tuitt, F. (2006). *Black achievers' experiences with and responses to stereotype threat and racial microaggressions.* Black Scholars and the Study of Black Folks: Setting Interdisciplinary Research Policies and Agendas for the 21st Century, Proceedings of the 2006 BOTA Think Tank. Atlanta, GA: Stylus.

Castenell, L., & Pinar, W. (Eds.). (1993). *Understanding curriculum as racial text: Representations of identity and difference in education.* Albany: State University of New York Press.

Constantine, M. G., Willon, L., Gainor, K. A., & Lewis, E. L. (2002). Religious participation, spirituality, and coping among African American college students. *Journal of College Student Development, 43,* 605–613.

Cook, B. J., & Cordova, D. I. (2007). *Minorities in higher education, 22nd annual status report: 2007 supplement.* Washington, DC: American Council on Education.

Daresh, J., & Playko, M. (1995, October). *Alternative career formation perspectives: Lessons for educational leadership from law, medicine, and training for the priesthood.* Paper presented at the annual meeting of the University Council for Educational Administration, Salt Lake City, UT. (ERIC Document Reproduction Service No. ED387090)

Feagin, J., & Imani, N. (1993). Black in a White world. In J. R. Feagin & M. P. Sikes, *Living with racism: The Black middle-class experience.* Boston: Beacon Press.

Franklin, A. (1999). Invisibility syndrome and racial identity development in psychotherapy and counseling African American men. *Counseling Psychologist, 27*(6), 761–793.

Galbraith, M. W., & Cohen, N. H. (Eds.). (1995). *New strategies and challenges.* San Francisco: Jossey-Bass.

Gay, G. (2004). Navigating marginality en route to the professoriate: Graduate students of color learning and living in academia. *International Journal of Qualitative Studies in Education, 17*(2), 265–288.

Granados, R., & Lopez, J. M. (1999). Student-run support organizations for underrepresented graduate students: Goals, creation, implementation, and assessment. *Peabody Journal of Education, 74*(2), 135–149.

Guido-DiBrito, F., & Batchelor, S. W. (1988). Developing leadership potential for minority women. In M. D. Sagaria (Ed.), *Empowering women: Leadership development strategies on campus.* San Francisco: Jossey-Bass.

Gutmann, A., Bacow, L., Brody, W., Hoffman, E., Swygert, P., Tarver, L., et al. (2006). *Presidential forum—Graduate training and the pathway to the academic workforce*. Retrieved February 10, 2008, from The Leadership Alliance Web site: http://www.theleadershipalliance.org/matriarch/MultiPiecePage.asp_Q_PageID _E_116_A_PageName_E_PresForumTrend2.

Herrera, R. R. (2003). Notes from a Latino graduate student at a predominantly White university. In J. Castellanos & L. Jones (Eds.), *The majority in the minority* (pp. 111–125). Sterling, VA: Stylus.

Hoffer, T. B., Welch, V., Jr., Williams, K., Hess, M., Webber, K., Lisek, B., et al. (2005). *Doctorate recipients from United States universities: Summary report 2004 (Appendix A, Table A-1)*. Chicago: NORC, University of Chicago.

Hughes, M. S. (1988). Developing leadership potential in minority women. In M. D. Sagaria (Ed.), *Empowering women: Leadership development strategies on campus*. San Francisco: Jossey-Bass.

Johnson-Bailey, J., & Cervero, R. M. (2004). Mentoring in Black and White: The intricacies of cross-cultural mentoring. *Mentoring and Tutoring, 12*(1), 7–19.

Kalbfleisch, P. J., & Davies, A. B. (1991). Minorities and mentoring: Managing the multicultural institution. *Communication Education, 40*(3), 266–271.

Kerckhoff, A. C. (1976). The status attainment process: Socialization or allocation? *Social Forces, 53*, 368–381.

Locke, M. E. (1997). Striking the delicate balances: The future of African American women in the academy. In L. Benjamin (Ed.), *Black women in the academy: Promises and perils*. Gainesville: University Press of Florida.

Long, B. T. (2003). Diversity by any other name: Are there viable alternatives to affirmative action in higher education? *Western Journal of Black Studies, 27*(1), 30–35.

Marx, D. M., Brown, J. L., & Steele, C. M. (1999). Allport's legacy and the situational press of stereotypes. *Journal of Social Issues, 55*(3), 491–502.

Mattis, J. S. (2002). Religion and spirituality in the meaning-making and coping experiences of African American women: A qualitative analysis. *Psychology of Women Quarterly, 26*, 309–321.

McCormick, T. (1997). An analysis of five pitfalls of traditional mentoring for people on the margins in higher education. In H. T. Frierson (Ed.), *Diversity in higher education: Examining protégé-mentor experiences* (Vol. 1, pp. 187–202). Stamford, CT: JAI Press.

Milem, J., Chang, M., & Antonio, A. (2005). *Making diversity work on campus: A research-based perspective*. Washington, DC: Association of American Colleges and Universities.

Myers, S. L., & Turner, C. S. (2001). Affirmative action retrenchment and labor market outcomes for African-American faculty. In B. Lindsay & M. J. Justiz (Eds.), *The quest for equity in higher education* (pp. 63–94). Albany: State University of New York Press.

Patton, L., & Harper, S. (2003). Mentoring relationships among African American women in graduate and professional schools. In M. F. Howard-Hamilton (Ed.), *New Directions for Student Services, Vol. 104: Meeting the needs of African American women* (pp. 67–78). San Francisco: Jossey-Bass.

Pierce, C., Carew, J., Pierce-Gonzalez, D., & Wills, D. (1978). An experiment in racism: TV commercials. In C. Pierce (Ed.), *Television and education* (pp. 62–88). Beverly Hills, CA: Sage.

Pope, R. L., Reynolds, A. L., & Mueller, J. A. (2004). *Multicultural competence in student affairs*. San Francisco: Jossey-Bass.

Redd, K. (2007). *Graduate enrollment and degrees: 1996 to 2006*. Washington, DC: Council of Graduate Schools.

Robinson, C. (1996, April). *One solution to minority graduate students' discontent at Peabody College*. Paper presented at the annual meeting of the American Educational Research Association, New York.

Seymour, E., & Hewitt, N. (1997). *Talking about leaving: Why undergraduates leave the sciences*. Boulder, CO: Westview Press.

Solórzano, D., Ceja, M., & Yosso, T. (2000). Critical race theory, racial microaggressions, and campus racial climate: The experiences of African American college students. *Journal of Negro Education, 69*(1/2), 60–73.

Spence, M. (1973). Job market signaling. *Quarterly Journal of Economics, 87*(3), 355–374.

Spence, M. (2002, June). Signaling in retrospect and the informational structure of markets. *American Economic Review, 92*(3), 434–459.

Steele, C. M. (1997). A threat in the air: How stereotypes shape intellectual identity and performance. *American Psychologist, 52*(6), 613–629.

Stewart, D. L. (2002). The role of faith in the development of an integrated identity: A qualitative study of Black students at a White college. *Journal of College Student Development, 43*, 579–596.

Thomas, D. A. (1990). The impact of race on managers' experiences of mentoring and sponsorship: An intra-organizational study. *Journal of Organizational Behavior, 11*(6), 479–492.

Tierney, W. G., & Rhoads, R. A. (1993). *Enhancing promotion, tenure and beyond: Faculty socialization as a cultural process*. ASHE-ERIC Higher Education Report 6. Washington, DC: George Washington University, School of Education and Human Development.

Tillman, L. (2001). Mentoring African American faculty in predominantly White institutions. *Research in Higher Education, 43*(3), 295–325.

Trower, C. A., & Chait, R. P. (2002, March/April). Faculty diversity: Too little for too long. *Harvard Magazine, 104*(4), 33–37.

Tuitt, F. (2003a). *Black souls in an ivory tower: Understanding what it means to teach in a manner that respects and cares for the souls of African American graduate students*. Unpublished doctoral dissertation, Harvard Graduate School of Education.

Tuitt, F. (2003b). Realizing a more inclusive pedagogy: Meeting the challenge of teaching racially diverse college classrooms. In A. Howell & F. Tuitt (Eds.), *Race in higher education: Rethinking pedagogy in racially diverse college classrooms*. Cambridge, MA: Harvard Education Publishing Group.

Tuitt, F. (in press). Removing the threat in the air: Teacher transparency and the creation of identity safe graduate classrooms. *Journal of Excellence in College Teaching.*

Tuitt, F., Danowitz, M., & Sotello-Turner, C. (2007). Signals and strategies in hiring faculty of color. In J. C. Smart (Ed.), *Higher education: Handbook of theory and research* (Vol. 22, pp. 497–536). Norton, MA: Kluwer Academic.

Watt, S. K. (2003). Come to the river: Using spirituality to cope, resist, and develop identity. In M. F. Howard-Hamilton (Ed.), *New Directions for Student Services, Vol. 104: Meeting the needs of African American women* (pp. 29–40). San Francisco: Jossey-Bass.

Weidman, J. C., Twale, D. J., & Stein, E. L. (2001). *Socialization of graduate and professional students in higher education: A perilous passage?* ASHE-ERIC Higher Education Report, 28(3). Washington, DC: George Washington University, Graduate School of Education and Human Development.

Welch, O. (1997). An examination of effective mentoring models in academe. In H. T. Frierson (Ed.), *Diversity in higher education: Examining protégé-mentor experiences* (Vol. 1, pp. 41–62). Stamford, CT: JAI Press.

Williams, D. A., Berger, J. B., & McClendon, S. A. (2005). *Towards a model of inclusive excellence and change in postsecondary institutions.* Washington, DC: Association of American Colleges and Universities.

Enakshi Bose is pursuing a Ph.D. in foundations and practices of education (specialization in teaching, learning, and curriculum) at the Graduate School of Education, University of Pennsylvania. Her research interests focus on mathematics education and teacher education, with an emphasis on teacher learning and interaction with reform-oriented mathematics curricula. Currently she is a doctoral fellow with MetroMath: The Center for Mathematics in America's Cities, a National Science Foundation–funded Center for Teaching and Learning devoted to improving mathematics teaching and learning in urban communities and classrooms. With a postsecondary background in electrical engineering, Bose is interested in the learning that occurs at different points along the STEM education pipeline.

Ghangis D. Carter is Director of Recruitment and Retention and a Ph.D. student in higher education administration at Indiana University–Bloomington's School of Education. He earned a B.A. in journalism/public relations from San Diego State University and an M.Ed. in higher education administration from Peabody College of Vanderbilt University. Carter has held student affairs positions at the University of Illinois–Chicago, Vanderbilt University, the University of Georgia, Northern Illinois University, California State Polytechnic University–Pomona, and the University of California–Riverside.

Linda DeAngelo is a postdoctoral research scholar at the University of California, Los Angeles. She received her B.A. in American literature and culture and her M.A. and Ph.D. in higher education and organizational change at UCLA. She has studied issues regarding the pipeline to the Ph.D. since 2002, and her dissertation research focused on this area. Her other research interests include issues of diversity, student learning and change in diverse environments, and faculty.

Noah D. Drezner is a Ph.D. candidate in higher education at the University of Pennsylvania. Drezner's research interests include philanthropy and fundraising as it pertains to higher education. In addition, Drezner's research focuses on the ways in which minority and special serving institutions contribute to the nation. Drezner has published numerous articles and given several presentations on related topics. Recently, Drezner published "Recessions & Tax-Cuts: The Impact of Economic Cycles on Individual Giving, Philanthropy, and Higher Education" in the *International Journal of Educational Advancement* (2007) and "New Orleans's Black Colleges: Rebuilding After Disaster" in *Multicultural Review* (2007, with Marybeth Gasman).

Shannon Gary is the assistant dean of Pennoni Honors College at Drexel University in Philadelphia. He is currently completing his doctoral work in higher education management at the University of Pennsylvania's Graduate School of Education. His research focuses on historically Black colleges and universities, STEM education, and graduate education. He is a member of the National Association of Student Personnel Administrators and the National Collegiate Honors Council.

Marybeth Gasman is an assistant professor of higher education at the University of Pennsylvania. She is a historian who focuses on African American higher education, specifically Black colleges, fund-raising, philanthropy, and leadership. Her most recent books are *Envisioning Black Colleges: A History of the United Negro College Fund* (Johns Hopkins University Press, 2007) and *Understanding Minority Serving Institutions* (SUNY Press, 2008). In 2006, she received the Association for the Study of Higher Education's Promising Scholar/Early Career Achievement Award.

Keon Gilbert is a doctoral candidate at the University of Pittsburgh Graduate School of Public Health, Department of Behavioral and Community Health Sciences. His interdisciplinary training in biology, African American studies, public affairs, and behavioral and community health sciences provides a foundation to investigate rigorously the connections among genetic, behavioral, environmental, economic, and social determinants of health, which affect multiple factors of health, and the health care system, including education and training of minority health professionals.

Juan Carlos González is an assistant professor in the School of Education at the University of Missouri–Kansas City. He received his B.A. from California State University–Bernardino, his M.A. from The Ohio State University, and his Ph.D. from Arizona State University. He recently coedited a special issue of the journal *Educational Studies* entitled *Can't We All Get Along?/*

¿Pueden Convivir Todas Las Razas? The 15th Anniversary of the Los Angeles Riots and the Status of Urban Schooling.

Valerie Grim is chair of the African American and African Diaspora Studies Department at Indiana University. Valerie holds a B.A. from Tougaloo College and M.A. and Ph.D. degrees in history from Iowa State University. Her area of expertise concerns African Americans in the United States and Blacks in the Rural Diaspora. She is currently completing a book on African American rural life and culture in the Mississippi Delta, 1910–1970.

Kandace G. Hinton is an assistant professor in the Educational Leadership, Administration, and Foundations Department's Higher Education Leadership Program at Indiana State University. Hinton holds a master's and a Ph.D. in higher education administration from Indiana University and a B.A. from Jackson State University. Her research interests include African American women in higher education, multicultural identity development, and institutional support of community-based programs. She recently co-edited a book entitled *Unleashing Suppressed Voices on College Campuses: Diversity Issues in Higher Education and Student Affairs.*

Mary F. Howard-Hamilton is a professor of higher education at Indiana State University. She received her B.A. and M.A. degrees from the University of Iowa and an Ed.D. from North Carolina State University. She is an accomplished author and has received numerous awards including the Robert S. Shaffer Award for Academic Excellence as a Graduate Faculty Member from the National Association of Student Personnel Administrators and the University of Iowa Albert Hood Distinguished Alumni Award in 2002.

Shirley Hune is a visiting professor in educational leadership and policy studies at the University of Washington. Previously, she was a professor of urban planning and an associate dean in the Graduate Division at UCLA. She holds a B.A. in history and a Ph.D. in American civilization. She has published in the areas of Asian American history, Asian American educational access and equity, the global issues of nonaligned countries, and the human rights of international migrant workers.

Ted N. Ingram is an assistant professor of student development at Bronx Community College of the City University of New York. He received his B.A. from the University at Albany, State University of New York; his M.A. from Rowan University; and his Ph.D. from Indiana University. His research interests include examining the experiences of African American students at predominantly White institutions.

Susan D. Johnson is a research analyst for the Office of University Planning, Institutional Research, and Accountability at Indiana University. Her research interests include ethnic and gender identity development, issues of access and equity in higher education, and institutional research as it relates to strategic planning at universities and colleges. She earned her B.S., M.S., and M.Ed. degrees from the University of Florida and her Ph.D. in higher education and student affairs at Indiana University. In 2008, she was the recipient of the National Association of Student Personnel Administrators Hardee Dissertation of the Year Award.

John A. Kuykendall III is an assistant professor in the School of Education at Marquette University. He received his B.S. from the University of Arkansas at Pine Bluff, his M.S. from Christian Brothers University, and his Ph.D. from Indiana University. His scholarly research focuses on African American undergraduate degree attainment rates and access to college for students of color.

Valerie Lundy-Wagner is a doctoral student in the Higher Education Program at the University of Pennsylvania. A former engineer, she is interested in the role that institutions of higher education play in promoting the success of science, technology, engineering, and mathematics (STEM) students. Overall, Lundy-Wagner seeks to use qualitative and quantitative methodological approaches to investigate institutional attitudes, policies, and practices that both contribute to and hinder degree completion for underrepresented groups.

Carla L. Morelon-Quainoo is the director of assessment and dean of honors at Dillard University. She received her B.A. from Grambling State University, her M.Ed. from Vanderbilt, and her Ph.D. from Indiana University. She has received the Robert H. Wade Fellowship and the Cangemi Dissertation Research Award.

Laura W. Perna is an associate professor of higher education at the University of Pennsylvania. Formerly she was on the faculty at the University of Maryland, College Park. She serves as a member of the technical review group for the GEAR UP evaluation; the technical work group of the Upward Bound Program evaluation; the technical review panels for the National

Postsecondary Student Aid Study, Beginning Postsecondary Student Survey, and the Baccalaureate and Beyond Survey; and the Lumina Foundation for Education's Research Advisory Committee. In 2003 she received the Association for the Study of Higher Education's Promising Scholar/Early Career Achievement Award.

Oiyan A. Poon is a Ph.D. candidate in education at the UCLA Graduate School of Education & Information Studies. Previously, she served as the first director of Asian American student affairs at both UC Davis and George Mason University. As a graduate student, she assisted in the establishment of the University of California Asian American & Pacific Islander Policy Multicampus Research Program. Her research interests include critical race theory, Asian American studies, and education policy.

Raechele L. Pope is an associate professor of higher education in the Department of Educational Leadership and Policy at the University at Buffalo. She earned her doctorate at the University of Massachusetts at Amherst and her M.A. and B.A. at Indiana University of Pennsylvania. She is the author of the Jossey-Bass best seller *Multicultural Competence in Student Affairs* and several book chapters and refereed journal articles.

Lilia Santiague is a graduate of the Educational Leadership and Policy Studies Department at Indiana University with a concentration in higher education and student affairs. Her research interests include the college experiences of Haitian and Haitian American students and access and retention issues faced by minority and Caribbean students. She earned a master's degree in student personnel in higher education at the University of Florida. While at the University of Florida, she served as coordinator and adviser for the Decision & Information Sciences Department in the College of Business.

Dwyane G. Smith is a doctoral candidate at Indiana University School of Education, Educational Leadership and Policy Studies, concentrating in higher education and student affairs. He received a B.M.E. and an M.M.E. from the University of Oklahoma. He is currently an instructor at Indiana University in the African American/African Diaspora Studies program, teaching African American history in the 20th century and the history of higher education and the civil rights movement.

Terrell Lamont Strayhorn is Associate Professor of Higher Education and Special Assistant to the Provost at the University of Tennessee, Knoxville, where he also serves as Adjunct Assistant Professor of Sociology. He earned his B.A. and M.Ed. degrees from the University of Virginia and a Ph.D. from Virginia Tech. He has published extensively on Black collegians and has received numerous awards recognizing his early career success including the Outstanding Junior Scholar Award from the Association for the Study of Higher Education Council on Ethnic Participation, the Benjamin L. Perry Award from the National Association of Student Affairs Professionals, and the Annuit Coeptis and Emerging Scholar Awards from the American College Personnel Association.

Venice Thandi Sulé, M.S.W., is a doctoral candidate at the Center for the Study of Higher and Postsecondary Education at the University of Michigan. She uses critical theory to analyze how women access and persist within higher education settings. In addition, her work interrogates notions of diversity by exploring how intersecting identities and social practices promote educational equity. As a social worker, Sulé has worked with women and girls in areas of HIV/AIDS advocacy and higher education access.

Frank Tuitt is an assistant professor and the director of the higher education program in the Morgridge College of Education at the University of Denver. He is a 2003 Ed.D. graduate from the Harvard Graduate School of Education. Tuitt's research explores a range of topics related to access and equity in higher education, teaching and learning in racially diverse college classrooms, and diversity and organizational transformation. Tuitt is also a coeditor of and contributing author to the book *Race and Higher Education: Rethinking Pedagogy in Diverse College Classrooms*.

Rachelle Winkle-Wagner is an assistant professor of higher education at the University of Nebraska. She received both her B.A. and M.A. from the University of Nebraska and her Ph.D. from Indiana University. Her research focuses on the sociological aspects of race, gender, and identity in higher education, with an emphasis on the college experiences of African American women. She was an Association for the Study of Higher Education–Lumina dissertation fellow in 2005–2006.

Susan Yoon is an assistant professor at the University of Pennsylvania Graduate School of Education specializing in the fields of science education, technology education, and the learning sciences. She investigates learning outcomes that emerge from the use of social network analyses and complex systems theory on decision making about socioscientific issues. She also uses complex systems approaches in teacher professional development programs and studies affordances and constraints to access and retention of students in STEM fields of study. She is the principal investigator of two NSF grants both aimed at developing content knowledge and interests in STEM for students in grades 4–10.